The Paul Mellon Centre *for Studies in British Art*

A HISTORY

1970–2010

Copyright

Privately printed for The Paul Mellon Centre for Studies in British Art in Italy.

ISBN: 978-0-300-17571-4

Photographic Credits

page 5 © Virginia Museum of Fine Arts
page 17 © Michael Marsland (Duncan Robinson, Patrick McCaughey, Amy Meyers)
page 23 © Ian Parry
All other photography © The Paul Mellon Centre for Studies in British Art (Institutional Archive)
Jacket photograph and new photography on pages 15, 19, 47, 49 and 53 by Martine La Roche.

Contents

PREFACE

FORTY YEARS is not long in terms of institutional history but since the Centre's foundation in 1970 the study of historic British art has undergone considerable change and development and it is easy to forget that matters were very different half a century ago when Paul Mellon began to collect British art (see page 8). It therefore seemed to be a propitious moment to take stock of our activities to date.

Although in its early years the Centre's available funds for supporting scholarship were very modest and the grants awarded were comparatively few (see graphs on page 75) the spectacular growth of Yale University's endowment (of which the Centre's funds are part) over the past twenty years has enabled a rapid growth in support in all areas of the Centre's activities. It is interesting to note, for example, that the total sum awarded in grants between 1970 and 1997 is less than two-thirds of that now awarded in an average year. To date over £6,000,000 has been awarded in funding for grants and fellowships and more than £850,000 has been expended on academic activities such as conferences, seminars and lectures organised or co-organised by the Centre in collaboration with museums, galleries and universities. Perhaps the most public aspect of the Centre's activities has been its own publications programme (in collaboration with Yale University Press) which has resulted in the publication of nearly two hundred and fifty titles (see pages 47–52). It is not possible to calculate exact sums expended but it is estimated that some £15,000,000 has been spent in underwriting these publications over the past four decades.

The building up of a specialist library and photographic archive containing tens of thousands of images unavailable elsewhere has been a comparatively invisible aspect of the Centre's activities since its foundation but very considerable sums have also been expended on these important resources (see pages 23–28). Increasingly, too, the Centre has become a repository for scholars' archives and many of the leading figures of the past generation of historians of British art have bequeathed or given their working papers and photographs (see pages 27–28).

The Centre is of course owned by Yale University and the presence of small groups of Yale undergraduates in the spring and summer months is a reminder of the important role the Centre has in encouraging the study of historic British art on the home campus and in helping to form the next generation of scholars. Similarly, the increasing number of graduate students from all over the world who are beneficiaries of the Centre's grants and fellowships programme, or who simply use the Centre's facilities when in London, is testament to the ambassadorial role that the Centre has taken on over the past four decades.

This short history is the result of a careful examination and reorganisation of the Centre's institutional archives which was led by Charlotte Brunskill, Archivist and Records Manager of the National Portrait Gallery. Charlotte was seconded to the Centre for a year from November 2008 and we are immensely grateful to the National Portrait Gallery and its Director Sandy Nairne for agreeing to this arrangement. It was Charlotte Brunskill's professionalism, clarity of mind and enthusiasm for the daunting task that confronted her that made what follows in these pages possible. With the able assistance of the Centre's own Archivists, Victoria Lane and Emma Lauze, its Librarian Emma Floyd, and the Grants Administrator Mary Peskett Smith, the task of compiling the extensive lists of grants, publications and academic activities was finally achievable. Much assistance was also provided by Ella Fleming, Administrative Assistant at the Centre and her predecessor Lucy Nixon whose quiet tenacity led to many apparent gaps in our records being plugged. Guilland Sutherland, who has designed and edited many of the Centre's most significant publications over the past fifteen years, undertook the challenging task of designing a publication that consisted mainly of lists. In one way or another all my colleagues, especially Kasha Jenkinson and also Martin Postle, Viv Redhead and Maisoon Rehani, have contributed to this document and I thank them for sharing my enthusiasm for the task.

At Yale University the Centre has been governed since its foundation with benign good grace and wisdom by a Board of Governors which has always understood the importance of allowing the staff of the Centre in London to create its programmes and manage its affairs with the minimum of interference. The encouragement and support of Richard C. Levin, President of Yale for most of the past two decades has been vital to the continuing success of the Centre; and without Jules D. Prown, Paul Mellon Professor Emeritus of the History of Art and first Director of the Yale Center for British Art, there would simply be no Paul Mellon Centre in London. Last, but by no means least, the active role of successive Directors of the Centre's sister institution, the Yale Center for British Art, has been central to its *modus operandi*. To the late Edmund Pillsbury, Duncan Robinson, Patrick McCaughey and the current incumbent, Amy Meyers, sincere thanks are due for all the time and effort they have given in support of their smaller overseas satellite.

BRIAN ALLEN, Director of Studies
December 2010

PAUL MELLON (1907–1999)

PAUL MELLON was one of the greatest American philanthropists of the twentieth century whose generosity was matched only by his modesty and avoidance of publicity. He devoted his life to supporting causes such as higher education, the arts, research in religion and psychiatry, and the environment. He dispersed more than one billion US dollars in his lifetime, and significantly more after his death, but rarely allowed his name to be attached to his benefactions. He believed deeply in the values of art, literature, thought and reflection and their power to shape individual lives. He was formed by them and wished that others could enjoy their life-enhancing effect.

He was the son of one of America's richest men, the financier and future Secretary to the US Treasury Andrew W. Mellon (1855–1937) and an English mother, Nora McMullen (1879–1973). Paul Mellon was christened in St George's Chapel, Windsor Castle and his associations with England were a feature of his childhood, especially after the bitter divorce of his parents in 1912. At the age of twelve he entered Choate School in Connecticut and moved on to Yale, from where he graduated in 1929. He remained devoted to the university throughout his life.

At Yale he was taught by a brilliant generation of scholars and developed there the deep love of English literature and British history which formed the basis of his later artistic and intellectual interests. After Yale he went to Clare College, Cambridge where, 'skimping on lectures and study for the pleasures of hunting and racing', as he put it in his autobiography, he was exceptionally happy and carefree; he graduated in 1931. It was at Cambridge that he discovered the joys of collecting prints and books on aspects of sporting life, passions which remained a lifelong interest and would lead to the breeding and racing of horses, including the great bay colt Mill Reef, which won the Derby in 1971, the King George VI and Queen Elizabeth Stakes and the French Prix de L'Arc de Triomphe. Throughout his life Paul Mellon would claim that horse-racing more than art provided his most treasured moments.

The 1930s were a crucial period for him. He never shared his father's dedication to business and a brief period working in the family bank was a conspicuously unhappy time. In 1935 he married Mary Conover and together they developed an abiding interest in the work and thought of Carl Gustav Jung which led to the creation in 1941 of the Bollingen Foundation and its series of publications both of Jung's work and of other major scholarly works of analytical psychology, myth, religion, literature and archaeology.

With the death of his father in 1937 the mantle of leading and directing the family, both its fortune and philanthropy, fell to him. The National Gallery of Art in Washington, entirely the gift of his father, was still under construction. Paul Mellon took over his father's responsibilities as a trustee and saw the building through to its completion, presenting it together with Andrew Mellon's remarkable collection of Old Master paintings to President Franklin D. Roosevelt in 1941.

Paul Mellon's commitment to the National Gallery of Art was profound. He was president of the board from 1963 until 1985, during which time he, with some assistance from other members of the Mellon family, provided all the $95 million to build the east wing. Designed by I. M. Pei, it has become a

Paul Mellon by Yousuf Karsh 1980

national landmark. He and his sister, Ailsa Mellon Bruce (1901–1969), gave generously of their remarkable collections of French and American paintings to enhance the gallery. He was richly supported in his work both there and at his local museum, the Virginia Museum of Fine Arts in Richmond, by his second wife, Rachel (Bunny) Lambert (b.1910) whom he had married in 1948 following the death of his first wife.

Throughout his life, he was deeply attracted to Britain and in 1936 he bought his first British oil painting, a masterpiece *Pumpkin with a Stable Lad* by the artist to whom he retained a lifelong devotion, George Stubbs. It was his first step towards becoming the greatest collector and benefactor of British art in the twentieth century and for these services and for his generosity to numerous British institutions and universities, he was awarded an honorary knighthood in 1974.

Beginning in the late 1950s, he began to assemble what was to become the finest and most comprehensive collection of British art in the world outside the national collection of British art at the Tate Gallery in London. In December 1966 he announced the gift of the collection to Yale University with the pledge of a building to house it and an endowment to sustain operations in perpetuity. The Yale Center for British Art, designed by Louis Kahn, is a landmark of modern architecture with a matchless collection and is also an emblem of Yale's excellence in art and scholarship. The impetus and inspiration of these gifts was truly philanthropic. Just as he had delighted in British art, Paul Mellon wanted succeeding generations of Yale students to share in and benefit from the experience.

Mellon's interest and devotion to Yale University extended well beyond the creation of the Center for British Art. One of his earliest gifts to the university enabled it to acquire the legendary Boswell Papers, now a precious part of the Beinecke Library, and he made generous gifts of works of art to the Yale University Art Gallery. His gifts have reached down to the very substance of the university with the endowment of professorships as well as college buildings. Among numerous gifts, he provided funds which enable Yale to be 'admissions blind', attracting to the university gifted students of whatever economic background.

In all this, Paul Mellon was a true philanthropist. He enjoyed great wealth all of his life: his driving concern was to make it possible for others to enjoy and be enriched by the experiences of the mind and spirit which had shaped and delighted him. He wished to privilege others as he had been privileged.

THE PAUL MELLON FOUNDATION FOR BRITISH ART

ALTHOUGH in his youth Paul Mellon briefly contemplated an academic career his intellectual bent was always towards the intuitive rather than the analytical when it came to looking at works of art. 'One of my failings as a collector may be my lack of curiosity about the lives of the artists, their social and political backgrounds, and their places in history. I am also little interested in their techniques, their materials, or their methods of working. I sometimes worry about it, but then I say to myself, "Why should I have to?" '[1] These words by Paul Mellon from his autobiography might seem somewhat at odds with his extraordinary legacy but they do nothing if not emphasise that his prime interest was always in the work of art itself. Although, objectively, and as a result of his education at Yale and Cambridge, Paul Mellon always understood the significance of scholarship, its results usually left him unmoved. 'I find most critical writing, most statements about art, to be totally misleading' he wrote. 'Critical analysis of art is quite different from literary criticism. You can translate Sanskrit into English and analyse the meaning, but when you try to sum up the meaning of [Raphael's] "Alba Madonna" or Cezanne's "Boy in a Red Waistcoat" in words, it all seems to go off the rails.'[2]

It is worth remembering that scholarship in the history of British art was woefully underdeveloped during Paul Mellon's formative years and before he began to collect British art seriously at the end of the 1950s. Unlike today, in pre-Second World War England the Tate Gallery played virtually no role in promoting the study of British art. The situation was barely better at the National Gallery because, according to Ellis Waterhouse, its Director Sir Augustus Daniel (1866–1950) 'actually disliked British painting of the eighteenth century.'[3] The curator at the National Gallery who specialised in British art, C.H. Collins Baker (1880–1959) was soon to depart for the Huntington Library in California and it fell to his young assistant, Ellis Waterhouse (1905–1985), to make British painting one of his areas of expertise at the National Gallery before he left to become Librarian of the British School at Rome in 1933. At the National Portrait Gallery its Director Henry Hake (1892–1951) and colleagues Henry Isherwood Kay (1893–1938) and C.K. Adams (1899–1971) conducted research on rather more specialist lines but before the outbreak of war that was about it as far as contributions from the official art establishment in Britain were concerned.

Much of what was written about British art in the first decades of the twentieth century was, in fact, penned by the 'librarians' of London's leading art dealers. Usually in the form of elaborate pamphlets produced by the dealers about individual works for sale, these now rather rare and often sumptuous publications are invariably anonymous but were undoubtedly sometimes written by scholars who were cautious about protecting their anonymity. It was a curious fact that since the beginning of the twentieth century the study of historic British painting had been almost entirely in the hands of the art trade.

The establishment of the Courtauld Institute in London in 1932, under the directorship of W.G. Constable (1887–1976), was undoubtedly a significant moment since a number of the first PhD theses to emerge from this new body were on English eighteenth-century painters, although they remained unpublished. Another important landmark at this date was the series of exhibitions held at the London house in Park Lane of Sir

38 Bury Street premises

THE PAUL MELLON FOUNDATION

Philip Sassoon (1888–1939), Chairman of the National Gallery's Trustees, in aid of the Royal Northern Hospital. The catalogues of the exhibitions on Gainsborough in 1936 and Reynolds in 1937, both written by Ellis Waterhouse, were important milestones in the study of eighteenth-century British painting and it might be argued that the interest in painters like Devis, Zoffany and Wheatley resulted from the first of these loan exhibitions, *English Conversation Pieces*, held in 1930.[4]

Paul Mellon had purchased a few British sporting pictures before the 1950s but most of his collecting activity had been confined to acquiring sporting and colour plate books, such as the magnificent Abbey collection purchased between 1952 and 1955. Although it seems quite probable, we do not really know if on his regular visits to England in the 1950s Paul Mellon ever saw the winter exhibitions at the Royal Academy, such as those devoted to the institution's first hundred years held in the winter of 1951–52 or the exhibition of British portraits shown in the winter of 1956–57.

It was a chance meeting between the English art historian Basil Taylor (1922–1975) and Paul Mellon in the spring of 1959 that led to the establishment of the Paul Mellon Foundation for British Art. Their joint interest in Stubbs and sporting art in general was the happiest of coincidences for it set in train a sequence of events that was to have a profound bearing on the creation of opportunities for new scholarship in the history of British art. Basil Taylor soon became Paul Mellon's adviser as he began to build up his collection of British art. Taylor had always insisted on not taking any remuneration but late in 1961 when he resigned his position at the Royal College of Art his continuing refusal to accept payment for his services effectively left him without an income. At about this time it came to Paul Mellon's attention that a lengthy and comprehensive manuscript on the history of watercolour painting in Britain by the deceased former Keeper of the Prints and Drawings Department at the Victoria & Albert Museum, Martin Hardie (1875–1952), remained unpublished, essentially because the cost of editing and publication were prohibitive to any British publisher. Since Paul Mellon had just purchased Martin Hardie's own fine collection of English watercolours he perhaps felt some sense of responsibility towards this project. After lengthy discussions with his friend Herbert Read, who was also a director of the publisher Routledge & Kegan Paul, he not only decided to underwrite the revision of Hardie's manuscript, which eventually appeared in three volumes published by Routledge between 1966 and 1968, but also asked Basil Taylor to draw to his attention any other writings on British art that faced the same predicament. From this almost accidental beginning, late in 1961, grew the concept of establishing a publishing venture that, to use Paul Mellon's own words, 'would promote a wider knowledge and understanding of British art'.[5] A non-profit Charitable Trust was then established with 'independent self-governing British status and with its own board of trustees, to publish a series to be entitled "Studies in British Art".'[6] This new project started under the wing of another of Paul Mellon's charitable trusts, the Bollingen Foundation, which he had established with his first wife Mary in December 1945 as the Bollingen Foundation for British Art and was officially incorporated as a Company Limited by Guarantee on 13th June 1963. Shortly after, having experienced complications operating as a Limited Company, it was reformed as a Trust and on 4th May 1964 received Charitable Status. Financial control was transferred to another Mellon charitable trust, the Old Dominion Foundation, which Paul Mellon had established in 1941.[7] The new Foundation in London was renamed the Paul Mellon Foundation for British Art and Basil Taylor was persuaded to take on the directorship from rented premises at 38 Bury Street, St James's. Its first Board of Trustees consisted of Basil Taylor; the scholar/connoisseur/art dealer James Byam Shaw (1903–1992) of Colnaghi's; Sir Herbert Read (1893–1968), the writer and friend of Paul Mellon; and (as Chairman) Charles Whishaw (1909–2006), a lawyer and trustee of the Gulbenkian Foundation.

The first results of the Foundation's activities were a series of short 'supplements' which began publication in *Apollo* magazine in 1964, consisting of short scholarly notices about previously unpublished works of art (for a full list see p.11). The first of these appeared some months before the first exhibition in England of Paul Mellon's collection which opened to the public at the Royal Academy on 12th December 1964. When the collection was shown at the Yale University Art Gallery in the following year a three-day conference was held (April 21–23) with the aim of bringing together the leading scholars in the field to debate the state of knowledge and to draw attention to those areas that were most in need of new research. Basil Taylor described the occasion as 'a most useful, but perhaps a little discouraging occasion, as hour by hour we were being reminded how much we did not know, how much remained to be discovered.'[8]

It is now all too easy to forget that in 1960s Britain there was still remarkably little confidence about the art of its past compared to that of mainland Europe. Denys Sutton (1917–1991), editor of *Apollo* magazine, even went as far as challenging his readers in an editorial in June 1967 entitled 'Let's Blow our Own Trumpet for a Change' to stop being so diffident, and posing the question whether the French Impressionists could 'rival Turner with his poetical blending of delicacy and strength'. He went on to note that 'British art was neglected for years, except by a few enthusiasts, but, largely thanks to the munificence of Mr Paul Mellon, it is marching ahead'.[9]

Sutton's editorial coincided with the publication in 1967 of the Paul Mellon Foundation's first three books. Robert Raines's monograph on Marcellus Laroon, Roy Strong's *Hans Holbein at the Court of Henry VIII* and Oliver Millar's *Zoffany and his Tribuna* all received the kind of widespread, lengthy reviews and publicity in the national press that would now be inconceivable for academic books. The books were edited by Basil Taylor and were designed by a staff member, Paul Sharp, and many of the photographs reproduced were taken by the Foundation's photographer Douglas Smith. A few months later, in an article published in the *Contemporary Review*, Basil Taylor offered a progress report on the Foundation's activities to date and noted that although the primary aim of the Foundation was to advance the knowledge, understanding and enjoyment of British painting, sculpture and graphic arts through publications – 'by increasing the authoritative literature of the subject' – it was recognised at the start 'that if such a programme of publishing was to have continuity, ambition and any intellectual drive, the study of British art itself would have to be nourished in other ways. As a contribution to that end', Taylor wrote, 'the Foundation has endowed two lectureships, one in British Medieval Art at the University of York and the other in Post-Medieval Art at the University of Leicester.'[10] In addition to offering modest grants to individual scholars for research purposes, financial support for mounting exhibitions was an important part of the Foundation's brief, with exhibitions devoted to Bonington, Wheatley, Brooking, Mortimer, Laroon and Mercier, to name but a few, all receiving significant help.[11]

Basil Taylor argued forcefully that, simply by virtue of its creation, the Paul Mellon Foundation asserted that British painting was worthy of intelligent consideration. He was however quick to point out that for the student of British art in 1967 'the very fundaments of knowledge are still missing', noting that catalogues raisonnés of most of the greatest British painters such as Turner and Constable simply did not exist and that if 'our writers had been as inadequately published and presented there would surely have been an outcry'.[12] In this interim report Basil Taylor also drew attention to what was to prove to be the Foundation's nemesis, a proposed multi-volume Dictionary of British Art. The Dictionary, in its planning stages since the Foundation's inception, was, as Taylor admitted, 'perhaps too ambitious for the present resources of British art scholarship. Time will tell'.[13] Indeed, the project eventually proved too ambitious, and the enormous estimated cost of the Dictionary was one of the prime reasons for the Foundation's demise in 1969. An indignant editorial entitled 'The Future of the Mellon Foundation' appeared in the *Burlington Magazine* in May 1970, after the Foundation's closure and the announcement that a newly constituted organisation, under the aegis of Yale University, named the Paul Mellon Centre for Studies in British Art had been established. The *Burlington* editorial noted that at a meeting held in London on 9th December 1969 'to which a number of outside art historians were invited to give their advice, it transpired that the ten or twelve volumes projected would cost nearly £1,400,000' – an enormous sum for the proposed, rather over-optimistic print run of five thousand copies.[14] This sum was way beyond the means of the newly established Centre: tighter financial controls under Yale's management meant that it was not prepared to countenance such extravagance. The Foundation had employed a research team for the Dictionary that, at its peak, numbered twenty and many young scholars cut their professional teeth on the venture at the beginning of their careers.

This is not the place to give a detailed account of the demise of the Paul Mellon Foundation but suffice it to say that Basil Taylor's fragile, self-destructive personality and his weakness in managing the Foundation's financial resources were certainly a significant factor. In his autobiography Paul Mellon gives a full account of these events during which Basil Taylor's mental state led him to test his friendship with him to breaking point.[15] Paul Mellon regretted that the Dictionary never appeared and years later remarked that 'if things had been handled differently and if Basil had had a more equable nature, it might have been possible to overcome the problems'.[16] Basil Taylor resigned as director of the Foundation towards the end of 1968 and his mental health deteriorated thereafter. He became increasingly isolated from his friends and family and, tragically, committed suicide in 1975. Despite this terrible ending it should always be remembered that without Basil Taylor's friendship with Paul Mellon neither the Foundation nor its successor might ever have been created.

Basil Taylor (1922–1975)

By the time Basil Taylor resigned, the planning of the Yale Center for British Art, designed to house Paul Mellon's collection of British art, the gift of which to Yale was announced on 9th December 1966, was progressing apace and it was decided, in large part due to Jules Prown (b.1930), the Center's first director, that a London outpost would be highly desirable. It was also abundantly clear that the present setup was not running satisfactorily and that both Paul Mellon and Yale University would require significant changes if the organisation was to survive in any form. Basil Taylor's two assistants, Angus Stirling (b.1933) and Colin Sorensen (1930–2001), took over in January 1969 as co-Directors, with the former in charge of administrative matters and the latter focused on publications. Charles Whishaw and James Byam Shaw continued as Trustees and were joined in February 1969 by Sir John Witt (1907–1982), a lawyer, and David Piper (1918–1990), Director of the Fitzwilliam Museum, Cambridge, replacing Herbert Read, who had died. Jules Prown, as first director of the embryonic Yale Center for British Art, also became a Trustee. At this point Paul Mellon was concerned that the London Foundation had become an open-ended financial commitment, especially since the long-term costs of the proposed Dictionary were spiralling. Paul Mellon therefore asked Yale University if it would be prepared to take over the Foundation if he donated $5,000,000 for the purpose. In April 1969 Yale's President Kingman Brewster approved the idea as long as it did not involve any incremental expenditure of university funds. At a meeting of the Foundation's Trustees in October 1969 Jules Prown informed them that the Andrew W. Mellon Foundation, successor to the Old Dominion Foundation, did not intend to continue annual funding but that Paul Mellon was considering endowing a new body under the auspices of Yale University. By the end of the year events had moved rapidly and on 1st December 1969 Paul Mellon and his lawyer Stoddard Stevens met with the Trustees in London and told them of his intention of endowing a Centre in London. A conference also took place on 9th December about the future of the Dictionary after which it was concluded that, despite its desirability, Yale would not be prepared to make a commitment to the project. Yale received the gift of $5,000,000 at the end of December 1969. It was envisaged that the new organisation would have substantially the same aims as those of the Foundation but that it would in due course become a sister institution to the Yale Center for British Art. In-house design of books would be discontinued in favour of a contractual arrangement with Yale University Press and it would no longer be involved with mounting exhibitions.

By the time the Foundation closed late in 1969 three more books had been published: Benedict Nicolson's *Joseph Wright of Derby, Painter of Light*; a beautiful facsimile of Richard Wilson's Italian Sketchbook edited by Denys Sutton; and Roy Strong's ground-breaking study of sixteenth-century painting, *The English Icon*. Mary Webster's monograph on Francis Wheatley appeared the following year under the Foundation's imprint, despite its demise. Many more books that were in preparation under the Foundation eventually, sometimes decades later, came to fruition under the auspices of the Paul Mellon Centre for Studies in British Art and Yale University Press but there is no doubt that the closure of the Foundation caused, as Ellis Waterhouse diplomatically put it, 'considerable bruised feelings.'[17]

1 *Reflections in a Silver Spoon: A Memoir* by Paul Mellon with John Baskett (New York, 1992), p. 294.
2 *Ibid.*, p. 294.
3 Ellis Waterhouse, *British Art & British Studies, Remarks by Ellis Waterhouse At the Inauguration of the Yale Center for British Art 16 April 1977* (New Haven, Yale Center for British Art, 1979), p. 5.
4 Peter Stansky, *Sassoon: The Worlds of Philip and Sybil* (New Haven & London, 2003), pp. 196–97.
5 *Reflections in a Silver Spoon*, p. 328.
6 *Ibid.*, p.328.
7 *Ibid.*, pp. 171–77, 357.
8 Basil Taylor, 'The Paul Mellon Foundation for British Art: a report on progress' *Contemporary Review*, November 1967, p. 267.
9 [Denys Sutton] *Apollo*, LXXXV (June 1967), p. 399.
10 Taylor, *loc. cit.*, p. 264.
11 Unfortunately no complete record of the Foundation's grants survives in its existing records.
12 Taylor, *loc. cit.*, p. 266
13 *Ibid.*, p. 267
14 *Burlington Magazine*, Vol. CXII (May 1970), p. 267.
15 *Reflections in a Silver Spoon*, pp. 329–36.
16 *Ibid.*, p. 332
17 Ellis Waterhouse, *British Art & British Studies*, p. 28.

Paul Mellon Foundation Staff

Colin Sorensen	1963–70	Co-Director
Basil Taylor	1964–69	Director
Douglas Smith	1964–69	Photographer
Dudley Snelgrove	1964–70	Senior Research Assistant
Kenneth Sharpe	1964–74	Archivist/ Senior Research Assistant
Patricia Barnden	1964–78	Associate Archivist
Mrs G. Sharpe	1965–70	Receptionist
Marion Spencer	1965–74	Senior Research Assistant
Paul Sharp	1967–70	Designer
Angus Stirling	1967–70	Co-Director
Mary Dougal	1968–71	Secretary to Angus Stirling
Patricia Butler	–1970	Secretary to Colin Sorensen
Mrs B. Girelli	–1970	Assistant Archivist
Belinda Loftus	–1970	Senior Research Assistant

PAUL MELLON FOUNDATION PUBLICATIONS

NOTES ON BRITISH ART: SUPPLEMENTS TO *APOLLO* MAGAZINE

June 1964

'The Paul Mellon Foundation for British Art'
John Hayes, 'Holker Gainsboroughs'
Roy Strong, 'Portrait miniature of Queen Elizabeth I by Nicholas Hilliard'

January 1965

Oliver Millar, 'Three little-known seventeenth-century paintings'

May 1965

Kenneth Sharpe, 'A view of the Tower of London by Samuel Scott'
Basil Taylor, 'Portraits of George Stubbs'

October 1965

Luke Herrmann, 'Samuel Palmer's earliest painting'
Robert Raines, 'Drawings by Marcellus Lauron – "Old Laroon" – in the Pepysian Library'

March 1966

W.A. Smeaton, 'Thomas Richard Underwood, 1772–1835: painter and naturalist'
Peter S. Walch, 'Nathaniel Dance's "Cleopatra and the dying Marc Antony" '

August 1966

Arthur S. Marks, 'The source of John Martin's "The Bard" '
Basil Taylor, 'A forgotten "pre-Raphaelite": Robert Bateman's "Pool of Bethesda" '
'Charles Brooking'
'Johann Zoffany'
'Francis Wheatley'

February 1967

Luke Herrmann, 'A Samuel Palmer sketch-book of 1819'

July 1967

Robert Raines, 'Two paintings and a drawing by Marcellus Laroon'

October 1967

Ann Hope, 'Cesare Ripa's iconology and the neoclassical movement'

April 1968

Lionel Lambourne, 'A portrait by Benjamin Marshall, 1768–1835'
Miklos Rajnai, 'Robert Paul, the non-existent painter'
Basil Taylor and Benedict Nicolson, 'A caricature group by John Hamilton Mortimer'

August 1968

H. A. Hammelmann, 'Shakespeare's first illustrators'

November 1968

Benedict Nicolson, 'Addenda to Wright of Derby'

January 1969

John Hayes, 'The ornamental surrounds for Houbraken's "Illustrious heads" '
Basil Taylor, 'George Stubbs and a drawing by Carle Vernet'

BOOKS AND EXHIBITION CATALOGUES

1965

Mary Webster, *Francis Wheatley RA 1747–1801* (Catalogue of an exhibition held Aldeburgh, Suffolk; City Art Gallery, Leeds)

1966

Colin Sorenson *Charles Brooking 1723–1759: Paintings, Drawings & Engravings* (Catalogue of an exhibition held Aldeburgh, Suffolk; Bristol City Art Gallery)
Robert Raines, *Marcellus Laroon* (in association with Routledge & Kegan Paul Ltd)
Oliver Millar, *Zoffany & his Tribuna* (in association with Routledge & Kegan Paul Ltd)

1967

Robert Raines *Marcellus Laroon* (Catalogue of an exhibition held Aldeburgh, Suffolk; Tate Gallery,)
Roy Strong *Holbein & Henry VIII* (in association with Routledge & Kegan Paul Ltd)

1968

Ed. Denys Sutton, catalogue by Ann Clements, *Richard Wilson RA, An Italian Sketchbook: Drawings Made by the Artist in Rome* (in association with Routledge & Kegan Paul Ltd)
Dudley Snelgrove and Angus Stirling, *Norwich School Prints Paintings & Drawings by the Rev E T Daniell 1804–1842* (Catalogue of an exhibition held Aldeburgh, Suffolk)
Benedict Nicolson, *John Hamilton Mortimer ARA 1740–1779: Paintings, Drawings and Prints* (Catalogue of an exhibition held Towner Art Gallery, Eastbourne; Iveagh Bequest, Kenwood)
Benedict Nicolson, *Joseph Wright of Derby: Painter of Light* Vol. 1, Vol. 2 (in association with London: Routledge & Kegan Paul; New York: Pantheon Books)

1969

Robert Raines and John Ingamells, *Philip Mercier 1689–1760: An Exhibition of Paintings and Engravings* (Catalogue of an exhibition held City Art Gallery, York; Iveagh Bequest, Kenwood)
Basil Taylor, *The Prints of George Stubbs* (Catalogue of an exhibition held Festival Gallery, Aldeburgh, Suffolk; Victoria and Albert Museum, London)
Anne Crookshank and the Knight of Glin, *Irish Portraits 1660–1860* (Catalogue of an exhibition held National Gallery of Ireland, Dublin; National Portrait Gallery, London; Ulster Museum, Belfast)
Roy Strong, *The English Icon: Elizabethan & Jacobean Portraiture* (in association with Routledge & Kegan Paul Ltd)

1970

Mary Webster, *Francis Wheatley* (in association with Routledge & Kegan Paul Ltd)

THE PAUL MELLON CENTRE FOR STUDIES IN BRITISH ART

IN MAY 1970, unhappy at the demise of the Paul Mellon Foundation, the editor of the *Burlington Magazine*, doubtless expressing the views of many British scholars who feared that the putative 'Golden Age' that the Foundation heralded might founder before it could even begin to flourish, predicted that the new Paul Mellon Centre, by then established with an endowment given to Yale by Paul Mellon, would 'have a tough time standing up to its American counterpart.' Since a new Director had yet to be appointed, it was hoped that such a figure would be someone of 'high standing and with a will of iron.' By a stroke of good fortune it transpired that in the summer of 1970 Professor Ellis Waterhouse was about to retire after eighteen years as Director of the Barber Institute of Fine Arts at the University of Birmingham and Jules Prown shrewdly persuaded him to take the helm of the new Centre until a longer-term successor could eventually be found. Waterhouse's international reputation immediately commanded respect in the London art world and he undoubtedly established the character of the new Centre, in its premises at 20 Bloomsbury Square, a building shared with Yale University Press's then very modest London operation.

In its early years the Paul Mellon Centre for Studies in British Art, although no less ambitious in its aims than its predecessor, operated under much tighter financial control. In order to win the confidence of institutions in Britain it was decided that the Centre should be completely disassociated with the building up of the Mellon collection: when the collection was shown at the Royal Academy in the winter of 1964–65 headlines such as that in the *Daily Telegraph* on 11th December 1964 – 'MELLON SHOW AROUSES DELIGHT AND DISMAY' – reminded the British art establishment and the public just how many good British pictures had left the United Kingdom over the previous five years.

Although the Foundation had been active in building up an archive of black and white photographs of British paintings, drawings and engravings during its few brief years of existence, under the directorship of Waterhouse, who had an unrivalled knowledge of British art in both public and private collections, the new Centre made photography of works passing through the auction houses and those in private collections a high priority. From his early days as a young curator at the National Gallery in London and later as Director of both the National Gallery of Scotland (1949–52) and the Barber Institute of Fine Arts at the University of Birmingham (1952–70), Waterhouse had always made a practice of establishing photographic archives and he recognised the vital importance of new photography to the art historian. Thanks to the excellent work of the photographer Douglas Smith (1920–2006), who was employed from 1964 successively by both the Foundation and the Centre until his retirement in 1996, this targeted approach, compared to the Witt Library's more comprehensive gathering of images, led to tens of thousands of works of art which might otherwise have remained unrecorded being photographed and catalogued in the Centre's archive. Ellis Waterhouse was Director of the Centre for less than three years but in that short time, with the support of Jules Prown at Yale and a distinguished Advisory Council comprised of leading scholars and museum directors from the British art world, he rapidly managed to

20 Bloomsbury Square

Christopher White and other members of the Centre staff in the backyard of the Bloomsbury Square premises, 1982

establish the Centre as a viable force and to dispel the unease which accompanied the Centre's foundation (for a full list of members see pp. 19–20).

Any doubts that the Centre might not continue the Foundation's policy of supporting scholarly books were dispelled with the publication for the Centre by Yale University Press of Ronald Paulson's magisterial two-volume *Hogarth, His Life, Art and Times* in October 1971, on the day the Centre opened its new premises in Bloomsbury Square. This was the first of the Centre's books published under a new contractual arrangement with Yale University Press and the sheer scale of this study (when it was completed in the late-1960s it was planned as a three-volume work) made the Centre's ambitions abundantly clear. Since then a steady stream of important publications (well over two hundred to date) have appeared under the Paul Mellon Centre and Yale University Press's imprint and the publications programme was given real impetus in 1973 when John Nicoll (b. 1944), a promising young publisher who was making a name for himself at Oxford University Press, was persuaded to join Yale University Press's London office, housed in the Paul Mellon Centre's premises, to handle production of its art books. In the following years the publication of catalogues raisonnés of Turner, Constable, Blake and Whistler all received substantial personal support from Paul Mellon, over and above the budgeted sums from the Centre's endowment income.

Since the turn of the new century further catalogues raisonnés of the work of Reynolds, Ramsay, Van Dyck, Sickert, Stubbs, Bonington, Holman Hunt, Madox Brown and Sargent have been published and Hogarth, Romney, Wilson, Gainsborough's portraits and Beardsley are all in preparation. These books have provided a solid base for a new generation of scholars of British art, and changing approaches to the discipline of art history are also reflected in the Centre's publication of many more discursive texts and books of essays. The Centre's support of architectural history should also be noted since the Paul Mellon Foundation had excluded architecture and the applied and decorative arts from its remit. Standard reference works such as the third and fourth editions of Howard Colvin's *A Biographical Dictionary of British Architects 1600–1840* have been published under the Centre's imprint and groundbreaking works such as Eileen Harris's *The Genius of Robert Adam: His Interiors*, John Cornforth's *Early Georgian Interiors* and Mark Girouard's *Elizabethan Architecture* have set the highest standards in both scholarship and in the sumptuous presentation of the material.

Ellis Waterhouse retired in 1973 and Christopher White (b. 1930) was recruited as the second Director of Studies from his post as Curator of Graphic Arts at the National Gallery in Washington. Christopher White had considerable experience in the museum world and the art trade, having worked for eleven years in the Department of Prints and Drawings at the British Museum before joining the dealers Colnaghi in 1965. Although a specialist in Dutch rather than British art, White was a distinguished and respected figure and during his twelve years as Director of Studies at the Centre he forged closer links with the sister institution, the Yale Center for British Art, after it opened in April 1977. One of his innovations was the introduction of the Yale-in-London programme in the summer of 1977. Although initially a summer course, it was extended in 1981 to two full semesters that provided study abroad opportunities for Yale and occasionally undergraduates from other American universities who were interested in pursuing a series of courses offered under the umbrella of what was then Yale's British Studies department. This gave the Paul Mellon Centre a definable role in Yale's undergraduate life, and daily life at 20 Bloomsbury Square was certainly enhanced by the presence of groups of lively and intelligent Yale undergraduates, whose experience of studying British art during a term in London enabled them to make greater use of Paul Mellon's collections at the Yale Center for British Art on their return to New Haven. Increasingly, too, the London Centre was becoming a base for the stream of Yale graduate students (and, indeed, those from other universities) who wished to pursue advanced research in historic British art in London. The presence of a London base, whence introductions to the London art world could be made, has undoubtedly provided a vital point of entry for students at what can sometimes be an isolated stage in their professional lives.

When Christopher White was appointed Director of the Ashmolean Museum at Oxford in 1985, he was succeeded by the Deputy Director of the Courtauld Institute of Art, Professor Michael Kitson (1926–1998). Although not a prolific author, Michael Kitson was a hugely influential figure within academic circles and he brought a wealth of experience and authority to the Paul Mellon Centre. The seven years of his directorship witnessed a greater engagement with history of art departments in the universities and also with national museums with whom closer academic links were forged. His successor, Brian Allen, began his career at the Centre in 1976 and he has been most fortunate to be in post at a time when the Centre's funds have grown significantly as a result of Yale University's careful investment of Paul Mellon's endowment. As a result, not only was the Centre able to move in 1996 to its larger current premises in Bedford Square but the modest sum available in grant aid from the Centre before 1998 has grown very considerably resulting in a hugely beneficial impact in the field. The Centre is now able to support the publication of, on average, twelve new titles each year and, through its grants programme, it is able to offer significant support to other academic publishers for scholarly books on British art.

16 Bedford Square (at right of picture)

In addition to support for publications, a new expanded Fellowship programme was instituted with the enthusiastic support of the Yale Center for British Art's then Director, Patrick McCaughey (b.1943), and this has provided far greater opportunities for supporting research in British art than had ever previously been available. One suspects that when the Centre was founded in 1970 Paul Mellon was, given the short and turbulent history of its predecessor, somewhat circumspect about its future prospects but by the time of his death in 1999 he was able to see that from comparatively modest beginnings the Centre had slowly begun to fulfil what he and Basil Taylor had first conceived thirty years earlier.

PREMISES

AFTER the founding of the Centre in June 1970 the newly constituted organisation continued to occupy the premises of the Paul Mellon Foundation at 38 Bury Street, St James, in the heart of London's commercial art world but it was thought that a move to a more academic quarter of London would be desirable and would help to dispel any associations between the Centre and the building up of Paul Mellon's collection of British art. A Georgian townhouse on the Bedford Estate in Bloomsbury was identified for rental late in 1970 and the Centre moved into its new home at no.20 Bloomsbury Square during the summer of 1971. The building was officially opened on 26th October of that year with a reception attended by three hundred guests. No.20 was on the north side of the square, one of a terrace of houses built *c.*1800–1 to the designs of the most enterprising and successful London builder of his time, James Burton (1761–1837). These houses were on the former site of Southampton House, built by the 4th Earl of Southampton in 1657 and renamed Bedford House in 1734. Bedford House was demolished in 1800 when the 5th Duke of Bedford obtained two Acts of Parliament for developing his estate to the north of Bloomsbury Square. Although the possibility of Mr Mellon's purchasing a freehold property for the Centre was explored in the Autumn of 1977 and Spring of 1978, and several potential properties were examined, it was eventually decided to continue as tenants on the Bedford Estate.

In 1994, as the Centre's twenty-five year lease from the Bedford Estate was drawing to an end and the Centre was informed that refurbishment of the entire terrace was being planned, the Director of Studies asked the Steward of the Bedford Estate to find other suitable premises to rent nearby and in the autumn of 1994 the Centre was offered a handsome house in Bedford Square, the only complete Georgian square left in Bloomsbury. At the Board of Governors meeting early in 1995 the relocation plans were approved and the Centre moved into no.16 Bedford Square early in June 1996. The property had been empty for almost two years and was comprehensively refurbished by the Bedford Estate in consultation with the Centre. The houses in Bedford Square are today listed as Grade I, placing them in the top five per cent of Britain's listed building stock, and great care was taken to ensure that the decorative paint schemes and furnishings of the building were as sympathetic as possible to its architectural grandeur. The most significant addition of space at Bedford Square was the large room at the rear of the house which could not only accommodate a large part of the Centre's library but was also suitable for hosting lectures and small conferences.

BOARD OF GOVERNORS

Although the Paul Mellon Foundation was an independent self-governing body, managed by its own Board of Trustees in London, from 1970 the newly formed Paul Mellon Centre for Studies in British Art operated under the aegis of Yale University. Four members of the Centre's Governors comprise the Trustees of the Centre and are usually the Director of the Centre's sister institution (the Yale Center for British Art) and the chief officers of Yale University (President, Provost and the Vice-President for Finance and Administration). The other members of the governing body are usually the Dean of Yale College, the chair of Yale's Art History department and senior professors in the fields of history or English literature. The four Trustees have legal responsibility for the Centre. The Director of the Yale Center for British Art is also ex-officio Chief Executive of the Paul Mellon Centre for Studies in British Art.

Jules Prown
Director YCBA 1970–76

Edmund Pillsbury
Director YCBA 1978–81

Duncan Robinson
Director YCBA 1981–95

Patrick McCaughey
Director YCBA 1996–2001

Trustees & Governors

Kingman Brewster Jr. (President, Yale University)
1970–77

Jules Prown (Director, Yale Center for British Art)
1970–76

John Ecklund (Secretary of the Board of Governors and Treasurer, Yale University)
1970–78

Louis Martz (Acting Director, Yale Center for British Art)
1970–74, 1980–81

Charles Taylor (Provost, Yale University)
1970–72

Richard Cooper (Provost, Yale University)
1972–74

Hanna Gray (President, Yale University)
1974–78

A. Bartlett Giametti (President, Yale University)
1978–86

Abraham Goldstein (Provost, Yale University)
1978–80

Edmund Pillsbury (Director, Yale Center for British Art)
1978–81

Jerald Stevens (Vice-President for Finance and Administration)
1978–84

Duncan Robinson (Director, Yale Center for British Art)
1981–95

William Brainard (Provost, Yale University)
1982–86

Michael Finnerty (Vice-President for Administration)
1984–88

John Buckman (Vice-President for Finance)
1985–88

William Nordhaus (Provost, Yale University)
1986–88

Benno Schmidt Jr (President, Yale University)
1987–92

Amy Meyers
Director YCBA 2003–present

BOARD OF GOVERNORS

Michael Finnerty (Vice-President for Finance and Administration)
1988–93

Frank Turner (Provost, Yale University)
1989–92

Howard Lamar (President, Yale University)
1993–93

Richard Levin (President, Yale University)
1993–present

Patrick McCaughey (Director, Yale Center for British Art)
1996–2001

Judith Rodin (Provost, Yale University)
1993–94

Joseph Mullinix (Acting Vice-President for Finance and Administration)
1993–2001

Alison Richard (Provost, Yale University)
1995–2002

Robert Culver (Vice-President for Finance and Administration)
2002–4

Amy Meyers (Director, Yale Center for British Art)
2003–present

Susan Hockfield (Provost, Yale University)
2003–4

John Pepper (Acting Vice-President for Finance and Administration)
2004–6

Andrew Hamilton (Provost, Yale University)
2005–8

Peter Salovey (Dean of Yale College; from 2009 Provost of Yale University)
2005–present

Bruce Alexander (Acting Vice-President for Finance and Administration)
2006–7

Shauna King (Vice-President for Finance and Administration; from 2008 Vice-President for Finance and Business Operations)
2007–present

Members of the Board of Governors

Chester Kerr (Managing Director, Yale University Press)
1970–75

Louis Martz (Department of English)
1974–85

Ronald Paulson (Department of English)
1976–85

Jules Prown (Department of the History of Art)
1980–present

Robin Winks (Department of History)
1984–2004

Martin Price (Department of English)
1984–87

Frank Turner (Department of History)
1992–2010

Linda Peterson (Department of English)
1994–present

Richard Brodhead (Dean of Yale College)
1994–2004

Constance Clement (Acting Director, Yale Center for British Art)
1995–96, 2001–2

Thomas Crow (Department of History of Art)
1999–2000

Edward Cooke (Department of History of Art)
2001–6

Keith Wrightson (Department of History)
2004–present

Barbara Shailor (Deputy Provost for the Arts)
2005–present

David Joselit (Department of History of Art)
2007–9

Alexander Nemerov (Department of History of Art)
2009–present

Mary Miller (Dean of Yale College)
2009–present

Lloyd Suttle (Deputy Provost for Undergraduate and Graduate Programs)
2009–present

ADVISORY COUNCIL

With the establishment of the Centre an Advisory Council was set up to consider applications for financial support and to provide advice to the Board of Governors concerning general matters relating to the history of British art. In accordance with the Centre's Articles of Association which stated that 'the number of members of the Council shall not be less than four nor more than twelve' the first Advisory Council was comprised of nine distinguished representatives from the British academic and museum community. The twice-yearly meetings of the Council are chaired by the Director of Studies and are also usually attended by the Director of the Yale Center for British Art. The primary purpose of the Advisory Council is to make recommendations on grants and fellowships to be awarded by the Centre. In the first two years of the Centre's history, the Advisory Council was also used as a forum to discuss and determine other areas of the Centre's activities, including in particular the Centre's publications, staffing (appointments and salaries), accommodation and general policy decisions. The Council meets twice a year in March and October.

Advisory Council meeting October 2010 in the Seminar Room, 16 Bedford Square

Francis Haskell
Oxford University
1970–72, 1972–77, 1980–84, 1987–92, 1992–97

Michael Jaffé
Fitzwilliam Museum
1970–72, 1972–77, 1983–88

Anthony Blunt
Courtauld Institute of Art
1970–72, 1972–77

John Pope-Hennessey
British Museum
1970–72, 1972–77

Oliver Millar
Surveyor, Queen's Pictures
1970–74, 1974–79, 1982–87

Norman Reid
Tate Gallery
1970–75, 1975–78

Roy Strong
Victoria & Albert Museum
1970–73, 1973–78, 1985–90

Ellis Waterhouse
British Library
1970–85

Francis Watson
Wallace Collection
1970–75

Michael Kitson
Courtauld Institute of Art
1972–75?, 1980–85

Peter Lasko
Courtauld Institute of Art
1975–80

Graham Reynolds
Victoria & Albert Museum
1976–81, 1981–84

John A. Gere
British Museum
1977–1982

Alan Bowness
Tate Gallery
1977–1982, 1984–1989

ADVISORY COUNCIL

Michael Levey
National Gallery
1977–82, 1982–87, 1987–90

John Gage
Cambridge University
1978–83

John Hayes
National Portrait Gallery
1978–83, 1989–94

Martin Butlin
Tate Gallery
1979–84

John Steer
Birkbeck College, London
1982–87

Richard Ormond
National Portrait Gallery
1983–88

John Ingamells
Wallace Collection
1984–89

Joseph Mordaunt Crook
Royal Holloway College
1985–90

Terry Friedman
Leeds City Art Gallery
1987–92

David Bindman
University College, London
1987–92, 1994–99, 2002–7

Michael Kauffmann
Courtauld Institute of Art
1988–93

Neil MacGregor
National Gallery
1988–93, 1994–99

William Vaughan
Birkbeck College, London
1989–94

Mark Girouard
Architectural Historian
1990–95

Andrew Wilton
Tate Gallery
1990–95

Caroline Elam
The Burlington Magazine
1993–98

Robin Simon
Apollo Magazine
1993–98

Lisa Tickner
Middlesex University
1993–98

Christopher White
Ashmolean Museum
1993–98

Antony Griffiths
British Museum
1995–2000

Charles Saumarez Smith
National Portrait Gallery
1995–2000

Nicholas Serota
Tate Gallery
1997–2002

Duncan Robinson
Fitzwilliam Museum
1997–2002, 2005–10

Linda Colley
London School of Economics
1998–2003

Marcia Pointon
University of Manchester
1998–2003, 2006–present

David Solkin
Courtauld Institute of Art
1998–2003

Andrew Saint
University of Cambridge
1999–2004

Desmond Shawe-Taylor
Dulwich Picture Gallery
1999–2004

Richard Cork
Art critic
2000–5

Shearer West
University of Birmingham
2000–5

Malcolm Baker
Victoria & Albert Museum and University of Southern California
2001–6

Stephen Deuchar
Tate Britain
2002–7

Giles Waterfield
Royal Collection
2002–7

Lynda Nead
Birkbeck College, London
2003–8

Kim Sloan
British Museum
2003–8

Julius Bryant
Victoria & Albert Museum
2004–9

Maurice Howard
University of Sussex
2004–9

Joseph Koerner
Courtauld Institute of Art
2004–9

Andrew Causey
Manchester University
2005–10

Michael Rosenthal
University of Warwick
2005–10

Sandy Nairne
National Portrait Gallery
2007–present

Elizabeth Prettejohn
University of Bristol
2007–present

Caroline Arscott
Courtauld Institute of Art
2008–present

Paul Binski
University of Cambridge
2008–present

Philippa Glanville
Honorary Fellow of the Victoria & Albert Museum
2008–present

Mark Hallett
University of York
2008–present

Gavin Stamp
Architectural Historian
2009–present

Christine Stevenson
Courtauld Institute of Art
2009–present

Penelope Curtis
Tate Britain
2010–present

Nigel Llewellyn
Tate Britain
2010–present

Andrew Moore
Norwich Castle Museum
2010–present

PAUL MELLON CENTRE STAFF

Ellis K. Waterhouse
Director of Studies
1970–73

Jenny Henschel
Personal Assistant to the Director
1971

Veronica Boswell
Personal Assistant to the Director
1971–74

Frank Simpson
Librarian
1971–76

James Read
Assistant Photographer
1972–77

Christopher White
Director of Studies
1973–85

Penelope Somerville
Assistant Photographic Archivist
1974–75

Robin Vousden
Assistant Photographic Archivist
1974–75

Laurie Walker
Archivist
1974–75

Sarah Marsh
Administrative Assistant
1974–76

Frances Butlin
Assistant Photographic Archivist
1974–79

Diana Norman
Assistant Photographic Archivist
1975

Jeanette Brandon
Secretary to the Director of Studies
1975–76

Pamela Eyres
Assistant Photographic Archivist
1975–78

Evelyn Newby
Photographic Archivist
1975–84
Indexing of *Farington Diary*
1984–98

Antonia Yates
Photographic Archivist
1975–91

Zophia Hawes
Receptionist
1976–77

Catherine Firth
Secretary to the Director of Studies
1976–78

Brian Allen
Assistant Director and Librarian
1976–87
Deputy Director of Studies
1987–92
Director of Studies
1993–present

Zara Muirhead
Assistant to Photographic Archivist
1976–?81

Louise Wynne-Williams
Photographic Archivist
1978

Julie Semere
Secretary to the Director of Studies
1978–80

Ann Mytton
Secretary to the Director of Studies
1980–81

Vivien Knight
Administrative Assistant
1981–82

Carolyn Vaughan
Assistant Photographic Archivist
1981–82

Juliet Collings-Wells
Assistant Photographic Archivist
1981–94

Amanda Kavanagh
Assistant Photographic Archivist
1982–86

Kasha Jenkinson
Administrator
1982–2000
Assistant Director for Administration
2001–present

Clare Logan
Assistant Photographic Archivist
1982–c.1985

Clare Lloyd-Jacobs
Index of exhibition reviews in London newspapers
1983–94

Sheila O'Connell
Assistant Photographic Archivist
1986–87

Ellis K. Waterhouse
Director of Studies 1970–73

Christopher White
Director of Studies 1973–85

Michael Kitson
Director of Studies 1986–92

Brian Allen
Director of Studies 1993–present

PAUL MELLON CENTRE STAFF

Michael Kitson
Director of Studies
1986–92

Kim Sloan
Editor, *Dictionary of British and Irish Travellers to Italy 1701–1800 (DB&I)*
1986–92

Alice Warden
Junior Administrative Assistant
1987

Philippa Brown
Junior Administrative Assistant
1988–89
1991–91

Fenella Taylor
Junior Administrative Assistant
1989–91

Carol Blackett-Ord
Assistant Editor *DB&I*
1989–94

Arabella Sim
Junior Administrative Assistant
1991–93

Joanne Elvins
Assistant Editor *DB&I*
1992–94

Sophie McKinlay
Administrative Assistant
1993–94

Elizabeth Powis
Librarian
1993–97

Victoria Sharp
Assistant Editor *DB&I*
1993–98

Guilland Sutherland
Editor, PMC Publications
1993–present

Emma Lauze
Administrative Assistant/Publications
1994–98
Director's Assistant
1998–2001
Photographic Archivist
2001–present

Steven Parissien
Assistant Director
1995–2001

Amanda Robinson
Information Officer
1995–2002

Vivienne Redhead
Receptionist
1996
Yale-in-London Coordinator
1996–present

Kathryn Cureton
Receptionist
1996–97

Dawn Goddard
Receptionist/Administrative Assistant
1997–98

Emma Floyd
Librarian
1997–present

Natasha Held
Library Assistant
1998
Acting Librarian
2001–2
2005–6

Alexandra Finch
Receptionist/Administrative Assistant
1998–2001

Mary Peskett Smith
Special projects
2000–4
Grants Administrator
2004–present

Louise Thacker
Receptionist
2001–2

Frank Salmon
Assistant Director for Academic Activities
2001–6

Maisoon Rehani
Information Officer
2002–present

Lydia Marçal
Receptionist
2003

Ebony Francis
Administrative Assistant
2003–4

Lucy Nixon
Administrative Assistant
2004–8

Martin Postle
Assistant Director for Academic Activities
2007–present

Ella Fleming
Administrative Assistant
2008–present

Charlotte Brunskill
Project Archivist
2008–9

Victoria Lane
Project Archivist
2010–present

Senior Research Fellows

John Ingamells, 1992–2010
Dictionary of British and Irish Travellers to Italy 1701–1800; Allan Ramsay: A Complete Catalogue of his Paintings; Letters of Sir Joshua Reynolds; Mid-Georgian Portraits; 1760–1790; Dulwich Picture Gallery: British; Later Stuart Portraits 1685–1714

Judy Egerton, 1998–2007
George Stubbs, Painter

Elizabeth Einberg, 1998–present
William Hogarth catalogue

Hugh Belsey, 2006–present
Thomas Gainsborough portraits catalogue

Maria-Dolores Sánchez Jáuregui Alpañés, 2006–present
The Westmorland Project

Eric Shanes, 2008–present
J.M.W. Turner biography

Alex Kidson, 2009–present
George Romney catalogue

Paul Spencer-Longhurst, 2009–present
Richard Wilson catalogue

Staff formerly at the Paul Mellon Foundation

Kenneth Sharpe
Senior Research Assistant (PMF)
1964–69
Archivist (PMC)
1969–74

Douglas Smith
Photographer (PMF, PMC)
1964–96

Marion Spencer
Senior Research Assistant (PMF, PMC)
1965–74

Mary Dougal
Secretary to the Director (PMF, PMC)
1968–71

COLLECTIONS: THE LIBRARY

IN THE FIRST YEARS of the Paul Mellon Centre's existence, the library did not play a pivotal role since its prime use was in providing information for annotating mounts in the photographic archive. When the Centre was established in 1970 the first Director of Studies, Professor Ellis Waterhouse (1905–1985) appointed a librarian, Frank Simpson (1911–2002) who over the course of a long career had previously been employed at the Courtauld Institute of Art, at the art dealer Knoedler's London office and (alongside Waterhouse) at the Barber Institute of Fine Arts at the University of Birmingham. The purchasing policy was primarily limited to acquiring monographs, catalogues raisonnés and collection catalogues and, initially, little attempt was made to purchase more discursive texts. The proximity of the British (Museum) Library and the University of London library at Senate House meant that additional needs could be provided elsewhere.

By the mid-1970s however it was decided that the library should be built up as a resource for visiting scholars rather than simply being a resource for photographic archive staff. The decision was made in 1973 to purchase as far as possible all recently published books on British art, an aim that continues to this day. The introduction of the Yale-in-London programmes in 1977 gave further impetus to expansion with the needs of Yale undergraduates also having to be met. Over subsequent years approximately 300–500 books and exhibition catalogues were purchased each year. When Frank Simpson retired in October 1976, a new position of Assistant Director and Librarian was created which combined both librarian and academic duties, a post filled by Brian Allen, and in the following years the library continued its steady growth. In 1983 Clare Lloyd-Jacob was employed on a project to collect photocopies of reviews of art exhibitions in 18th-century British newspapers. This resource, eventually covering the years 1760–1793, has become a much-used asset. By the late 1980s the growth of the photographic archive had slowed primarily because so many auction sale catalogues were copiously illustrated but the library continued to expand. This inevitably created pressure on the limited space in the Centre's modest premises at 20 Bloomsbury Square. The need for a properly qualified full-time librarian had long been apparent and when Brian Allen was appointed Director of Studies in 1992 he created the new post of librarian with Elizabeth Powis, formerly librarian of the Barber Institute of Fine Arts at the University of Birmingham, as

The Library, shortly after moving to 16 Bedford Square in 1996

the first incumbent. By the time of the move to 16 Bedford Square in May 1996, the library had grown to contain approximately 10,000 books and exhibition catalogues as well as periodicals and thousands of auction sale catalogues. One of the advantages of the new building was the existence there of a large room that could serve as the Centre's first dedicated library reading room. Emma Floyd, former Librarian of the National Portrait Gallery, succeeded Elizabeth Powis early in 1997 and began the process of automating the library catalogue. By the middle of 1998 and with the help of Natasha Held the library was classified and catalogued onto a computerised library management system.

Over the years a steady flow of donations and large purchases have augmented the library's collections. A large collection of sale catalogues was acquired from the art dealers Tooth in the mid-1970s and a significant collection of annotated sales catalogues was purchased from the estate of Ellis Waterhouse in 1985. From the late 1990s onwards the library began to attract donations and bequests from art historians, usually closely connected with the Centre. In 1999, David Bindman donated books on Westminster Abbey and the 18th-century sculptor Louis-François Roubiliac in memory of the Centre's third Director of Studies, Professor Michael Kitson, as well as a further donation in 2005 on his retirement from University College London. Perhaps most notable was the very significant bequest of 800 books from the library of the late architectural historian John Cornforth, bequeathed by him to the National Trust but subsequently transferred to the Centre in August 2004. This added considerably to the Centre's holdings on the history of the country house and 18th-century decorative arts. By 2007 the library was growing at a considerable pace: a collection of books and guides on 17th-century painting from the collection of the late Sir Oliver Millar (1923–2007) was donated in the summer of that year. The following year a number of exhibition catalogues on 20th-century artists and on the subject of the grand tour were donated by the family of the late Sir Brinsley Ford (1908–1999) and the late Sir Howard Colvin (1919–2007) bequeathed a collection of PhD theses, annotated copies of his *Dictionary* and a collection of modern country-house guides.

The library's strengths had now begun to become more publicly apparent. Alexandra Finch embarked on a project to assemble guide books to all country houses in England and to ensure the collection was as comprehensive as possible. A programme of visits from the staff of other libraries was organised as a means of publicising the collection to the wider scholarly community, including a visit from ARLIS/UK & Ireland in 2004, the members of AKMB (the Working Group of Art and Museum Libraries) from Germany in June 2001 and Librarians from Flanders, the Netherlands and Finland in 2006, and INHA (Institut national d'histoire de l'art), Paris in 2008. In 2003 the library's web OPAC was developed and launched allowing much wider access to the Centre's collections. The Centre's journals were also listed on arlis.net periodicals database. In late 2003 work began on adding to the library catalogue the collection of auction sales catalogues acquired from the estate of the late Sir Ellis Waterhouse. These are to be added to the SCIPIO database. The library was slowly developed in these years to create separate rooms for archival material, and for sales and periodical collections, culminating in the redevelopment of the mews garage into a library store with mobile shelving units. Wi-Fi wireless technology was installed in Spring 2007 and the library catalogue was adapted to allow online issuing, renewals and returns of books. These developments have resulted in increased visitor numbers, and the library being used by the Centre's staff, fellows, and Yale-in-London students as well as students and academics from the United Kingdom and abroad. Subject coverage has also broadened to encompass fine art and architecture and garden history as well as some decorative arts from the post-medieval period to the present day.

THE ARCHIVE

The Centre has attracted a steady stream of archive collections which are mainly the working papers of art historians who have been associated with the Centre's activities. The strength of the archives is the study of 17th- and 18th-century British art, although the range extends from the 16th to the 20th century and includes papers on foreign artists in England. The archives were gradually accumulated in a piecemeal way. Some, such as the Daphne Haldin (1899–1973) and Gilbert Benthall (1880–1961) archives, were probably donated at the time of the Paul Mellon Foundation but the first active acquisition was in 1977 from the art historian and gallery director, W.G. Constable (1887–1976) relating to his research for his monograph on Richard Wilson (1714–1782). The next major acquisition was the extensive photographic and research papers of Ellis K. Waterhouse in 1985.

Many archives were acquired for the purpose of producing publications. In 1988 Sir Brinsley Ford (1908–1999) gave his enormous archive of papers on the Grand Tour, which he had accumulated over the course of 40 years, with this specific intent. Brian Allen recommended that John Ingamells edit the mass of papers for publication and this began a long and continuing relationship between Ingamells and the archives. *A Dictionary of British and Irish Travellers in Italy, 1701–1800* was published in 1997. After publication, it was anticipated that the archive would be in less demand but the opposite was the case. The book served to generate more interest in the subject and researchers are keen to go back to the original Brinsley Ford papers in order to glean further material. Ingamells went on to edit Alastair Smart's (1922–1992) papers to complete the publication *Allan Ramsay: A Complete Catalogue of his Paintings* (1999) and he was instrumental in the acquisition of the research papers of his colleague and friend, Robert Raines (1909–1986). He has recently given his personal archives on Philip Mercier (c.1689–1760) and Andrea Soldi (1703–1771) to the archive.

In 1997, the Librarian, Emma Floyd, took on responsibility for the care of these collections which had continued to increase steadily. It was at this juncture that they started to be recognized as a discrete collection of archives and were brought together in one room. In 2007, when the Centre acquired the substantial and important archive of Sir Oliver Millar (1923–2007), the extent of the archives became apparent. It became evident that a professional archivist was needed to manage and catalogue the archives.

Charlotte Brunskill, Archivist & Records Manager at the National Portrait Gallery, was recruited on a one-year placement from November 2008 to begin this task but with the Centre's 40th anniversary fast approaching her attentions were diverted to the Centre's own records. Following consultation with staff, she started the process of creating an institutional archive for the Centre by reviewing and sorting the records, retaining or destroying material as appropriate, and cataloguing the records with long-term historic value. She also began to introduce a comprehensive Records Management programme as well as establishing retention schedules and devising plans for the electronic management of the Centre's records. Towards the end of the year, Charlotte Brunskill made a survey of the scholars' archives which were renamed the 'Collected Archives' so that they were seen as distinct from the institutional records of the Centre. She suggested that in order to make these resources more accessible they should be catalogued by a professionally qualified archivist. Victoria Lane was appointed to undertake this three-year project in July 2010. Meantime Krzysztof Adamiec continued to catalogue the Institutional Archives from October 2009 to April 2010 and Emma Lauze took over responsibility for them in July 2010.

An automated archive database, CALM, has been installed and the cataloguing project is starting to reveal the richness and sometimes unexpected content of the archives. The papers of John Hayes (1929–2005), for example, predictably include his research on Thomas Gainsborough (1727–1788) but also contain

John Ingamells working with the Brinsley Ford archive in 1994 at 20 Bloomsbury Square

correspondence with the artist Graham Sutherland (1903–1980). What is becoming apparent is that the Collected Archives expose the network of scholars, curators, dealers, collectors, publishers, museums and societies that have shaped discourses on artistic practice. As well as containing important original research and information on artists, they also chart the historiography of British art history.

THE PHOTOGRAPHIC ARCHIVE

THE PHOTOGRAPHIC ARCHIVE was begun in 1964 as part of the Paul Mellon Foundation which closed in 1969 (see pp.7–11). The Foundation's director Basil Taylor initially employed an in-house photographer, Douglas Smith, and when the Paul Mellon Centre was established in 1970 the photographic archive and its photographer transferred to the new organisation. The Centre set out to augment the Foundation's photographic archive and to provide a photographic service for scholars. By 1972, such was the scale of photographic work that the Centre had employed another photographer, James Read (1972–77). Both Read and Douglas Smith worked from a photographic studio in St John's Wood. In the 1970s and early 1980s the scale of acquisition of material in comparison to more recent years was impressive. In 1973–74, for instance, the photographers visited 137 collections, took 3,189 photographs, produced 15,945 prints and made 789 reprints.

PHOTOGRAPHIC ARCHIVE

In the early days the focus was on new photography of works in the salerooms, temporary exhibitions and private collections. Works that were difficult to find reproductions of elsewhere (such as at the Courtauld Institute's Witt Library) and that might potentially disappear from view (if on the art market) were given priority. The Centre worked closely with individual scholars to photograph specific works that they required for their research or for publications and, in effect, these were grants-in-kind.

By 1973 when the archive was almost ten years old certain idiosyncrasies had developed and Christopher White, the new Director of Studies, laid out in his first Annual Report a fresh focus and direction for the archive. The use of photographic archives was at that time more or less restricted to advanced students and established scholars but no interested member of the public was ever turned away. Although the archive was never intended to provide a comprehensive overview of all British art, by 1973 it was felt that its contents often gave an eccentric view of an artist's oeuvre because it was so heavily dependent on what happened to have passed through the art market or on whatever works individual scholars had requested to be photographed for their research. As a result, steps were taken to acquire photographs from public collections where negatives existed. This view was reinforced with the foundation of the Yale-in-London programme in 1977 when the Director of Studies decided that students should be able to find all the basic works of art in the Centre's boxes of photographs as well as some of the more obscure. He also noted that the emphasis had been placed on acquiring images to the detriment of mounting and filing them into boxes. As a result a full-time and two part-time assistants were hired to work on this area.

A gradual shift away from original photography to the acquisition of photographs from existing negatives had taken place by the mid-1970s. Most London auction sales continued to be viewed in search of good, unusual or documented works. Increasingly however, the salerooms by this date took their own photographs and this relieved the Centre of some part of this burden. The Centre sought to avoid duplicating material at the Courtauld Institute, whose Photographic Survey department was increasingly meeting the demand for new photography in larger private collections and country houses, by purchasing prints from the Photographic Survey rather than commissioning new photography. It was also decided that the Centre should avoid acquiring 20th-century works as the Tate Gallery was building a photographic collection in this area. After the opening of the Yale Center for British Art in 1977 the Centre in London supplied prints from its own negatives and has acted as an agent for the Yale Center's embryonic photographic archive.

Responsibility for the photographic archive always lay with successive Librarians. Frank Simpson (1971–1976) and subsequently Brian Allen (1976–1992) were in overall charge with assistance from key personnel, Evelyn Newby (1975–98) who acquired photographs from exhibitions and Antonia Yates (1975–1991) who acquired photographs from the salerooms. In the early years Patricia Barnden (1964–1978) planned the various expeditions of the Centre's two photographers. In 1998, Emma Lauze took over responsibility for the archive. By 1980 Douglas Smith had left St John's Wood and had established a photographic studio in the basement of 20 Bloomsbury Square. Since the late 1970s a number of collections of photographs have been bequeathed or acquired by the Centre from leading scholars and these holdings complement the existing collections (see p.28).

During the 1980s and 1990s the photographic archive continued to acquire photographs from the Courtauld's Photographic Survey, from salerooms and for Paul Mellon Centre publications. In recent years however there have been enormous changes in the photographic world with the increasing predominance of digital imagery and the strictures of copyright legislation. All the saleroom images added to the archive are now colour cuttings from auction catalogues since as a result of copyright legislation the salerooms will no longer supply images. Images acquired for the Centre's own publications are now almost exclusively digital and are not stored as part of the main sequence of boxes of the photographic archive.

The current size of the photographic archive is estimated to be about 90,000 reference photographs with about 30,000 of those emanating from the Centre's own negatives. The 18th century remains the focus of the archive with particularly strong holdings for key artists such as Reynolds, Gainsborough, Ramsay, Richard Wilson, Wright of Derby, Turner and Constable. Currently about 300, mostly colour, images are added to the archive each year.

The photographic archive in 20 Bloomsbury Square in the 1980s

SPECIAL COLLECTIONS

Library Collections

The Rev. Eric Baker
Temporary exhibition catalogues and dealers' catalogues.
Late 1970s. Gift of the Rev. Eric Baker.

Arthur Tooth & Sons
Auction catalogues.
1977. Gift of the Tooth family.

Sir Ellis K. Waterhouse
Auction catalogues.
September 1985. Purchased from Lady Waterhouse.

Duncan Bull
Country-house guidebooks and exhibition catalogues.
February 1999. Gift of Duncan Bull.

David Bindman
Books on Westminster Abbey and Louis-François Roubiliac in memory of Michael Kitson.
July 1999. Gift of David Bindman.

Christopher C. Lack
Twentieth-century exhibitions catalogues.
August 2003. Gift of Christopher Lack's son.

British Council
Books on 20th-century art.
2003. Donated by British Council.

John Cornforth
Books on decorative arts, architecture and especially the country house.
August 2004. John Cornforth bequest to National Trust.

David Bindman
Books and offprints on Romanticism and late 18th-/early 19th-century art.
August 2005. Gift of David Bindman.

Antonia Yates
Country-house guidebooks.
February 2006. Gift of Antonia Yates.

Warburg Institute
Country-house and castle guidebooks and other books.
May 2007. Donated by the Warburg from the collection of Joan Alcock.

Sir Oliver Millar
Books and exhibition catalogues on 17th- and 18th-century art, especially Anthony Van Dyck; country-house guidebooks; antiquarian books from the 17th and 18th centuries.
July 2007. Gift of Sir Oliver Millar's family.

Gilbert collection
Books on silver.
February 2008. Gift of Timothy Stevens.

Sir Howard Colvin
Theses on British architectural history. The interleaved copies of the first three editions of *Biographical Dictionary of British Architects*. A collection of modern guides to English country houses.
May 2008. Bequest of Sir Howard Colvin via his son Hugh Colvin.

Sir Brinsley Ford
Books on the Grand Tour, exhibition catalogues on 18th- and 20th-century artists.
June 2008. Gift of Sir Brinsley Ford's family.

Central St Martin's College of Art
Issues of *Art Bulletin*.
June 2008. Donated by Central St Martin's College of Art.

Geffrye Museum
Books on furniture and interior decoration.
July 2008. Donated by the Geffrye Museum.

David Solkin
Reviews of genre painting compiled by Hamish Miles, David Solkin and Greg Smith.
July 2008. Gift of David Solkin.

Sir Nicholas and Lady Goodison
Royal Academy pictures catalogues from the 1890s.
October 2008. Gift of Sir Nicholas and Lady Goodison via the Courtauld Institute.

English Heritage
Issues of *Country Life*.
May 2010. Gift of English Heritage.

Museum of London
Collection of books and back issues of *Country Life*.
October 2010. Donated by Museum of London.

Archive Collections

Gilbert Benthall
Three volumes of notebooks that contain drafts and notes for Benthall's unpublished account of English Art Schools in London, 1626–1780.
[*c.*1960s]. Source unknown.

Daphne Haldane
Material concerning her work on an unpublished 'Dictionary of Women Artists'.
[c. 1970]. Source unknown.

Frank Herrmann
Material concerning his publication *The English As Collectors.*
Early 1970s. Donor Frank Simpson.

William George Constable
Papers and photographs relating to Richard Wilson.
1977. Gift of W.G. Constable's family.

Sir Ellis K. Waterhouse
Collection of photographs of British paintings, drawings, watercolours and prints, correspondence and cuttings.
1985. Purchased from Lady Waterhouse.

Robert Raines
Material concerning foreign artists working in Britain in the early 18th century including, in particular, Peter Tillemans; Simon Verelst; Marcellus Laroon; Egbert van Heemskerck.
1986. Presented by John Ingamells.

Sir Brinsley Ford
Material on British & Irish travellers in Italy in the 18th century.
1988. Gift of Sir Brinsley Ford.

Alastair Smart
Material concerning Allan Ramsay, including photographs.
1992. Bequest of Alastair Smart.

Hugh Macandrew
Material concerning John Talman.
1999. Gift of Graham Parry.

Malcolm Stewart
Material concerning Guy Head.
2004. Gift of Malcolm Stewart.

Sir Roy Strong
Material concerning mainly Tudor and Jacobean art.
2004. Gift of Sir Roy Strong.

John Hayes
Material concerning Thomas Gainsborough; also Graham Sutherland, Thomas Rowlandson & Cincinnati Art Collection.
2005. Bequest of John Hayes.

Sir Oliver Millar
Material concerning British art, particularly the 17th & 18th centuries.
2007. Acquired from the estate of Sir Oliver Millar.

Sir Howard Colvin
Papers relating to church and country-house architecture, either associated with or inserted into Colvin's books.
2008. Bequest of Sir Howard Colvin via his son Hugh Colvin.

Christopher Wright
Material concerning British and Irish paintings in public collections.
2009. Gift of Christopher Wright.

John Ingamells
Research papers on Philip Mercier (c.1689–1760) and Andrea Soldi (1703–1771)
2010. Gift of John Ingamells

Photographic Archive Collections

William George Constable
Collection of photographs relating to Richard Wilson; also to John Constable and John Flaxman.
1977. Gift of Professor Giles Constable.

Dudley Snelgrove
Nine hundred negatives made of L.G. Duke collection of British drawings and watercolours.
1985/86. Gift.

David Solkin
Collection of c. 200 photographs of works by Richard Wilson.
1992–93. Purchased.

Joan Coutu
Two hundred and seventy-nine photographs of 18th-century West Indian architecture and sculpture.
1994. Gift.

The British Museum
Collection of black and white reference photographs of works in the Department of Prints and Drawings.
February 2009. Gift.

Tate Photographic Collection
Curatorial collection of reference photographs and cuttings of British Art.
March 2009. Gift.

Mary Bennett
Collection of 800 reference photographs on Ford Madox Brown.
September 2010. Gift.

William Packer
Collection of original typescript articles by the painter and critic relating to his work for the *Financial Times* and other journals.
2010. Gift.

YALE IN LONDON

When the Centre was founded it was not envisaged that undergraduate teaching would be part of the organisation's activities but by the mid-1970s it was increasingly apparent that it would be desirable for the Centre to establish a much closer rapport with Yale University. After extensive discussions between the Centre, the Yale Center for British Art and the university administration in 1975–76 it was decided to introduce an intensive Summer Term, the equivalent to a full semester at Yale and eligible for full credit. It was proposed that three courses would be offered by a combination of Yale faculty, Paul Mellon Centre staff and distinguished British academics, to take place over ten weeks and to examine various aspects of the history of British art and architecture with a significant part of each course involving visits to museums, galleries, buildings and landscapes. The first group of students arrived in London in late May 1977.

In 1979, after much discussion by Faculty, the Yale Summer Term at the Paul Mellon Centre became an independent programme offered to the undergraduate body under the aegis of a Yale committee. Under this new arrangement, the Yale Summer Programs Committee (which had originally been formed to oversee the use of the Yale campus during the summer for various programmes) had the authority to approve the Paul Mellon Centre Summer Term budget. Academic authority remained with the Yale faculty, with all course proposals (then as now) requiring approval by the Course of Study Committee.

From 1977 to 1981 the Centre offered each year a fully credited ten-week Yale Summer Programme. The 1982 Summer Term was cancelled because enrolment was affected by the introduction in the Fall of 1981 of the Centre's full-year programme. From 1983 the Summer Term was reduced to six weeks and consisted thereafter of two courses. In order to meet growing demand for places in the summer a second Summer Term was introduced in 2002. Since the majority of the students are not art history majors it was decided in 1985 (as with the longer Spring and Fall Yale in London programmes) gradually to offer courses in British literature, history or drama in addition to art and architectural history, to accommodate the academic requirements of many undergraduates.

In the early years students found their own short-term accommodation in London with help from the Paul Mellon Centre's staff but with the advent and timing of the six-week programme students could thereafter be accommodated at University of London dormitories during the summer vacation.

Early in 1981 the Provost of Yale appointed a committee to consider the possibility of establishing new programmes of study to be conducted at the Paul Mellon Centre. The committee recommended the establishment, on a trial basis, of a regular Yale College programme of interdisciplinary study in England throughout the academic year. It was proposed that the programme be approved for a period of three years, at which point a report would be submitted to Faculty recommending either its continuance on a permanent basis or its termination. The programme was offered as part of the Special Undergraduate Programmes in the Humanities, and was administered by the British Studies Programme. Thus Yale in London was established as a full-year programme of interdisciplinary studies in British Culture and Society, carrying Yale College credit. Students were able to enrol for one semester or an entire academic year and, in

Yale in London Summer 1977 students outside 20 Bloomsbury Square. Standing back row (right to left) Brian Allen, Ronald Paulson, Christopher White, Deborah Howard and Catherine Firth.

the first year, took three courses at the Paul Mellon Centre with the option of enrolling for one or two courses at the University of London. The latter arrangement, however, proved unsatisfactory primarily because of the inevitable timetable clashes with courses at the University of London but also because the nature of the courses at a British university was often significantly different from the American model. From September 1982, four courses were offered at the Centre, taught by a visiting Yale professor (who was expected to teach two of them) with the other courses taught by Paul Mellon Centre staff and local scholars. Up to eighteen students could be enrolled although, typically, groups of twelve to fifteen students were the norm. For almost two decades students had found it comparatively easy to find appropriate and affordable accommodation in central London, but by the mid-1990s the burgeoning property market was forcing up rents and students were increasingly being pushed to less desirable locations. As a result, the Board of Governors decided in 1999 that students should be charged Yale room rate for their accommodation and the Paul Mellon Centre would subsidise the rent for good quality central London apartments. This did much to increase the quality of life for students enrolled for a full semester.

In 1984 the Yale Committee declared the Yale in London programme a success and recommended that it continue. There have been only minor administrative changes since this date with one notable exception. From the late 1990s onwards recruitment for the Fall Semester began to falter whilst demand for the Summer Term dramatically increased. As a result it was decided in 2002 to abandon the Fall semester and to replace it with the additional six-week Summer Term.

1977, Summer
British Painting in the Age of Hogarth (non-credit)
Ronald Paulson, Yale University
English Landscape, 1630–1850 (double credit)
Christopher White, Paul Mellon Centre
Seventeenth- and Eighteenth-century Architecture
Deborah Howard, University College London

1978, Summer
English Art, 1526–1851
Jules Prown, Yale University
English History Painting
Jules Prown, Yale University
The English Country House, 1520–1840
John Harris, Royal Institute of British Architects

1979, Summer
English Landscape Painting, 1630–1850
Christopher White, Paul Mellon Centre
English Sculpture of the 18th and Early 19th Centuries
Nicholas Penny, University of Manchester
The Classical Tradition in English Architecture from Inigo Jones to John Nash
John Newman, Courtauld Institute of Art

1980, Summer
British Painting from Holbein to Turner
Ronald Paulson, Yale University
English Architecture, 1530–1830
Deborah Howard, University College London
British Drawings and Watercolours of the 18th and early 19th Century
Christopher White, Paul Mellon Centre

1981, Summer
Patrons, Art and Architecture in England in the 17th Century
Christopher White, Paul Mellon Centre
English Architecture from Wren to Nash
Nicholas Penny, University of Manchester
British Painting of the 19th Century
Teri Edelstein, Yale Center for British Art

1981, Fall
Art, Politics and Literature in the Tudor Age
Christopher White, Paul Mellon Centre
London in History and Literature
Lawrence Manley, Yale University

1982, Spring
Art, Politics and Literature in the Stuart Age
Christopher White, Paul Mellon Centre
Drama and Society in England: A Study of Four Periods
Lawrence Manley, Yale University

1982, Fall
Drama and Society in England: A Study of Four Periods
Dwight Culler, Yale University
Painting in England in the Age of Hogarth and Reynolds
Brian Allen, Paul Mellon Centre
The Rise and Fall of the Whig Supremacy
Derek Jarrett, Goldsmiths College, London
The Dialectic of Victorian Culture
Dwight Culler, Yale University

1983, Spring

Patrons, Art and Architecture in the 17th Century
Christopher White, Paul Mellon Centre

The Complexities of Change: The 'Long Revolution' in British Politics and Society from James I to Walpole
Penelope Corfield, Bedford College London

The Bloomsbury Group
Dwight Culler, Yale University

Britain's Decline as a World Economic Power and Its Effect on British Society 1914–1945
Donald Cameron Watt, London School of Economics

1983, Summer

The English Cathedral in the Middle Ages
Walter Cahn, Yale University

The Mediaeval Revival and Victorian Art
William Vaughan, University College London

1983, Fall

Drama and Society in England: A Study of Four Periods
Bryan J. Wolf, Yale University

Tudor Art and Architecture
Christopher White, Paul Mellon Centre

The Romantic Experience in England
Bryan J. Wolf, Yale University

Reality and Myth of the Industrial Revolution
Lisanne Radice, Brunel University, London

1984, Spring

English Poetry of the Middle Ages
Eric Gerald Stanley, University of Oxford

Revolution or Counter-Revolution? England under the Stuarts
Roger Lockyer, Royal Holloway College, London

Stuart Art and Architecture
Christopher White, Paul Mellon Centre

Drama and Society in Modern England
Donna Smith Vinter, Yale College

1984, Summer

Painting in Britain in the 18th Century
Brian Allen, Paul Mellon Centre

18th-century British Sculpture: Setting and Context
David Bindman, University of London

1984, Fall

England in the Age of Chaucer and the Pastons
F.R.H. Du Boulay, University College London

British Painting in the Age of Hogarth and Reynolds
Brian Allen, Paul Mellon Centre

Architecture and the Applied Arts in 18th-century England
Duncan Robinson, Yale Center for British Art

The 19th-century Novel, 1813–1872
Leonée Ormond, University of London

1985, Spring

Poetry and Politics in the English Tradition
Thomas Hyde, Yale University

Studies in Shakespeare and his Contemporaries
Thomas Hyde, Yale University

The Rise and Fall of the Whig Supremacy
Derek Jarrett, Goldsmiths College, London

Tudor and Stuart Domestic Architecture
Christopher White, Paul Mellon Centre

1985, Summer

Anglo-Saxon England
Charles McClendon, Yale University

Painting in Britain in the 18th Century
Brian Allen, Paul Mellon Centre

Shakespeare and the Modern Dramatic Tradition
Donna Smith Vinter, Yale College

Stonehenge, Spring 2003 students with Frank Salmon

Imperial War Museum, Salford, Spring 2007 students with William Vaughan

YALE IN LONDON COURSES

1985, Fall

Drama and Society in England: A Study of Four Periods
Alan Bewell, Yale University
British Painting in the 18th Century
Brian Allen, Paul Mellon Centre
The Complexities of Change: the Long Revolution in British Politics and Society from James I to Walpole
Penelope Corfield, Royal Holloway College, London
The Romantic Experience in England
Alan Bewell, Yale University

1986, Summer

British Romantic Landscape Painting
Michael Kitson, Paul Mellon Centre
British 18th-century Sculpture
David Bindman, University College London

1986, Fall

Revolution or Counter-Revolution? England under the Stuarts
Roger Lockyer, Royal Holloway College, London
Augustan Literary Theory and Practice
Derek Alsop, St Mary's College, London
British Art and Italy (double course)
Michael Kitson and Brian Allen, Paul Mellon Centre

1987, Spring

The Baroque Age in England
Brian Allen, Paul Mellon Centre
The British Monarchy 1714–1830: Power, Patronage and Public Image
Linda Colley, Yale University
Topics in British History from the Glorious Revolution of 1688 to the Loss of America in 1783
Linda Colley, Yale University
Drama and Society in Modern Britain
Donna Smith Vinter, Yale College

1987, Summer

City and Country in Anglo-American Literature and Art in the 19th and 20th Centuries
Alan Trachtenberg, Yale University
The Medieval Revival and Victorian Art
William Vaughan, London University

1987, Fall

British Painting from the Romantics to the Early Victorians
Michael Kitson, Paul Mellon Centre
Individualism and Society: Writing in England 1840–1890
Timothy Hilton, Norwich School of Art
Anglo-American Relations during World War II
John M. Blum, Yale University
Westminster Abbey and the Court Style
Pamela Z. Blum, Yale University

1988, Spring

British Painting from the Romantics to the Early Victorians
Michael Kitson, Paul Mellon Centre
Individualism and Society: Writing in England 1840–1890
Timothy Hilton, Norwich School of Art
Anglo-American Relations during World War II
John M. Blum, Yale University
Westminster Abbey and the Court Style
Pamela Z. Blum, Yale University

1988, Summer

Architecture in the Age of Wren
Michael Kitson, Paul Mellon Centre
The 18th-century Landscape Garden
Judith Colton, Yale University

1988, Fall

Painting and Sculpture in the Age of Hogarth
Brian Allen, Paul Mellon Centre
Sir Joshua Reynolds and late 18th-century British Painting
Michael Kitson, Paul Mellon Centre
Britain in the Era of the World Wars
John Turner, Royal Holloway College, London
The Idiom of 20th-century British Drama
John Northam, University of Bristol

1989, Spring

The Baroque Age in England
Brian Allen, Paul Mellon Centre
Complexities of Change: The Long Revolution in British Politics and Society from James I to Walpole
Penelope Corfield, Royal Holloway College, London
British Drama
Linda Peterson, Yale University
Studies in the Novel: City and Country in 19th-century Fiction
Linda Peterson, Yale University

1989, Summer

British Art in the 20th Century
Richard Humphreys, Tate Gallery
The English Country House in the 18th Century
Brian Allen, Paul Mellon Centre

1989, Fall

British Drama: Text and Performance
Gordon Turnbull, Yale University
The Novel and the City
Gordon Turnbull, Yale University
Britain in the 18th Century: Commerce, Consumers and Culture
Roy Porter, Wellcome Institute, London
Turner and Constable
Michael Kitson, Paul Mellon Centre

1990, Spring
British Painting in the 18th Century
Brian Allen, Paul Mellon Centre
Critics of Colonial Policy
Diana Wylie, Yale University
Britain in South Africa
Diana Wylie, Yale University
Shakespeare and Renaissance England
Timothy Kidd, Gonville and Caius, Cambridge

1990, Summer
English Medieval Architecture
Paul Binski, Yale University
The Age of Hogarth
Brian Allen, Paul Mellon Centre

1990, Fall
England and Britain, 1603–1660
Conrad Russell, University of London
British Art and Italy (double course)
Michael Kitson, Paul Mellon Centre
The Idiom of 20th-century British Drama
John Northam, University of Cambridge

1991, Spring
Shakespeare and his Theatrical Contemporaries
Murray Biggs, Yale University
Contemporary British Drama and Society
Murray Biggs, Yale University
British Romantic Painting
Michael Kitson, Paul Mellon Centre
Britain in the Era of the World Wars
John Turner, Royal Holloway College, London

1991, Summer
The English Country House in the 18th Century
Brian Allen, Paul Mellon Centre
British Art of the 20th Century
Richard Humphreys, Tate Gallery

1991, Fall
Art and Architecture in Britain: The 17th Century
Michael Kitson, Paul Mellon Centre
Revolution or Counter-Revolution? England under the Stuarts
Roger Lockyer, Royal Holloway College, London
The Age of Hogarth
Brian Allen, Paul Mellon Centre
Modern Drama: Text and Performance
Timothy Kidd, Gonville and Caius, Cambridge

1992, Spring
Art and Architecture in Britain: The 18th Century
Brian Allen, Paul Mellon Centre
Britain in the 18th Century: Commerce, Consumers and Culture
Roy Porter, Wellcome Institute, London
Victorian Social Criticism
David Bromwich, Yale University
British Theatre from Shakespeare to Shaw
David Bromwich, Yale University

1992, Summer
The English Country House in the 18th Century
Brian Allen, Paul Mellon Centre
British Art of the 20th Century
Richard Humphreys, Tate Gallery

Rievaulx Abbey, Spring 2005 students with Gillian Forrester

Bath, Summer 2004 Session 1 students

YALE IN LONDON COURSES

1992, Fall
British History, c.1688–1815
Linda Colley, Yale University
Turner and Constable
Michael Kitson, Paul Mellon Centre
The Culture of Empire under Queen Victoria
Linda Colley, Yale University
Modern Drama
Sheila Fox, independent critic and BBC producer

1993, Spring
Drama in Britain, 1590–1990
Ian Duncan, Yale University
British Painting in the 18th Century
Brian Allen, Paul Mellon Centre
Poverty, Philanthropy and Social Reform in Britain, 1750–1950
Franklyn Prochaska, Wellcome Institute, London
Dickens and His Age
Ian Duncan, Yale University

1993, Summer
Art and Architecture of the English Country House
Duncan Robinson, Yale University
The British Mystery Novel
Robin Winks, Yale University

1993, Fall
Seventeenth-century Art and Architecture in Britain
Brian Allen, Paul Mellon Centre
Revolution or Counter-Revolution? England under the Stuarts
Roger Lockyer, Royal Holloway College, London
The 19th-century Novel
Leonée Ormond, University of London
Drama and Theatre in Britain, 1593–1993
Timothy Kidd, Gonville and Caius, Cambridge

1994, Spring
Britain in the Era of the World Wars
John Turner, Royal Holloway College, London
Twentieth-century British Art
Frances Spalding, independent scholar
Jacobean Drama
Kevin Dunn, Yale University
Courtly Culture in Renaissance England
Kevin Dunn, Yale University

1994, Summer
Studies in the English Novel: City and Country
Linda Peterson, Yale University
Fantasy and Reality in Victorian Art
Robyn Asleson, Huntington Library

1994, Fall
British Painting in the 18th Century
Brian Allen, Paul Mellon Centre
Britain in the 18th Century: Commerce, Consumers and Culture
Roy Porter, Wellcome Institute, London
Victorian Fiction
Andrew Sanders, Durham University
Modern Drama
Sheila Fox, independent critic and BBC producer

1995, Spring
Shakespeare and his Theatrical Contemporaries
Murray Biggs, Yale University
Contemporary British Drama and Society
Murray Biggs, Yale University
Britain in the Era of the World Wars
John Turner, Royal Holloway College, London
Seventeenth-century Art and Architecture in Britain
Brian Allen, Paul Mellon Centre

1995, Summer
Landscape, Power and Representation
Esther da Costa Meyer, Yale University
The Novel and the City
Gordon Turnbull, Yale University

1995, Fall
Shakespeare and British Drama
John Rogers, Yale University
Revolution or Counter-Revolution? England under the Stuarts
Esther da Costa Meyer, Yale University
Studies in 17th-century English Literature
John Rogers, Yale University
The Baroque Age in England
Steven Parissien, Paul Mellon Centre

1996, Spring
The Age of Hogarth
Brian Allen, Paul Mellon Centre
Victorian Fiction
Andrew Sanders, Durham University
The British Empire 1783–1982
Richard Drayton, Lincoln College, Oxford
Modern Drama
Sheila Fox, independent critic and BBC producer

1996, Fall
Neoclassical Architecture in the Augustan Age
Steven Parissien, Paul Mellon Centre
Britain in the 18th Century: Commerce, Consumers and Culture
Roy Porter, Wellcome Institute, London
The 19th-century Novel: 1813–1872
Leonée Ormond, University of London
Drama and Society in England
Sheila Fox, independent critic and BBC producer

1997, Spring

British Painting in the 18th Century
Brian Allen, Paul Mellon Centre

Revolution or Counter-Revolution? England under the Stuarts
Roger Lockyer, Royal Holloway College, London

Literature and Religious Controversy, 1530–1640
Laura King, Yale University

Tradition and Theory in Contemporary English Theatre
Laura King, Yale University

1997, Summer

The Art and Architecture of the English Country House in the 18th Century (double course)
Brian Allen and Steven Parissien, Paul Mellon Centre

1997, Fall

Italy and the Arts in Britain, 1500–1800 (double course)
Brian Allen and Steven Parissien, Paul Mellon Centre

English Romance
Elizabeth Fowler, Yale University

Shakespeare and the English Theatre
Elizabeth Fowler, Yale University

1998, Spring

Architecture and Design in Regency Britain
Steven Parissien, Paul Mellon Centre

Politics and Society in Great Britain, 1688–1832
Leslie Mitchell, University College, Oxford

Victorian Fiction
Andrew Sanders, Durham University

Modern British Drama
Sheila Fox, independent critic and BBC producer

1998, Summer

The Metropolitan Culture of London
Andrew Saint, University of Cambridge

British Drama
Murray Biggs, Yale University

1998, Fall

Building Victorian Britain
Steven Parissien, Paul Mellon Centre

Tradition and Innovation in British Theatre
Blakey Vermuele, Yale University

Manners, Morals, Culture and Society, Behn to Dickens
Blakey Vermuele, Yale University

The British People and the State, 1789–1901
Katherine Prior, University of Cambridge

1999, Spring

The Age of Hogarth
Brian Allen, Paul Mellon Centre

Revolution or Counter-Revolution? England under the Stuarts
Roger Lockyer, Royal Holloway College, London

Shakespeare and his Contemporaries
Katherine Rowe, Yale University

Sixteenth-century Lyric and Long Poem
Katherine Rowe, Yale University

1999, Summer

Interpreting England's Historic Built Environment
Steven Parissien, Paul Mellon Centre

Modern British Drama
Sheila Fox, independent critic and BBC producer

Liverpool, Summer 2006 Session 2 students with Angus Trumble

Stourhead, Summer 2005 Session 2 students

YALE IN LONDON COURSES

1999, Fall

Patronage, Design and the Anglo-French Wars, 1660–1714
Steven Parissien, Paul Mellon Centre

Sites and Spaces of Renaissance Poetry
Ramie Targoff, Yale University

Tradition and Innovation on the London Stage
Ramie Targoff, Yale University

Politics and Society in Great Britain, 1688–1832
Leslie Mitchell, University College, Oxford

2000, Spring

Art and Architecture in Romantic England
Brian Allen and Steven Parissien, Paul Mellon Centre

An Introduction to British Drama
Nigel Alderman, Yale University

From Romantic to Victorian: British Literature, 1814–1850
Nigel Alderman, Yale University

Modern Empires: A Comparative History
Robin Winks, Yale University

2000, Summer

Building Victorian Britain
Steven Parissien, Paul Mellon Centre

Modern British Drama
Sheila Fox, independent critic and BBC producer

2000, Fall

London in Fiction, Poetry and Biography, 1700–1999
Traugott Lawler, Yale University

Shakespeare and the British Theatre
Traugott Lawler, Yale University

Georgian London
Steven Parissien, Paul Mellon Centre

The British People and the State, 1780–1901
Katherine Prior, University of Cambridge

2001, Spring

The Baroque Age in England (double course)
Brian Allen and Steven Parissien, Paul Mellon Centre

Politics and Society in Great Britain, 1688–1832
Leslie Mitchell, University College, Oxford

Modern British Drama
Sheila Fox, independent critic and BBC producer

2001, Summer

Interpreting England's Historic Built Environment
Steven Parissien, Paul Mellon Centre

Orwell and English Culture 1930–1950
David Bromwich, Yale University

2001, Fall

Italy and the Arts in Britain, 1530–1830 (double course)
Brian Allen, Paul Mellon Centre and Richard Hewlings, English Heritage

Revolution or Counter-Revolution? England under the Stuarts
Roger Lockyer, Royal Holloway College, London

Modern British Drama
Sheila Fox, independent critic and BBC producer

2002, Spring

The British People and the State, 1780–1901
Katherine Prior, University of Cambridge

Victorian Fiction
Andrew Sanders, Durham University

Patronage, Design and the Anglo-French Wars, 1660–1714
Richard Hewlings, English Heritage

Modern British Drama
Sheila Fox, independent critic and BBC producer

2002, Summer Session 1

Nation and Metropolis in Early Modern England, c.1500–c.1750
Keith Wrightson, Yale University

British Architecture and Culture, 1714–1753: The Rule of Taste
Frank Salmon, Paul Mellon Centre

2002, Summer, Session 2

British Art of the Georgian Era
Martin Postle, Tate Britain

Truth and Masquerade: Performing Gender, Performing Identity
Elizabeth Dillon, Yale University

2003, Spring

British Literature and the Modern Metropolis
Laura Frost, Yale University

Contemporary British Drama
Laura Frost, Yale University

Revolution or Counter-Revolution? England under the Stuarts, 1603–1714
Roger Lockyer, Royal Holloway College, London

Enlightenment and Revolution: Architecture and its Contexts, c.1750–1840
Frank Salmon, Paul Mellon Centre

2003, Summer, Session 1

Modern British Drama
Sheila Fox, independent critic and BBC producer

British Architecture and Culture 1714–1753: The Rule of Taste
Frank Salmon, Paul Mellon Centre

2003, Summer, Session 2

British Art in London, 1815 to the Present
Tim Barringer, Yale University

The Literature of London in Crisis
John Rogers, Yale University

2004, Spring

Revolution or Counter-Revolution? England under the Stuarts 1603–1714

Roger Lockyer, Royal Holloway College, London

Modern British Drama

Sheila Fox, independent critic and BBC producer

British Landscape 1750–1850: Representation, Interpretation and Intervention

Scott Wilcox, Yale Center for British Art

2004, Summer, Session 1

British Art of the Georgian Era

Martin Postle, Tate Britain

Poetry and the City

Claude Rawson, Yale University

2004, Summer, Session 2

Modern British Theatre

Laura King, Yale University

British Architecture and Culture 1714–1753: The Rule of Taste

Frank Salmon, Paul Mellon Centre

2005, Spring

London Artists

Gillian Forrester, Yale Center for British Art

Modern British Drama

Sheila Fox, independent critic and BBC producer

London and the Country

Tim Fulford, Nottingham Trent University

British Architecture and Culture 1714–1753: The Rule of Taste

Frank Salmon, Paul Mellon Centre

2005, Summer, Session 1

William Morris: The Theory and Practice of Craft

Edward Cooke, Yale University

Contemporary British Drama

Sheila Fox, independent critic and BBC producer

2005, Summer, Session 2

British Art of the Georgian Era

Martin Postle, Tate Britain

London: Modern British Urban Fiction

Nigel Alderman, Yale University

2006, Spring

Revolution or Counter-Revolution? England under the Stuarts 1603–1714

Roger Lockyer, Royal Holloway College, London

Italy and the Arts in Britain 1530–1830 (double course)

Brian Allen and Frank Salmon, Paul Mellon Centre

Nineteenth-century Writings on Landscape

Leonée Ormond, University of London

2006, Summer, Session 1

Shakespeare, History, Nationality and Identity

Elliott Visconsi, Yale University

British Architecture and Culture 1714–1753: The Rule of Taste

Frank Salmon, Paul Mellon Centre

2006, Summer, Session 2

Nation and Metropolis in Early Modern England, c.1500–c.1750

Keith Wrightson, Yale University

Public Monuments in Victorian and Edwardian London

Angus Trumble, Yale Center for British Art

2007, Spring

Politics and Society in Great Britain, 1688–1832

Leslie Mitchell, University College, Oxford

Modern British Drama

Sheila Fox, independent critic and BBC producer

The Country and the City 1785–1943

Tim Fulford, Nottingham Trent University

Artists and Society in Britain c.1790–1900

William Vaughan, University of London

Spring 2009 students at a London landmark

Spring 2003 students at Holkham in Norfolk

YALE IN LONDON COURSES

2007, Summer, Session 1
British Art of the Georgian Era
Martin Postle, Paul Mellon Centre
English Comic Fiction from the 18th to the 20th Century
Andrew Sanders, Durham University

2007, Summer, Session 2
Modern British Drama
Joseph Roach, Yale University
Modern British Architecture
Sandy Isenstadt, Yale University

2008, Spring
Revolution or Counter-Revolution? England under the Stuarts 1603–1703
Roger Lockyer, Royal Holloway College, London
Dream-Vision in the Middle Ages and Renaissance
Jessica Brantley, Yale University
Modern British Drama
Jessica Brantley, Yale University
British Art of the Georgian Era
Martin Postle, Paul Mellon Centre

2008, Summer, Session 1
British Art of the Georgian Era
Martin Postle, Paul Mellon Centre
English Comic Fiction from the 18th to the 20th Century
Andrew Sanders, Durham University

2008, Summer, Session 2
The Origins of the British Empire
Steven Pincus, Yale University
Monuments and Memory 1600–1945
Roger Bowdler, English Heritage

2009, Spring
Victorian Fiction
Andrew Sanders, Emeritus, Durham University
Modern British Drama
Sheila Fox, independent critic and BBC producer
Politics and Society in Great Britain, 1688–1832
Leslie Mitchell, University College, Oxford
The Gothic Revival in British Architecture from the 17th to the 20th Century
Gavin Stamp, architectural historian

2009, Summer, Session 1
British Art of the Georgian Era
Robin Simon, Editor *British Art Journal*
Modern British Drama
Sheila Fox, independent critic and BBC producer

2009, Summer, Session 2
Modernist London: Literature and the Arts
Pericles Lewis, Yale University
William Morris: The Theory and Practice of Art
Edward Cooke, Yale University

2010, Spring
Americans Abroad
Susan Chambers, Yale University
The London Stage
Susan Chambers, Yale University
Politics and Society in Great Britain 1688–1832
Leslie Mitchell, Oxford University
British Art and Landscape
Martin Postle, Paul Mellon Centre

2010, Summer, Session 1
British Art and Landscape
Martin Postle, Paul Mellon Centre
Modern British Theatre
Sheila Fox, independent critic and BBC producer

2010, Summer, Session 2
Society and Culture in London from Stow to Hogarth c.1560–1760
Keith Wrightson, Yale University
The History of Suburban Ideas and Practices in England from Regent's Park to Milton Keynes
Jay Gitling, Yale University

YALE IN LONDON STUDENTS

1977, Summer
Allan Chong
Sarah Fetherston
Christopher Goodrich
Catharine Long
Heather Macisaac
Laura Roe
Shelley Sadin
Mary Siliciano
James Stein
Ella Torrey
Susan Vernon

1978, Summer
Nancy Adelson
Robert Arnold
Deborah Binder
Sandra Carrithers
R. Anne Casscells
Joseph Goldstein
Cecily Horton
Avery Knox
Lisa Patten
Nicholas Smith
Archbold Vanebueuren
Clinton Wilder

1979, Summer
William Cross
Amy Feldhun
Elizabeth Frost
Sofia Haberman
Lisa Leinbach
Eugene Nesbit
Kirk Savage
Laurie Wallach
Tiana Wimmer
Michiko Yoshizawa

1980, Summer
Claudia Allen
Elizabeth B. Brainerd
Alexandra Claire Cohn
Christina Rose Gianelli
Beverley C. Graham
Kathleen A. James
Laurie McGovern
Christine Louise Olsen
Oliver W. Radford
Ralph W. Rose
Richard L. Selden
Claire Hardie Wadlington
Alexandra West

1981, Summer
Kathryn A. Brizzolara
Richard J. Burston
Lea Anne Copenheffer
Christopher DeRoetth
Sara E. Kaplan
Sharon Ann Livieri
Mark V. Morocco
Andrea S. Neil
Sarah B. Putney
William J. Quinn
Doreen Stoller
Joanna Wissinger

1981, Fall
Robin Cembalest
Brian Crawley
Edward Dumont
Michael P. Green
Lori Humphrey
Diane Ives
Tamar Katz
Stephanie Lowet
David Payne
Deidre Sullivan
Kristin Teergarden
Stephen Tomlin
Harold Wrobel

1982, Spring
Peter Brooks
Caroline J. Brown
Louise Burnham
Anne Debevoise
Diane Fox
Susan Yee-Shan Leung
Mary Sales
Landon Storrs
Glenn Sullivan
Julie Marie Sullivan
Kristin Teergarden
Stacy Wolf

1982, Fall
Gill Anav
Karen Cook
Andrea Diaz
Martha Foote
Kenneth Goldstein
Kenneth C. Handy
Brenda L. Jones
Karen Swanson

1983, Spring
Hilary Bennett
Laura Cutler
Roman Darmer
Maxine Eichner
Stephen Erhart
Jill Fisher
Laura George
Lorena Lopes
Amy Malsin
Bailey McClure
Pamela Puryear
Mary Solomons
Charlotte Sonnenblick
Jane Tillinghast
Mary Trokel
Cynthia Watts
Douglas Wayne
Sarah Reed

1983, Summer
Nancy Berkowitz
Gretchen Biggs
Gina Brown
Mary Anne Christy
Margaret Favretti
Elizabeth Gildea
Hilary Knittle
Peter Schmitz
Edward Vilga
Lauren Wojtyla

Summer 2009 Session 2 students on the steps of 16 Bedford Square

Seminar Room, 16 Bedford Square, Spring 2009 students with Andrew Sanders

YALE IN LONDON STUDENTS

1983, Fall
Emily Ballew
Joy Bochner
Marc Bousquet
Mary Christy
Tobias Emmerich
Stephen Erhart
Melisa Hall
Donna Kaiser
Eugenia Kelly
Mary Jane Mace
Joy McDougall
Mariangeli Miranda
Andrew Ritten
Alexandra Rockwell
Anne Rossheim
Elisabeth Roth
Margaret Russell
Katherine Van Den Blink

1984, Spring
Elizabeth Chew
Huntley Funsten
Jessamyn Jackson
Mary Kilkelly
Amy Ludwig
David Morgan
Margaret Russell
Ira Shapiro
Andrew Vasey
Richard Weiss
Karin Weng
Barbara Will
Margaret Wrinkle
Debra Zarlin

1984, Summer
Elizabeth Adams
John Dempsey
Sheryl Etergino
Michele Kenzie
Susan Lavine
Bruce McCashin
Stephen Reily
Becca Roth
Errol Small
Sarah Stephenson

1984, Fall
Steven Bailey
Michael Cavanaugh
Celia Converse
Karen Couch
Ellen Epstein
Sarah Gillman
Kim Heirston
Laura Hoffman
Sarah Hutt
Karen Hwa
Louise Kennelly
Katharine Kirkpatrick
Robert Klein
Dorothy Meek
Mark Simonoff
Elizabeth Wein

1985, Spring
Christopher Ashley
Ellen Epstein
Lauri Feldman
Ann Flower
Janice Friedman
Mary Grant
Phillip Hillhouse
Martin Hipsky
Karen Hwa
Hugh Kennedy
Lisa Kovetz
Elise Lemire
Martha McKnight
Maria Montoya
Paul Outka
Stephen Reily
William Shirky

1985, Summer
Timothy Albright
Mary Bing
Brenda Breslauer
Robert Claar
Kathy Collen
Sarah Donaldson
Amy Galper
Meredith Hyde
Susan Marotta
Paul McClure
Ellen Mendlow
Ellen Munson
Jonathan Rabb
Laura Spadone
Kara Stein
Jane Vernon
Anne Wallace
Serena Young

1985, Fall
Nicholas Avdellas
Holly Bowen
George Caulkins
Joyce Davis
Libby Driscoll
Noah Emmerich
Kate Goodale
Holly Hegener
Sarah Hickerson
Nicholas Johnson
Charlie Lord
Emmett Powell

1986, Summer
Elizabeth Arnold
Christopher Baker
William Barnett
Elizabeth Breyer
Diana Glassman
Astrid Hoffius
Sarah Hundley
Catherine Kennedy
Karen McKelvy
Charles Meyer
Katherine Meyer
William Shapard
Courtney H. Smith
Donna Thompson
Heidi Waterfield
Alexia Zerbinis

1986, Fall
Elizabeth Anscombe
Reed Brozen
Ravenel Curry
Beth Flanagan
Debra Gann
Katharine Gearhart
Eric Lee
Robert McIntosh
David Nichols
Steven Peikin
Robert Persing
Mary-Alice Pomputius
Eric Sorenson
Sarah Thailing
Pamela Thurschwell
Aileen Tsui
David Williamson

1987, Spring
Julie Applebaum
Elizabeth Blair
Lucile Bruce
Denise Byrd
Abigail Frank
Katharine Gearhart
Susan Kleckner
Matthew Levey
Beverly Lindh
Robert McIntosh
Jean McLoughlin
Joseph McMaster
David Snyder
Sophie Young

1987, Summer
Thomas Ahn
Jennifer Barrett
David Conant
Paul Fox
Holly Gates
Grace Glassman
Mary Ruffin Hanbury
Jennifer Lee
Tim Lewis
Elizabeth McCance
David Pollay
Rob Pyott
David Saltzman
Nadine Schaeffer
Susan Skrzypczak
Jonathan Warren
Torrance York

1987, Fall
Marc Ackerman
Catherine Aswumb
Alison Begner
Mary Bing
Sarah Burnes
Eliza Carlson
JoAnn Cohn
Margaret Driscoll
Margot Hoffman
Christopher Krentz
Benjamin Lipton
Amon Liu
David Martz
Melissa Palmer

Mary Beth Possomando
Claudia Taylor
Steven Young

1988, Spring

Andrea Allen
Rebecca Allen
Wylie Allen
Alison Ambach
Meredith Bennett
Lindsay Bullard
A. Marc Caplan
Rachel Carner
Sarah Friedman
Robert Losasky
Elizabeth Outka
Anne Robinson
Elizabeth Rosenkrantz
Richard Sargent
Laura Smith
Shelley Wilson

1988, Summer

Dorothy Alveizatos
Antonia Carew-Watts
Melissa Chung
Judith Federbush
Peter Giblin
Jeffrey Naiman
Adrienne Neff
Julie Ongaro
Michelle Pentz
Jon Seydl

1988, Fall

Liam Callanan
Laurie Conniff
Jane Hedreen
Anne Knott
Cynthia Lollis
Renee Romano
Amelia Starr

1989, Spring

Elizabeth Barcott
Heather Beatty
Holly Beatty
Sherrod Blankner
William Crosby
Caroline Curry
Robert Jackson
Jason Jacobs
Whitney Nelson
Katherine Riker
Jane Seiter
Allegra Shapiro
Hilary Trotman
Andrew Walvoord
Kristin Wolcott

1989, Summer

Daniel Bursky
Abigail Crozier
Louise Johnson
Jennifyr Lux
Robert Meinhardt
Marisa Nightingale
Stephen Pike
Shannon Summers
Douglas Webster
Stephen Youngwood

1989, Fall

Martin Acevedo
Laura Arrillaga
Jeremiah Carew
Sue Ann Gormley
Carol Hagan
Craig Kennedy
Jeremy Klee
Robert Koppell
Pamela Kroll
Sara Landis
Kenneth O'Flaherty
Elizabeth Reagad
Robert Schmults
Christopher Slowk
Andrew Smith
Chester Te
Richard Theobald

1990, Spring

Marshall Bartlett
Frank Dill
Raymond Kam
Melania Kasfir
Heather Kelly
Debra Loevy
Mark Miller
Nicholas Ross
David Seeberan
Brooks Taylor

1990, Fall

Elizabeth Barker
Elana Bober
Kristina Crothers
Adam Drucker
Steven Edward
Jonathan Hevenstone
Kristin Mattson
Jonathan Steckler
An-Dan Thi
Jean Turner
Paul Weinberger

1991, Spring

Reine Boyer
Jessica Buckley
John Cantarella
Rachel Dickstein
Elliot Grant
Rebecca Kramer
Fielder Lampkins
Rachel Murphy
Vanessa Peterson
Hillary Quarles
Lisa Ronthal
Jordan Schildcrout
David Seronas
Joshua Swiller

Summer 2005 Session 1 students in the Bodleian Library with Edward Cooke

On the River Thames at Greenwich, Summer 2007 Session 2 students with Sandy Isenstadt

YALE IN LONDON STUDENTS

1991, Fall
Hillary Blumberg
Timothy Carnes
Julia Ditelberg
Cynthia Elden
Julia Hayes
Suzanne Huber
Benjamin Justice
Jennifer Katz
Peter Menzies
Gabrielle Silver

1992, Spring
Ashley Fox
Jean Johnson
David Kovel
Geoff Lehman
Yoji Nimura
Janice Pomerance
Ari Shwedel
John Taylor
Melissa Wolff

1992, Summer
Ligia Bouton
Jessica Dawson
Alicia Gale
Callie Rogers
Jason Stavers
Kirsten Strotz
Belinda Tate
Sean Tobin
Perrin Wicks
Bethany Williston

1992, Fall
Kathryn Clippinger
Harper Montgomery
Sammy Redd
Hannah Ross
Catherine Schenker
Thomas Shakow
Alexandra Shapiro
Tristan Steel
Lorinda Wong

1993, Spring
Esther Choo
Alison Conlon
Elysa Engelman
Gregory Fontana
Claire Hall
Jennifer Hock
Karin Hoppmann
Meghan Klee
Jessica Lissy
Mary Peck
Antonious Porch

1993, Summer
Naja Armstrong
John Blouch
Nina Boulard
Melissa Brown
Robert Hodgson
Robin Kemper
Allison Randolph
Adrian Wolff

1993, Fall
Sarah Baldwin
John Contos
Elizabeth Dodge
Naomi Goguts
William Janensch
Brian Murphy
Meagan Ortega
Anne Paul
Jeanette Plourde
Raymond Rast
David Scarpelli
Nicole Sudberg
Andrew Zurcher

1994, Spring
Sheri-Ann Butterfield
Celia Curtis
Neva Daley
Natasha Farny
Katherine Keating
Miranda Kreitzer
Leora Maltz
Sharon Otterman
Melissa Plotkin
Alison Siegler
Paula Silverman
Emily Sklar
Lisa Wangsness

1994, Summer
Katherine Bell
Frederico Dautzenberg
Jason Finestone
Amina Hines
Stefanie Lieberman
Susan Meine
Carolyn Mockett
Jonathan Otting
Holly Sando
Elizabeth Silver
Colin Wexler
Randy Wexler

1994, Fall
Joseph Facciponti
Elizabeth Mahoney
Ellen Roberts
David Rohrbach
Mallory Rome
Adam Schupak
Sarah Shubert

1995, Spring
Jessica Bates
Michelle Chihara
Braden Cleveland
Dael Cohen
Jordana Dezeeuw
Eliot Dobris
Annie Dorson
Amy Duross
Mark Hanna
Karen Herbert
Cynthia Marion
Jenny Petrow
Amy Porter
Cheryl Thompson

1995, Summer
Kenneth Barry
Kellianne Bartlett
Rachel Carey
Alison Manges
Andrew Mondschein
Bertrand Navarette
Heather Nolan
Franklin Parker
Scott Rickert
Stanley Shepard
Loren Weinberg

1995, Fall
Nicholas Boggs
Molly Breen
Dael Cohen
Aaron Fleisher
Elizabeth Hines
Donya Levine
Priscilla Marshall
Thomas Miles
April Snyder
Kishma Tilley
Eliza Woolston

1996, Spring
Niki Eldridge
Melissa Gold
Tamar Gordon
Leila Jones
Katie McClancy
Asha Muldro
Dan O'Neil
Maria Ricciardone
Victoria Sancho
Adam Swire
Molly Woodroofe

1996, Fall
Allan Abinoja
Jenny Brevorka
Ben Carp
Natasha Gianvecchio
Joel Hafvenstein
Sarah Levy
Becky Lightman
Kirsten Magnuson
Anne Mosher
Sophie Schlondorff
Jill Simandl

1997, Spring
Caroline Adams
John Carroll
Dara Epstein
Sandra Farkas
Miguel Flores
Catherine Hilyard
Michael Horwitz
Dan McGarry
Cynthia Miller
Teri Niadna
Sara Nichols
Anupama Subramony
Heather Templeton
Karen Teoh

1997, Summer
Cordelia Carter
Sevra Davis
Casey Deloach
Emily Groom
Genevieve Groom
Dawn Hirokawa
Alice McCarthy
Eric Misiaszek
Jenny Nelson
David Penn
Rob Schlaff
Sara Schwebel
Sara Suleiman
Greg Vlacich
Kurtran Wright

1997, Fall
Rebecca Antoine
Alison Calabia
Elizabeth Carter
Jamie Ewing
Piper Fogg
Ted Huffman
Amanda Leff
Brian Levinson
Jessica Meyer
Chris Mooney
Elena Oxman
Ariel Pepple
Tyler Schnoebelen
Alisha Scrivens
Caroline Smith
Rob Stilling
David Weber
Tom Williams

1998, Spring
Ethan Bacon
Erin Bernau
Kate Fisher
Adam Giuliano
Ben Kalevitch
Kristen Kenney
Sarah Kinsley
Carmen Korehbandi
Bianca Levin
Natasha Lightfoot
William Lin
Brooke Richie
Alisha Scrivens
Mike Vermylen

1998, Summer
Dana Byrd
Amy Cerciello
Laura Chavkin
Elizabeth Cushingham
Rion Danjuma
Liz DeLuca
Andrew Eggert
Karen Go
Catherine Hinsdale
Dan Logan
Hannah McCaughey
Jeremy Melius
Mini Naidu
Karen Paik
Karen Rosenberg
Melissa Rouke
Allie Stenberg
Elizabeth Woyke

1998, Fall
Molly Dorozenski
Edgar Garcia
Kenyon Harbison
Stacey Haro
Hanna Janiszewska
Kapila Juthani
Caitlin Wheeler
Ashley Wisneski

1999, Spring
Mica Darley
Simone Davalos
Yani Indrajana
Sara Lester
Annelena Lobb
Tanya Loh
Zachary Mazur
Jacquie Ruppert
Shana Smith
Sumanthi Subbiah
Nathan Willard

1999, Summer
Begum Bengu
Dan Brodhead
Celina Bustamente
Adam De Havenon
Elizabeth Edmondson
Fitz Fitzpatrick
Heather Fletcher
Alex Greene
Emily Hertzer
Erin Johnson
Abha Khanna
Eric Klein
Brian Lizotte
Adam Marshall
Caroline Marvin
Annie McBeath
Sashank Prasad
Sarah Weeks
Anna Ziegler

1999, Fall
Nuala Droney
Steve Huff
Matthew Kennedy
Michelle Lee
Richard Yun

2000, Spring
Jen Arthur
Kate Baker
James Bickford
Christine Billy
Kelly Gittlein
Yung Kao
Andrew Nguyen
Megan Palmer
Kate Roach
Jennie Vogel
Caleb Weaver
Jessica Wolland

Summer 2009 Session 2 students on the Kings Cross 'Harry Potter' platform

Reception in the Paul Mellon Centre Library for Summer 2009 Session 1 and 2 students with Pericles Lewis and Edward Cooke

YALE IN LONDON STUDENTS

2000, Summer
Geoffrey Chepiga
Katie Cole
Laurel Grodman
Robert Hanson
Michael Horn
Alice Ko
Jeff Little
Ben Marcovitz
Claire Miller
Julie O'Connor
Ben Reiter
Margaret Rimsky
Monique Rose
Jen Russ
Margot Sanger-Katz
Maria Stookey

2000, Fall
Jennifer Fiedler
Jon Garland
Benjamin Gould
Brian Ivy
Ciara Lacy
Danielle Muniz
Kate Sands

2001, Spring
Amanda Brown
Nancy Holochwost
Julia Iyasere
Brad Lebow
Marina Lin
Lisa Marshall
Huy Nguyen
Warner Off
Erin Roberts
Sam Trepel
Sam Warshauer
Devon Williamson
Mollie Wilson
Mary Ruth Windham

2001, Summer
Li Yun Alvarudo
Jannifer Andress
Plem Bonython
Ravi D'Cruz
Melissa Doscher
Andrea Freyer
Deborah Friedell
Whitney Grace
Joanna Liberman
Michi Murao
Kara Nesburg
Nina Nuangchamnong
Naomi Pease
Will Perkins
Becky Rauth
Jamie Schuman
Stacey Sofka
Jeremy Stacy
Jessica Zachary

2001, Fall
Lillian Fish
Erica Forneret
Jami Harrison
Lindsay Kaden
Julie Marchesi
April Mohr
Javier Ramirez
Sarah Senk
Kristin Urquiza
Peter Varga

2002, Spring
Max Borenstein
Rand Dadasovich
Joanna Dolgin
Rebecca Felsenthal
Will Frazier
Tad Jachowicz
Becca Kelly
Jessica Leventhal
Heather Nelson
Kayla Nelson
Joshua Secrest
Alex Sullivan
Peter Varga
Mitch Webber

2002, Summer, Session 1
Catey Bradford
Zander Dryer
Brynn Gingras
Sean Kass
Lucy Kaufman
Lisa LeCointe
Bibi Lesch
TJ Lim
Anne Myers
Dan O'Neil
Andrew Roach
Nick Strohl

2002, Summer, Session 2
Becca Baneman
Chris Benson
Liz Carter
Julie Cohen
Kaitlyn Gumpper
Stephanie Jones
Caitlin Lonegan
Brooke Lyons
Natalia Payne
Sarah Sherblom
Michael Shulman
Kellie Sorenson
Megham Stack
Andrew Williams

2003, Spring
Momo Akade
Andrew Baroody
Rachel Burgess
Liz Chu
Eric Gilde
Aaron Goode
Katherine Hill
Molly Lewis
Taureen Newland
Kris Pieper
Ali Pruet
Lucinda Stamm
Megan Wall-Wolff

2003, Summer, Session 1
Anjanine Bonet
Jenny Carter
Carrie Coughlin
Abby Epstein
Olia Galenianou
Smita Gopisetty
Noah Heymann
Caroline Johnston
Jeff Morris
Diana Reiter
Dina Solomon
Catherine Stewart
Lauren Stripling
Stephanie Wei

2003, Summer, Session 2
Mike Atkins
Jordan Bass
Alex Bevan
Matt Fitzgerald
Bridget Henn
Jane Innis
Hye-Jin Kim
Yali Lewis
Toby Merrill
Alex Nemser
Brendan O'Sullivan
Mia Simpson
Hiromi Yoshida

2004, Spring
Leah Anderson
Jessie Goldhirsh
Diana Greenwold
Su Mon Han
Anna Kolontyrsky
Jackson Maier
Dan St Jean
Kati Stevens
James Suerken
Michal Towber
Jeff Yohalem

2004, Summer, Session 1
Catherine Brobeck
Erin Dress
Adam Eaker
Evgenia Hatzidakis
Xin Ma
Daniel Martinez
Farah Peterson
Laurel Peterson
Anne Pinedo
Joshua Platt
Julia Pudlin
Adriane Quinlan
Jeb Remus
Jonathan Sack
Christopher Wells

2004, Summer, Session 2
Melinda Delis
Russell Eida
Bahram Jahanbakhsh
Andy Kohler
Ashley Linnenbank
Gloria Loya
Priscila Martins
Maggie Moore
Tommy Ou
Jenni Park
William Trevor Rees
Jeremy Schmidt
Amy Seese
Lauren Taft-McPhee
Ting Ting Yan

2005, Spring
Lindsey Counts
Carl Fuldner
Anabel Gallegos
Erfun Geula
Sunny Kang
Sam Kendrick
Swarnameenakshi Manickam
Bristol Maryott
Jennifer Paton
Ricardo Sandoval
James Strom
Helen Vera
Julia Wallace
Victoria Wolcott

2005, Summer, Session 1
Ali Adler
Eugene Ashton-Gonzalez
Sage Galesi
Nicole Hallarman
Serena Hines
Brynne Lieb
Holly Mazar
Tamara Micner
Kasdin Miller
Christian Nakarado
Kate O'Brien
Jenny Reisner
Lydia Shook
Amanda Turner

2005, Summer, Session 2
Yohannes Abraham
Sarah Cortina
Melissa Doerken
Nate Hundt
Libby Irwin
Casey Littlefield
Maureen Miller
Marya Myers
Alison Stern
Kristen Von Hoffman
Rose Weill

2006, Spring
Matthew Armendariz
Alexander Borinsky
Sonia Cooke
Laura Heiman
Angel Hertslet
Mengmeng Huang
Jennifer Jaye
George Kalogeropoulos
Jeanny Lee
Moon Huei Lee
Jose Ramirez
Kristen Saruwatari
Nikolaus Wasmoen
Evan Wilson

2006, Summer, Session 1
Laura Aronsson
Kanya Balakrishna
Erin Dickerson
Leonora Higginbottom
Andrew Law
Andrew Lee
Rebecca Lee
Elise Panza
Alex Sassaroli
Chris Solga
Carly Zien

2006, Summer Session 2
Kate Arata
Elijah Barrett
Erin Cawley
Kate Cobb
Regina Goldman
JaeAnn Huh
Neli Lazarova
Robby Legg
David Lyons
Steve Miller
Lexi Newman
Aarthy Thamodaran
Meg Weeks

2007, Spring
Mark Beyersdorf
Samuel Chua
Katherine Dempsey
Ashley Fox
Nicole Green
Angela Hygh
Diana Mellon
Joshua Mukai
Rachel Rose
Cari Tuna
Elisabeth Walden
Alexander Weinstein

2007, Summer, Session 1
Mackenzie Asel
Jessica Balderston
Simone Berkower
Mariana Brandman
Marjorie De Witt
Elizabeth Dwyer
Nicole Espy
Marco Garcia
Alexandra Junewicz
Alana Riksheim
David Rudnick

Spring 2004 students in the Director's office at 16 Bedford Square

Avebury, Summer 2008 Session 2 students with Roger Bowdler

YALE IN LONDON STUDENTS

2007, Summer, Session 2

Bix Bettwy
Camille Gajewski
Amy Koenig
Liz Koenig
Jenny McClain
Cassie Mitchell
Sarah Naftalis
Jenny Nissel
Sophie Quinton
Ashley Rodboro
Ariel Shepherd-Oppenheim
Paul Spera
Jaime Totti
Alex Trow
Emmett Zackheim

2008, Spring

Laura Beavers
Joshua Blair
Andrea Bouchard
Sophia Cooper
Kate McCoubrey
Gerald McElroy
Courtney Sender
Tanya Whisant

2008, Summer Session 1

Erin Capistrano
Sarah Evans
Bill Kamens
Patty Lehtinen
Alex Marraccini
Marla Menninger
Alyssa Murphy
Nell Pach
Conor Robinson
Liz Rodrick
Hayley Zevenbergen

2008, Summer, Session 2

Rachel Cooke
Shayari DeSilva
Claudia Duncan
James Gleckner
Vince Granata
Matt Long
Charley Moore
Kate Philip
Natasha Sarin
Amy Watson
Ben Wescoe

2009, Spring

Kelly Cannon
Amanda Glassman
Michelle Glienke
Rebecca Hinkle
Becky Jaye
Elizabeth Kennedy
Claire Laudone

2009 Summer Session 1

Jordan Abergel
Hilary Cronin
Cory Finley
Peregrine Heard
Michele Keene
Elizabeth Kennedy
Mary Miller
Elizabeth Reeves
Caroline Reigeluth
Stephanie Rosenthal
Andrew Saviano
William Stephen
Ayana Sumiyasu
Ben Wexler
Isaac Wilson

2009 Summer Session 2

Whitney Barlow
Lauren Campbell
Nora Caplan-Bricker
Victoria Charette
Matthew Gerken
Emma Griffin
Katherine Grunzweig
Eve King
William Robles
Mercedes Rodriguez
Antonio Sirianni
Rachel Sturm
Murphy Temple
Tomas Unger
Laura Vrana

2010, Spring

Laura Blake
Ella Dershowitz
Erica Irving
Jamile Kadre
Eleanor Kenyon
Heeseung Kim
Yinshi Lerman-Tan
Taryn Nakamura
Stephanie Scaramella
Ian Sprague
Alexa Suarez
Adanna Ukah

2010 Summer Session 1

Alison Altman
Mary Attardo
Martha Burson
Andrew Freeburg
Rachel London
Jennifer Matichuk
Lauren Richards
Michael Singleton
Sage Snider
Oren Stevens
Virginia Waldrop

2010 Summer Session 2

John Eliasberg
Mana Ikebe
Timothy Kressman
Christina Lee
Liya Lomsadze
Courtney Peters
Joshua Scharff
Mia Thompson
Peter Vizcarrondo
Christina Wakefield
Cullinan Williams

ACADEMIC ACTIVITIES

PUBLICATIONS

WHEN the Centre was established in 1970 there was no formal procedure for approving publications inherited from the Paul Mellon Foundation, whose books were published through a contractual arrangement with Routledge & Kegan Paul. Soon after its establishment the Paul Mellon Centre entered a contractual arrangement with Yale University Press whose small London office was from 1973–79 housed in the Centre's premises in Bloomsbury Square before they eventually established their own independent premises at no. 13 Bedford Square in 1979. In 1990 the Press moved to offices in Pond Street, Hampstead, before relocating to 47 Bedford Square in 2002. Initially, after the establishment of the Centre in 1970, decisions relating to publications were discussed at the Advisory Council meetings but in 1974 Christopher White, with the encouragement of John Nicoll, the newly appointed art history editor at Yale University Press, established a sub-committee for Publications. This committee consisted of selected members of the Advisory Council and representatives of Yale University Press in London. The Publications Committee thereafter met two or three times each year to consider manuscripts submitted for publication. The manuscripts under consideration would already have been read and their suitability for publication assessed by leading experts in the appropriate field. If a manuscript was then approved for publication by the Publications Committee the proposal still had to be ratified by Yale University's Publications Committee in New Haven, Connecticut. In rare instances manuscripts may be submitted to the Centre without any prior warning but it is much more common for prospective authors to have discussed their book proposal with either the Director of Studies or the editorial staff of Yale University Press at an earlier stage. In some instances, publications such as dictionaries or catalogues raisonnés resulted from projects initiated by and supported from their inception by the Centre. Some projects started under the Paul Mellon Foundation in the 1960s, such as Alastair Smart's *Allan Ramsay: A Complete Catalogue of his Paintings* or *The Dictionary of British and Irish Travellers in Italy 1701–1800* compiled from the Brinsley Ford Archive by John Ingamells, eventually came to fruition many years later as Paul Mellon Centre publications.

1971

Ronald Paulson, *Hogarth: His Life, Art & Times*, 2 vols.
John Hayes, *The Drawings of Thomas Gainsborough* (published for the PMC in USA only; UK edition Zwemmer, 1970)

1972

John Hayes, *Gainsborough as Printmaker* (published for the PMC in the USA only; UK edition Zwemmer, 1971)

1973

Eric Adams, *Francis Danby: Varieties of Poetic Landscape*

PUBLICATIONS

1974
A. Charles Sewter, *The Stained Glass of William Morris & his Circle*, 2 vols.

1975
Leonée and Richard Ormond, *Lord Leighton*
Hans Hammelmann, *Book Illustrators in 18th-century England*

1976
M. H. Port, *The Houses of Parliament*
Edward Mead Johnson, *Francis Cotes* (Phaidon, published with support from the PMC)
Andrew Saint, *Richard Norman Shaw*
Rajnai Miklos and Mary Stevens, *The Norwich Society of Artists 1805–1833*

1977
Nicholas Penny, *Church Monuments in Romantic England*
Robin Gibson, *The Clarendon Collection* (published privately for PMC by BAS Printers Ltd)
Martin Butlin and Evelyn Joll, *The Paintings of JMW Turner* (rev. 1981), 2 vols.

1978–84
Ed. Kenneth Garlick and Angus MacIntyre, *The Diary of Joseph Farington*, Vols 1–16

1978
Peter Thornton, *Seventeenth-century Interior Decoration in England, France & Holland*

1979
Anthony Quiney, *John Loughborough Pearson*
William Vaughan, *German Romanticism & English Art*
George P. Landow, *William Holman Hunt and Typological Symbolism*

1980
Kathryn Moore Heleniack, *William Mulready*
Andrew McClaren Young, Margaret MacDonald, Robin Spencer, with the assistance of Hamish Miles, *The Paintings of James McNeill Whistler*, 2 vols.

1981
William L. Pressly, *The Life & Art of James Barry*
John Ingamells, *The English Episcopal Portrait 1559–1835: A catalogue* (published privately by the PMC)
Mansfield Kirby Talley, *Portrait Painting in England: Studies in the Technical Literature before 1700* (published privately by the PMC)
Martin Butlin, *The Paintings & Drawings of William Blake*, 2 vols.
Ed. Virginia Surtees, *The Diary of Ford Madox Brown*

1982
Hugh Brigstocke, *William Buchanan and the 19th-century Art Trade* (published privately by the PMC)
Benedict Read, *Victorian Sculpture*

1983
Susan Beattie, *The New Sculpture*
Louise Lippincott, *Selling Art in Georgian London: The Rise of Arthur Pond*

1984
Graham Reynolds, *The Later Paintings & Drawings of John Constable*, 2 vols.
Terry Friedman, *James Gibbs*

1985
Richard Dorment, *Alfred Gilbert*
Rudiger Joppien and Bernard Smith, *The Art of Captain Cook's Voyages* (4 vols.)

1987
Cecily Langdale, *Gwen John*
Michael McCarthy, *The Origins of the Gothic Revival*
Cecilia Powell, *Turner in the South: Rome, Florence, Naples*

1988
Felicity Owen and David Blayney Brown, *Collector of Genius: A Life of Sir George Beaumont*
Stephen Deuchar, *Sporting Art in 18th-century England: A Social & Political History*
Ed. Bernard Smith and Alwyne Wheeler, *The Art of the First Fleet & other Early Australian Drawings*
Iain Pears, *The Discovery of Painting: The Growth of Interest in the Arts in England 1680–1768*

1989
Clive Wainwright, *The Romantic Interior*

1991
Christopher Gilbert, *English Vernacular Furniture 1750–1900*

1992
Alastair Smart, *Allan Ramsay: Painter, Essayist & Man of the Enlightenment*

1993
David H. Solkin, *Painting for Money: The Visual Arts & the Public Sphere in 18th-century England*
Douglas D.C. Chambers, *The Planters of the English Landscape Garden*
Eds. D. Bindman and Gottfried Rienamm, K. F. Schinkel, *The English Journey: Journal of a visit to France and Britain in 1826*

Simon Thurley, *The Royal Palaces of Tudor England: Architecture & Court Life 1460–1547*
Marcia Pointon, *Hanging the Head: Portraiture & Social Formation in 18th-century England*

1994
Sam Smiles, *The Image of Antiquity: Ancient Britain & the Romantic Imagination*
Charles Harrison, *English Art and Modernism 1900–1939. With a new introduction*
John Schofield, *Medieval London Houses*
Nigel Everett, *The Tory View of Landscape*
Miles Glendinning and Stefan Muthesius, *Tower Block: Modern Public Housing in England, Scotland, Wales & Northern Ireland*

1995
Howard Colvin, *A Biographical Dictionary of British Architects 1600–1840* (3rd ed.)
David Bindman and Malcolm Baker, *Roubiliac & the 18th-century Monument*
Ed. B. Allen, *Towards a Modern Art World: Studies in British Art* (SBA1)
Ed. L. Gent *Albion's Classicism: The Visual Arts in Britain 1550–1660* (SBA2)
Jules Lubbock, *The Tyranny of Taste: The Politics of Architecture and Design in Britain 1550–1960*
M. H. Port, *Imperial London: Civil Government Building in London 1851–1915*
Giles Worsley, *Classical Architecture in Britain: The Heroic Age*
Paul Binski, *Westminster Abbey and the Plantagenets: Kingship and the Representation of Power 1200–1400*
Margaret F. MacDonald, *James McNeill Whistler: Drawings, Pastels and Watercolours. A Catalogue Raisonné*

1996
Ed. C. Chard and H. Langdon *Transports: Travel, Pleasure & Imaginative Geography 1600–1830* (SBA3)
Diana Donald, *The Age of Caricature: Satirical Prints in the Reign of George II*
Graham Reynolds, *The Early Paintings and Drawings of John Constable*, 2 vols.
Ian Bristow, *Interior House Painting: Colours & Technology 1615–1840*
Ian Bristow, *Architectural Colour in British Interiors 1615–1840*
Charlotte Klonk, *Science & the Perception of Nature*
Ed. B. Allen and Larissa Dukelskaya, *British Art Treasures from Russian Imperial Collections in the Hermitage*

1997
Ed. John Ingamells, *A Dictionary of British and Irish Travellers in Italy 1701–1800 Compiled from the Brinsley Ford Archive*
Anthony Wells-Cole, *Art and Decoration in Tudor England: The Influence of Continental Prints, 1558–1625*
Kay Dian Kriz, *The Idea of the English Landscape Painter: Genius as Alibi in the early 19th Century*
Timothy Clayton, *The English Print 1688–1802*
Ed. Jeffrey M. Muller and Jim Murrell, *Miniatura or the Art of Limning: Edward Norgate*
Ed. Ronald Paulson, *William Hogarth: The Analysis of Beauty*
Ed. Robert R. Wark, *Discourses on Art: Sir Joshua Reynolds*
Deborah Frizzell, *Humphrey Spender's Humanist Landscapes: Photo Documents, 1932–1942* (Published with the YCBA)
Ed. Michael Rosenthal, Christiana Payne and Scott Wilcox, *Prospects for the Nation: Recent Essays in British Landscape, 1750–1880* (SBA4)

PUBLICATIONS

1998

Richard Ormond and Elaine Kilmurray, *John Singer Sargent: The Early Portraits. The Complete Paintings: Volume I*
Evelyn Newby, *The Diary of Joseph Farington: Index*
Margaret Garlake, *New Art New World: British Art in Postwar Society*
James Ayres, *Building the Georgian City*
Ed. Elizabeth Prettejohn and Timothy Barringer, *Frederic Leighton: Antiquity, Renaissance, Modernity* (SBA5)

1999

Ellen D'Oench, *Copper Into Gold: Prints by John Raphael Smith*
Mark Hallett, *The Spectacle of Difference: Graphic Satire in the Age of Hogarth*
Howard Colvin, *Essays in English Architectural History*
Michael Rosenthal, *The Art of Thomas Gainsborough*
Ed. Katharine Lochnan, *Seductive Surfaces: The Art of Tissot* (SBA6)
Stephen Daniels, *Humphrey Repton: Landscape Gardening and the Geography of Georgian England*
Nicholas Cooper, *Houses of the Gentry 1480–1680*
Alastair Smart, ed. John Ingamells, *Allan Ramsay: A Complete Catalogue of his Paintings*

2000

Peter Fergusson and Stuart Harrison, *Rievaulx Abbey*
Ann Bermingham, *Learning to Draw: Studies in the Cultural History of a Polite and Useful Art*
Lisa Tickner, *Modern Life and Modern Subjects: British Art in the early 20th Century*
John Summerson, *Inigo Jones* (rev. ed.)
Ruth Bomberg, *Walter Sickert Prints*
Paul Edwards, *Wyndham Lewis: Painter and Writer*
Roy Strong, *The Artist and the Garden*
Ed. Chris Brooks, *The Albert Memorial*
Carol Gibson Wood, *Jonathan Richardson: Art Theorist of the English Enlightenment*
David Mannings and Martin Postle, *Sir Joshua Reynolds: A Complete Catalogue of his Paintings*, 2 vols.
Eds. John Edgcumbe and John Ingamells, *The Letters of Sir Joshua Reynolds*
Ed. John Hayes, *The Letters of Thomas Gainsborough*
Alastair Grieve, *Whistler's Venice*
Christine Stevenson, *Medicine and Magnificence: British Hospital & Asylum Architecture 1660–1815*

2001

Stefan Muthesius, *The Postwar University: Utopianist Campus and College*
John Bold, *Greenwich: An Architectural History of the Royal Hospital for Seamen and the Queen's House*
Todd Longstaffe-Gowan, *The London Town Garden 1700–1840*
Allen Staley, *The Pre-Raphaelite Landscape*
G. E. Bentley, *The Stranger from Paradise in the Realm of the Beast: A Biography of William Blake*
Eileen Harris, *The Genius of Robert Adam: His Interiors*
Edward McParland, *Public Architecture in Ireland 1680–1760*
James Hyman, *The Battle for Realism: Figurative Art and its Promotion in Britain during the Cold War 1945–59*
David Solkin, *Art on the Line*
Ed. Debra Mancoff, *John Everett Millais: Beyond the Pre-Raphaelite Brotherhood* (SBA7)
Ed. Pauline Croft, *Patronage, Culture and Power: The Early Cecils* (SBA 8)

2002

Ed. Alex Kidson, *Those Delightful Regions of Imagination: Essays on George Romney* (SBA 9)
Eds. David Peters Corbett, Ysanne Holt and Fiona Russell, *The Geographies of Englishness: Landscape and the National Past 1880–1940* (SBA 10)
Sara Stevenson, *The Personal Art of David Octavius Hill*
Anne Crookshank and the Knight of Glin, *Ireland's Painters*
Eds. Larissa Dukelskaya and Andrew Moore, *A Capital Collection: Houghton Hall and the Hermitage with a Modern Edition of Aedes Walpolianae*
Michael J. K. Walsh, *C.R.W. Nevinson: This Cult of Violence*
Susan Sloman, *Gainsborough in Bath*
Richard Ormond and Elaine Kilmurray, *John Singer Sargent: Portraits of the 1890s. The Complete Paintings: Volume II*
Vaughan Hart, *Nicholas Hawksmoor*

2003

Emmanuel Cooper, *Bernard Leach: Life & Work*
Colum Hourihane, *Gothic Art in Ireland 1169–1550*
Jonathan Scott, *The Pleasures of Antiquity: British Collectors of Greece & Rome*
John Summerson, *Georgian London*, ed. Howard Colvin
Ed. Robyn Asleson, *Notorious Muse: The Actress in British Art and Culture 1776–1812* (SBA 11)
Ed. Edward Chaney, *The Evolution of English Collecting* (SBA 12)
Kathryn A. Morrison, *English Shops and Shopping*
Simon Thurley, *Hampton Court: A Social and Architectural History*

2004

Richard Ormond and Elaine Kilmurray, *John Singer Sargent: The Later Portraits. The Complete Paintings: Volume III*
Anthony Quiney, *Town Houses of Medieval Britain*
G. E. Bentley, Jr., *Blake Records* (2nd edition)
Peter Guillery, *The Small House in 18th-century London*
Bruce Laughton, *William Coldstream*
S. Barnes, N. De Poorter, O. Millar and H. Vey, *Van Dyck: A Complete Catalogue of the Paintings*
Sanford Schwartz, *William Nicholson*
David J. Getsy, *Body Doubles: Sculpture in Britain, 1877–1905*
Sue Malvern, *Modern Art, Britain and the Great War*
Fiona Donovan, *Rubens and England*
Veronica Franklin Gould, *G.F. Watts: The Last Great Victorian*

Eds. Julian Holder and Steven Parissien, *The Architecture of British Transport in the 20th Century* (SBA 13)
Giles Worsley, *The British Stable*
Paul Binski, *Becket's Crown: Art and Imagination in Gothic England 1170–1300*
John Cornforth, *Early Georgian Interiors*
Tim Barringer, *Men at Work: Art and Labour in Victorian Britain*
Susan Foister, *Holbein and England*
Alastair Grieve, *Constructed Abstract Art in England: A Neglected Avant-Garde*
Paula Henderson, *The Tudor House and Garden*
Martin Hammer, *Bacon and Sutherland*

2005
Ed. Chris Miele, *From William Morris: Building Conservation and the Arts and Crafts Cult of Authenticity 1877–1939* (SBA14)
Richard Wendorf, *After Sir Joshua: Essays on British Art and Cultural History* (SBA 15)
Edward Morris, *French Art in 19th-century Britain*
Anne Middleton Wagner, *Mother Stone: The Vitality of Modern British Sculpture*
Daniel Abramson, *Building the Bank of England: Money, Architecture, Society 1694–1942*
C. Paul Christianson, *The Riverside Gardens of Thomas More's London*
Michael Levey, *Sir Thomas Lawrence*
Martin Myrone, *Body Building: Reforming Masculinities in British Art 1750–1810*
Matthew Hargraves, *Candidates for Fame: The Society of Artists of Great Britain 1760–1791*
Aileen Ribeiro, *Fashion and Fiction: Dress in Art and Literature in Stuart England*
Kate Retford, *The Art of Domestic Life: Family Portraiture in 18th-century England*
Angela Rosenthal, *Angelica Kauffman: Art and Sensibility*

2006
Ed. Frank Salmon, *Summerson & Hitchcock: Centenary Essays on Architectural Historiography* (SBA16)
Christopher Wright, with Catherine Gordon and Mary Peskett Smith, *British and Irish Paintings in Public Collections*
Judith Bronkhurst, *William Holman Hunt: A Catalogue Raisonné*, 2 vols.
Wendy Baron, *Sickert Paintings and Drawings*
Peter Draper, *The Formation of the English Gothic: Architecture and Identity*
Richard Ormond and Elaine Kilmurray, *John Singer Sargent: Figures and Landscapes 1874–1882. The Complete Paintings Volume IV*
Giles Worsley, *Inigo Jones and the European Classicist Tradition*
The Knight of Glin and James Peill, *Irish Furniture*
Ed. John Styles and Amanda Vickery, *Gender, Taste and Material Culture in Britain and North America 1700–1830* (SBA17)

2007
John Harris, *Moving Rooms: The Trade in Architectural Salvages*
Gill Perry, *Spectacular Flirtations: Viewing the Actress in British Art and Theatre 1768–1820*
Brian Foss, *War Paint: Art, War, State and Identity in Britain 1939–1945*
Judy Egerton, *George Stubbs. Painter*
Elizabeth Prettejohn, *Art for Art's Sake: Aestheticism in Victorian Painting*
Anna Gruetzner Robins, *A Fragile Modernism: Whistler and his Impressionist Followers*
Diana Donald, *Picturing Animals in Britain*
Thomas P. Campbell, *Henry VIII and the Art of Majesty: Tapestries at the Tudor Court* (Published by Yale University Press, New Haven)

2008
Ed. Julia Marciari Alexander and Catharine MacLeod, *Politics, Transgression, and Representation at the Court of Charles II* (SBA18, Published by Yale University Press, New Haven)
Maurice Howard, *The Building of Elizabethan and Jacobean England*
Matthew Craske, *The Silent Rhetoric of the Body: A History of Monumental Sculpture and Commemorative Art in England, 1720–1770*
Howard Colvin, *A Biographical Dictionary of British Architects 1600–1840* (4th ed.)
Ed. Philip Temple, *Survey of London Vol. XLVI, South and East Clerkenwell* and *Vol. XLVII, Northern Clerkenwell and Pentonville*
Kay Dian Kriz, *Slavery, Sugar and the Culture of Refinement*
Vaughan Hart, *Sir John Vanbrugh: Storyteller in Stone*
Andor Gomme and Alison Maguire, *Design and Plan in the Country House: From Castle Donjons to Palladian Boxes*
David H. Solkin, *Painting Out of the Ordinary: Modernity and the Art of Everyday Life in early 19th-century Britain*
Patrick Noon, *Richard Parkes Bonington: The Complete Paintings*

2009
Caroline Arscott, *William Morris and Edward Burne-Jones: Interlacings*
Judith A. Neiswander, *The Cosmopolitan Interior: Liberalism and the British Home, 1870–1914*
Helen Pierce, *Unseemly Pictures: Graphic Satire and Politics in Early Modern England*
Ed. Cinzia Sicca, *John Talman: An early 18th-century Connoisseur* (SBA 19)
Richard Ormond and Elaine Kilmurray, *John Singer Sargent Venetian Figures and Landscapes, 1898–1913. The Complete Paintings Volume VI*
Rachel Stewart, *The Town House in Georgian London*
Ingrid Roscoe, Emma Hardy and M.G. Sullivan, *A Biographical Dictionary of Sculptors in Britain 1660–1851*

PUBLICATIONS

Mark Girouard, *Elizabethan Architecture*
Robert Hewison, *Ruskin on Venice*
Jason M. Kelly, *The Society of Dilettanti*

2010

Celina Fox, *The Arts of Industry in the Age of Enlightenment*
Marcia Pointon, *Brilliant Effects: A Cultural History of Gem Stones and Jewellery*
Ilaria Bignamini and Clare Hornsby, *Digging and Dealing in 18th-century Rome* (2 vols)
Paula Murphy, *Nineteenth-century Irish Sculpture, Native Genius Reaffirmed*
Malcolm Jones, *The Print in Early Modern England: An Historical Oversight*
Christiana Payne, *John Brett: Pre-Raphaelite Landscape Painter*
Andrew Saint, *Richard Norman Shaw* (rev. ed.)
Mary Bennett, *Ford Madox Brown: A Catalogue Raisonné* (2 vols.)
Tomás Ó Carragáin, *Churches in Early Medieval Ireland*
Grace Brockington, *Above the Battlefield: British Modernism and the Peace Movement, 1900–1918*
Tara Hamling, *Decorating the 'Godly' Household: Religious Art in Post-Reformation Britain*
Richard Ormond and Elaine Kilmurray, *John Singer Sargent Figures and Landscapes, 1883–1899: The Complete Paintings Volume V*
Philip Temple, *Survey of London: The Charterhouse*
Eds. Morna O'Neill and Michael Hatt, *The Edwardian Sense: Art, Design, and Performance in Britain, 1901–1910* (SBA 20)
Morna O'Neill, *Walter Crane: The Arts and Crafts, Painting and Politics, 1875–1890*
Eds. Mark Crinson and Claire Zimmerman, *Neo-avant-garde and Postmodern: Postwar Architecture in Britain and Beyond* (SBA 21)
Terry Friedman, *The 18th-Century Church in Britain*

GRANTS

The grants administered by the Paul Mellon Foundation had been processed in an ad hoc fashion although all those disbursed were approved by the Trustees of the Foundation. There were no formal application guidelines or set budget and applicants approached the Foundation directly.

Under the aegis of the Paul Mellon Centre a more formal scheme was established with a fixed annual budget. Applications were reviewed at the twice-yearly meetings of the Advisory Council. The procedure however remained relatively informal until the mid-1980s with applicants submitting to the Centre an outline of their proposed project and its funding needs. As a matter of policy the Centre would not pay for or reimburse the photographic expenses of individual scholars but would instead offer the services (where appropriate) of the Centre's own photographer so that the negatives became the property of the Centre. Also the Centre would not support scholarship grants that effectively provided living expenses but was prepared to consider applications for specific research tasks such as visiting archives, libraries or collections both in the UK and overseas. It was further agreed that the Centre would not, with regard to institutions, finance whole exhibitions (as the Foundation had done) but would contribute towards the cost of scholarly exhibition catalogues. Although the Paul Mellon Foundation had supported lectureships in the history of art at the universities of York and Leicester, the Centre decided against providing funding for this purpose. Nor would it finance the formation of collections of research material by other academic bodies.

In the 1970s the sums dispersed were very modest with an average grant being between £250 and £750 and an annual budget of £10,000. During the later 1970s inflation was running at very high levels and the Centre's income could not sustain a commensurate growth in its grants budget. Indeed during the financial year 1979–80, when the dollar exchange rate plummeted to c.$2.50 to the pound and Yale's endowment (of which the Centre is part) was producing very low percentage returns and growth, there were fears that the Centre might not be able to meet its basic running costs and, as a result, in that year funding for grants was significantly diminished (see expenditure graph on p.75). By the later 1980s the gradual stabilising of the UK economy and steady growth of the Centre's endowment made it possible for the grants budget to be doubled to £20,000 per annum and within a decade the sum available annually had risen to £50,000.

By the mid-1990s the Centre's endowment invested at Yale had grown considerably and surpluses had accrued. The new Director of the Yale Center for British Art, Patrick McCaughey (in his capacity as Chief Executive Office of the Paul Mellon Centre) and the Director of Studies felt confident that surplus funds could be used to create a more ambitious grants and fellowships programme which would begin to meet the growing demand from a widening academic community. At the Annual Governors' meeting held on 25th February 1998 approval was given to implement the new grants and fellowships programme for a three-year trial period. Up to 1998 most of the grants awarded were to support publications (usually exhibition catalogues) since it was then (as now) thought inappropriate to support trade publishers or, at that date, even other academic publishers who might be deemed rivals to Yale University Press.

After 1998 the new grants programme introduced four distinct funding streams: Research Support, Educational Programmes, Curatorial Programmes and Publications, and funding for the programme has grown at a steady but sustainable level since then. Initially it was envisaged that the Centre would support Doctoral Fellowships at both Yale and at universities in the UK but it quickly became apparent that the cumulative effect of such largesse would have drained most of the available resources for the entire grants and fellowship programme and was therefore deemed unsustainable. Five doctoral students (see p. 77) received support before the scheme was abandoned.

With the steady growth in the number of applications it has been necessary to create a grants sub-committee (drawn from members of the Advisory Council) to reduce the burden on the full Advisory Council at its twice-annual meetings. The Council however still formally approves all recommendations from the sub-committee.

Books supported by the Publications Grants Programme, 2010

GRANTS 1998–

THE NEW GRANTS PROGRAMME

In 1998 the new grants programme introduced four distinct funding streams: Curatorial Research, Educational Programmes, Publications (Author, Publisher) and Research Support.

CURATORIAL RESEARCH GRANTS

1998

Courtauld Institute of Art, *The Royal Academy Exhibitions at Somerset House 1780–1836* (3 years)
Harewood House Trust, *Chippendale Exhibition at Harewood House*
Norfolk Museums and Archaeology Service, *Frederick Sandys, The Norwich Pre-Raphaelite* (2 years)
Tasmanian Museum and Art Gallery, *John Glover and the Colonial Picturesque*
Tate Britain, *British Art Project* (3 years)
Victoria and Albert Museum, *The Summary Catalogue of British Sculpture*

1999

Henry Moore Foundation, *Gunnis Dictionary of British Sculptors 1660–1851* (6 years)
Sir John Soane's Museum, *Dance Family Drawings* (2 years)
University of Cambridge, Kettle's Yard, *The Ede Collection and Development of the Study Centre* (2 years)

2000

National Museums Liverpool, *George Romney Exhibition*
Nottingham Castle Museum and Art Gallery, *Richard Parkes Bonington: Bicentenary Exhibition*

2001

National Portrait Gallery, *Catalogue of Works of Alexander Browne and John Smith* (2 years)
Royal Academy of Arts, *Database Catalogue of pre-1850 Drawings in the RA Collection* (2 years)
University of Cambridge, Kettle's Yard, *The Ede Collection and Development of the Study Centre* (2 years)

2002

National Maritime Museum, *William Hodges Exhibition*
Tate Britain, *Turner's Works on Paper (Vols. 1 and 2)* (2 years)

2003

Royal Academy of Arts, *British Drawings Cataloguing Project: Artists Born before 1850*
Royal Watercolour Society, *Royal Watercolour Society Bi-centenary Exhibition*
Ruskin Gallery, Sheffield Galleries and Museums Trust, *The Ruskin Collection of the Guild of St George*
Society of Antiquaries of London, *The Picture Collection of the Society of Antiquaries*
Temple Newsam House, Leeds, *Wallpapers at Temple Newsam*
York Museums Trust, *Urban Life in 18th-century York*

2004

Bodleian Library, *Illuminated British Manuscripts in the Bodleian Collection* (3 years)
Djanogly Gallery, University of Nottingham, *From Victorian to Modern: Laura Knight, Vanessa Bell, Gwen John 1890–1914*
Leighton House Museum, *On-line Catalogue of Lord Leighton Drawings*
Scottish National Portrait Gallery, *John Muir Wood*
Ruskin Gallery, Sheffield Galleries and Museums Trust, *The Ruskin Collection of the Guild of St George* (2 years)
Society of Antiquaries of London, *The Picture Collection of the Society of Antiquaries*
Whitechapel Art Gallery, *Whitechapel Archive Collection* (2 years)

2005

Ashmolean Museum, Oxford, *The Ashmolean Chantrey Project* (3 years)
British Museum, *British Reproductive Printmaking Project* (3 years)
British School at Rome, *Digging and Dealing in 18th-century Rome*
Henry Moore Foundation, *Gunnis Dictionary of British Sculptors 1660–1851*
National Portrait Gallery, *Catalogue of Later Victorian Portraits* (2 years)
The National Trust, *Paper Architecture: Architectural Drawings in National Trust Collections*
York Museums Trust, *The York Collection of Works on Paper (Phase II)*

2006

British School at Rome, *Digging and Dealing in 18th-century Rome*
Crafts Study Centre, Farnham, *Alastair Morton and Edinburgh Weavers: Textiles and Modern Art* (3 years)
Louvre Museum, *Database of British Works of Art in French Collections*
Nottingham Castle Museum and Art Gallery, *Paul Sandby 1730–1809: Picturing the Nation* (2 years)
Scottish National Gallery of Modern Art, *Paolozzi Archive* (3 years)
The Chapter of Peterborough Cathedral, *The West Front of Peterborough Cathedral*
The National Trust, *Paper Architecture: Architectural Drawings in National Trust Collections* (2 years)

2007

Beazley Archive, University of Oxford, *The Arundel and Marlborough Collections of Engraved Gems and Cameos* (2 years)
National Portrait Gallery, *Catalogue of Later Victorian Portraits*

Plymouth City Museum and Art Gallery, *Reynolds's Early Patrons and Reynolds's Collection of Works on Paper* (2 years)
The Chapter of Peterborough Cathedral, *The West Front of Peterborough Cathedral*

2008

Castle Howard Estate Ltd, *George Howard, 9th Earl of Carlisle (1842–1911)* (2 years)
Louvre Museum, *D'Outre Manche: British Art Database*
York Museums Trust, *William Etty Exhibition* (2 years)

2009

Bath Spa University, *Wyndham Lewis, 1882–1957*
British Museum, *Catalogue of Antiquarian Drawings in the British Museum* (3 years)
The National Trust, *Catalogue of the National Trust's Tapestry Collection* (3 years)
Royal Collection, *Revision of Oliver Millar's Catalogues of the Tudor, Stuart and Georgian Pictures in the Royal Collection* (3 years)
Greg Sullivan, *Gunnis Dictionary of British Sculptors 1660–1851*

2010

Hamilton Kerr Institute, University of Cambridge, *Crome and Cotman are the Glories of the Norwich School*
St Paul's Cathedral Foundation, *The Wren Drawings Project*
Royal Albert Memorial Museum and Art Gallery, *The South West in the Elizabethan Age*
Ruthin and District Civic Association and Ruthin Local History Group, *Edward Pugh, 1763–1813: A Bicentenary Exhibition*
Tate Britain, *Picasso and Britain: British Artistic, Cultural, Social and Political Responses to Picasso, 1910–73*
Whitechapel Art Gallery, *Art in the East End of London* (3 years)
University of York, *The London Art World 1660–1735: a new online database* (2 years)

EDUCATIONAL PROGRAMME GRANTS

1998

Castle Howard Estate Ltd, *Sir John Vanbrugh and Landscape Architecture*
University of Plymouth, *Edward Burne-Jones: Pre-Raphaelite, Aesthete, Symbolist*

1999

Djanogly Gallery, University of Nottingham, *The Artist's Model: Its Role in British Art and Society*
Kingston University, *British Drawing in the 20th Century*
Leighton House Museum, *Artists at Home: Artists' Houses in Europe, 1850–1900*
Queen Mary and Westfield College, *Georgian Geographies*
University of Northumbria, *Visual Culture in a Changing Society: Britain 1940–2000*
Maison Française, University of Oxford, *Crossing the Channel for Art's Sake: Anglo-French Attitudes to the Pictorial Arts in the 18th and 19th Century*

2000

Society of Architectural Historians of Great Britain, *The Place of Technology in Architectural History*
The Georgian Group, *British Colonial Architecture in India*
University of Chicago, *Natural Histories: Landscape and Antiquity in Britain 1770–1850*
University of Edinburgh, *Britannia, Italia and Germania: Taste and Travel 1815–1870*
University of York, *Anxious Flirtations: Homoeroticism, Art and Aestheticism in Late Victorian Britain*

2001

Richmond, Virginia, The American International University in London, *Occidents will Happen*
Scottish National Portrait Gallery, *The Miniature Portrait c.1500–1850*
Stowe House Preservation Trust, *Stowe: The Forgotten Treasure House*
University of Bristol, *Adrian Stokes Centenary Conference*
University of Greenwich, *C.R.W. Nevinson: Life, Art and Legacy*
University of Northumbria, *Post-War Visual Culture in Britain*

2002

Christ's College, University of Cambridge, *The Textures of Life at Penshurst Place, 1552–1743*
National Museums and Galleries of Wales, *Thomas Jones (1792–1803)*
Tate Britain, *The French Affair with British Art*
University of Birmingham, *Turner 2004: New Perspectives*

2003

Tate Britain, *The Art of Murder: Representation and Crime in Late Victorian Britain*
Victoria and Albert Museum, *Bill Brandt Centenary Symposium*
Wallace Collection, *Auctions, Agents and Dealers: The Mechanisms of the Art Market, 1660–1830*

2004

Northwestern University, Mary and Leigh Block Museum of Art, *William Morris in Context: The Public and Private Life of an Artist*
University of Leeds, *Newby Hall and the Yorkshire Country House*
University of York, *Art and the Islands: Centre and Periphery in British Art in the Time of William Orpen*
University of York, *The Aesthetic Interior: Neo-Gothic, Aesthetic, Arts and Craft*
Victoria and Albert Museum, *The Georgian Interior*

GRANTS 1998–

2005

Holburne Museum of Art, *The Art of Innocence: Children in Portraits from Hogarth to Lawrence*

National Portrait Gallery, *Shakespeare: Portraiture, Biography and the Material World*

The Emery Walker Trust, *Emery Walker's House: The Arts and Crafts Movement in London and the Cotswolds*

University of Birmingham, *Eighteenth-century Voices*

University of Birmingham, *Victorian Masculinities*

University of Warwick, *The Intellectual and Cultural World of the Early Modern Inns of Court*

Victoria and Albert Museum, *Sacred Silver*

2006

Leeds City Art Gallery, *Frank Brangwyn*

Leighton House Museum, *Leighton and his Contemporaries: Drawing in the late 19th Century*

Loughborough University, *The John Grace Memorial Conference*

National Portrait Gallery, *Between Worlds: Cultures, Biographies, Spectacle*

Scottish National Portrait Gallery, *Henry Raeburn (1756–1823)*

University of York, *Rethinking the Baroque*

Worcester College, University of Oxford, *Geometrical Objects: Architecture and the Mathematical Sciences 1400–1800*

2007

Leeds City Art Gallery, *Oil Prints by George Baxter*

National Portrait Gallery, *Brilliant Women: Gender and Intellect, Reputation and Representation*

Royal West of England Academy, *The Representation of Night in Art*

University of Birmingham, *Wyndham Lewis: Modernity and Critique*

University of Leeds, *Shugborough: Thomas Anson, James 'Athenian' Stuart and their contemporaries*

University of Liverpool, *Joseph Wright of Derby*

2008

Birmingham Museums and Art Gallery, *Matthew Boulton Bi-centenary*

Cambridge Victorian Studies Group, *From Plunder to Preservation: Britain and the 'Heritage' of Empire, c.1820–1940*

Cheltenham Art Gallery and Museum, *Surrealism Returns*

Roehampton University, *The 'Pictorial Turn' in History*

Serpentine Gallery, *Derek Jarman*

Tate Britain, *Van Dyck and the Aristocratic Image*

Université de Paris, *Diderot/William Blake Conference*

University of Westminster, *Capital Views: Aerial Vision and the Changing Image of London*

University of York, *Anglo-American: Artistic Exchange between Britain and the USA*

Whitworth Art Gallery, *Envisioning Utopia: The Urban and the Pastoral in British Art and Socialist Politics, 1870–1900*

2009

Courtauld Institute of Art, *New Approaches to British Art, 1939–1969*

Museum of London, *Pomp and Power: Carriages as Status Symbols*

National Portrait Gallery, *Tudor and Jacobean Painting: Production, Influences and Patronage*

Northwestern University, Mary and Leigh Block Museum of Art, *A Room of Their Own: The Bloomsbury Artists in American Collections*

Royal Cambrian Academy of Art, *An Artistic Inheritance: The Legacy of Welsh Artist Richard Wilson*

The Victorian Society, *Ecclesiology and Empire: Victorian Church Design outside the British Isles 1830–1910*

University College, Dublin, *The Fusion of Neoclassical Principles: Scholars, Architects, Builders and Designers in the Neoclassical Period*

University of Birmingham, *Boulton and Eginton's Mechanical Paintings (1777–1781): Defining the Mechanical rocess*

University of Birmingham, *Building the Future: Birmingham's Architectural Story*

University of Birmingham, *Modernism and Utopia: Convergences in the Arts*

University of Plymouth, *Sir Joshua Reynolds: The Acquisition of Genius*

2010

Birmingham Museums and Art Gallery, *Drawing and the Victorian Artist*

Centre for Research in the Arts, Social Sciences and Humanities, University of Cambridge, *William Henry Fox Talbot: Beyond Photography*

Christ Church Picture Gallery, Oxford, *Henry Aldrich (1648–1710): An Oxford Universal Man*

English Heritage, *Robert Adam Furniture: Designs for Kenwood and Osterley*

Northwestern University, Mary and Leigh Block Museum of Art, *Thomas Rowlandson: Pleasures and Pursuits in Georgian England*

University of Kent, *The Visual and the Verbal in the 18th Century*

University of Leicester, *Balancing the 'Account': The Study of English Medieval Sculpture a Century after Prior and Gardner*

University of St Andrews, *The Reception of Titian in Britain 1769–1877: Artists, Collectors, Critics*

University of York, Dept. of History of Art, *Cultural Landscapes*

PUBLICATION GRANTS (AUTHOR)

1998

Michael Bath, *Renaissance Decorative Painting in Scotland*
Christopher Webster, *The Cambridge Camden Society and its Influence on the Victorian Church*

1999

James Yorke, *The History of Lancaster House 1825–1913*

2000

Michael Kerney, *The Stained Glass of Frederick Preedy*
Gavin Stamp, *George Gilbert Scott Junior*

2001

M. E. Burkett, *Sutton and his Circle: The Cockermouth School of Painting 1750–1880*
Nicholas Goodison, *Ormolu: The Work of Matthew Boulton*

2002

Diana Burfield, *Edward Cresy, Architect and Civil Engineer*
Mark Duffy, *English Royal Tombs 1066–1509*
Anna Gannon, *The Iconography of Early Anglo-Saxon Coinage*
Cyndy Manton, *Practical Idealist: Henry Wilson (1864–1934)*

2003

Jeremy Barlow, *The Enraged Musician: Hogarth's Musical Imagery*
Ute Engel, *English translation of Die Kathedrale von Worcester*
Douglas Fordham, *Art and the British Empire*
Terry Friedman, *The Georgian Parish Church: Monuments to Posterity*
Luciana Gallo, *Lord Elgin and the Quest for Greek Architecture*
Anthony Geraghty, *A Catalogue of the Wren Drawings at All Souls College Oxford*
Stanley A. Shepherd, *The Stained Glass Windows of A. W.N. Pugin*
Vyacheslav P. Shestakov, *Pre-Raphaelites: Religion of Beauty*

2004

Jason Edwards, *Alfred Gilbert's Aestheticism: Gilbert amongst Whistler, Wilde, Leighton, Pater and Burne-Jones*
David Berkeley Elliott, *The Artist and the Critic: Marie Spartali Stillman and William James Stillman*
Kitty Hauser, *Landscape, Photography and the Archaeological Imagination: Britain 1927–1951*
Carol Jacobi, *William Holman Hunt: Painter, Painting, Paint*
Barbara Ravelhofer, *The Early Stuart Masque: Dance, Costume and Music*
S.H.M. Ricketts, *Piety and Power: The Evolution of the Country House Chapel in the 16th and 17th Century*
Dennis Sharp and Sally Rendel, *Connell, Ward and Lucas: English Modern Architecture and the Reappraisal of Technique*
William Whyte, *Oxford Jackson: Architecture, Education, Status, and Style 1835–1924*
Kim W. Woods, *Imported Images: Netherlandish Late Gothic Sculpture in England c.1400–1550*

2005

Anna Chalcraft and Judith Viscardi, *'A Castle built for Eternity': Interior Decoration of Strawberry Hill*
Valentine Gatrell, *The Passion of Laughter: Sex, Manners, and the Satirical Print in London 1770–1830*
Andor Gomme, *Chevening Confirmed*
Brian W. Harvey and Carole Fitzgerald, *Elgar, Vicat Cole and the Ghosts of Brinkwells*
Frédéric Ogée, *Henry Fielding: A Collection of Essays for the Bicentenary of his Death*
Denise Blake Oleksijczuk, *The First Panoramas: Vision, the Body and British Imperialism, 1787–1820*
John Peacock, *The Look of Van Dyck: The 'Self-Portrait with a Sunflower' and the Vision of the Painter*
Andrew Saint, *Architect and Engineer: A Study in Sibling Rivalry*
Vyacheslav P. Shestakov, *History of English Art from the Middle Ages to our Day*
Adam White, *Lady Anne Clifford: Culture, Patronage and Gender in 17th-century Britain*

2006

Peter Black, *My Highest Pleasures: The Fine Arts in Dr Hunter's Museum*
Timothy Brittain-Catlin, *The English Parsonage in the early 19th Century*
Bridget Cherry, *Dissent and the Gothic Revival*
Miles Glendinning, *Modern Architect: The Life and Times of Robert Matthew*
Elizabeth Goldring, *Court and Culture in the Reign of Queen Elizabeth I: A New Critical Edition of John Nichols's 'Progresses'*
Jennifer Graham, *Inventing Van Eyck: The Remaking of an Artist for the Modern Age*
Harriet Guest, *Empire, Barbarism and Civilisation: James Cook, William Hodges and the Return to the Pacific*
Lara Kriegel, *Grand Designs: Labour, Empire, and the Museum in Victorian Culture*
Joseph Monteyne, *The Printed Image in Early Modern London: Visual Representation, Urban Space, and Social Exchange*
André Rogger, *Landscapes of Taste: The Art of Humphry Repton's Red Books*
Catherine Tite, *Portraiture, Dynasty and Power: Art in Hanoverian Britain 1714–1756*
Nicholas Tromans, *David Wilkie: History and the Everyday*
Amelia Yeates, *'Keep the modern magazine and novel out of your girl's way': Ruskin on Women's Reading*

GRANTS 1998–

2007

Susan Bennett, *'Cultivating the human faculties': James Barry (1741–1806) and the Society of Arts*

Jonathan Black and Brenda Martin, *Dora Gordine: Sculptor, Artist, Designer*

Gill Clarke, *Representing the Women's Land Army*

Hanneke Grootenboer, *Treasuring the Gaze: Intimacy and Extremity of Vision in Eye Miniature Portraits*

Stanley Shepherd, *The Stained Glass Windows of A.W.N. Pugin*

2008

Tarnya Cooper, *Citizen Portrait: Portrait Painting and the Urban Elites of Tudor and Jacobean England and Wales*

Katy Deepwell, *Women Artists in Britain between the Two World Wars: 'A Fair Field and No Favour'*

Paul Dobrazczyk, *Into the Belly of the Beast: Exploring London's Victorian Sewers*

Magdalen Evans, *Utmost Fidelity: The Painting Lives of Marianne and Adrian Stokes*

Frances Fowle, *Dealing in Impressionism: A Biography of Alexander Reid*

Elizabeth Goldring, *The Intellectual and Cultural World of the Early Modern Inns of Court*

Michael Hunter, *Printed Images in Early Modern Britain: Essays in Interpretations*

Berta Joncus and Jeremy Barlow, *'The Stage's Glory': John Rich (1692–1761)*

John McAleer, *Representing Africa: Landscape, Exploration and Empire in Southern Africa, 1780–1870*

Matthew Payne and James Payne, *Regarding Thomas Rowlandson, 1757–1827: His Life, Work and Acquaintance*

William L. Pressly, *James Barry (1741–1806): History Painter*

Kevin Sharpe, *Representations and Revolutions: Images of Kings and Commonwealths, 1603–1660*

Sam Smiles, *Sir Joshua Reynolds: A Life in Art*

Banmali Tandan, *British Architecture in Calcutta in the Georgian Age: An Illustrated Gazetteer*

Kristina Taylor and Robert Peel, *Three Hundred Years of the Bute Family Landscapes*

2009

Alison Brisby, *George Howard, 9th Earl of Carlisle (1843–1911)*

Sarah Burnage and Laura Turner, *William Etty RA*

Elizabeth Chang, *Britain's Chinese Eye: Literature, Empire and Aesthetics in the 19th Century*

Martin Cook, *Edward Prior (1852–1932): Architect, Scholar and Gentleman*

Richard Cork, *Mercy, Madness, Pestilence and Hope: A History of Western Art and Hospitals*

Gordon Crosskey, *Old Sheffield Plate: A History of the 18th-century Plated Trade*

Elizabeth Eger, *Bluestockings Displayed: Portraiture, Performance and Patronage, 1730–1830*

Douglas Fordham, *Allegiance and Autonomy: British Art and the Seven Years' War*

Tim Fulford, *'The Banks of Wye': A Critical Edition of a Picturesque Sketchbook, Journal and Poem*

Hilary Grainger, *The Architecture of Sir Ernest George and Partners*

Albert Grimstone, *Building Pembroke Chapel: Wren, Pearce and Scott*

Christiane Hille, *In 'Britainnes glorious eye': Changing Images of the Courtly Body in Stuart Masque and Painting*

Holger Hoock, *Empires of the Imagination: Politics, War and the Arts in the British World, 1750–1850*

Alex Kidson, *Early British Paintings in the Walker Art Gallery and at Sudley House*

Leonée Ormond, *Linley Sambourne*

Lene Østermark-Johansen, *Walter Pater and the Language of Sculpture*

Christiana Payne, *John Brett*

Amy Sargeant, *'The Servant'*

Kevin Sharpe, *Rebranding Rule: Images of Restoration and Revolution Monarchy, 1660–1714*

Frances Spalding, *The Art of Prunella Clough: Regions Unmapped*

Margaret Willes, *Circles of Cultivation: Gardeners and Gardens 1560–1660*

2010

Jonathan Black, *The Face of Courage: Eric Kennington, Portraiture and the Second World War*

David Coke and Alan Borg, *Vauxhall Gardens 1661–1859: More Nightingales than Strumpets*

Jonathan Conlin, *Grounds for Pleasure: The Pleasure Garden in Britain and the United States, 1660–1914*

Peter Humfrey, *The Reception of Titian in Britain 1769–1877: Artists, Collectors, Critics*

Victoria George, *Whitewash: The New Aesthetic of the Protestant Reformation*

Shannon Hurtado, *Genteel Mavericks: Professional Women Sculptors in Victorian Britain*

Amanda Reeser Lawrence, *Revisionary Modernism: The Architecture of James Stirling, 1955–84*

Margaret MacDonald, *The Etchings of James McNeill Whistler*

Arthur MacGregor, *Animal Encounters. Episodes in a Millennium of Interaction with the Animal Kingdom*

Nancy Marshall, *City of Gold and Mud: Painting Victorian London*

Pauline Rose, *Henry Moore in America: Art, Business and the Special Relationship*

PUBLICATION GRANTS (PUBLISHER)

1998

Barber Institute of Fine Arts, *John Constable 'The Leaping Horse': Masterpieces from the Royal Academy of Arts*

Burlington Magazine, *Collecting Prints and Drawings in Europe 1550–1800*

Cheltenham Art Gallery and Museum, *Catalogue of Cheltenham Art Gallery Arts and Crafts Movement Collections*

National Museums Liverpool, *Earlier British Paintings in the Lady Lever Gallery*

Scolar Press, *Sir John Soane and the Country Estate*

Ruskin Gallery, Sheffield Galleries and Museums Trust, *The Portraits of John Ruskin*

Society of Antiquaries of London, *English Decorative Ironwork 1050–1500*

Walsall Museums and Art Galleries, *Catalogue of the Garman Ryan Collection*

Working Party on Jewish Monuments in the UK and Ireland, *Jewish Buildings and Sites in Britain and Ireland*

York City Art Gallery, *The Artist's Model: From Etty to Spencer*

1999

Ashgate Publishing Ltd, *God's House at Ewelme*

Ashmolean Museum, Oxford, *The Royal Society of Printmakers 1880–1999*

Bolton Museum and Art Gallery, *British Impressionism: Henry La Thangue and the 'Plein-air' Naturalist School 1880–1906*

British Museum, *A Noble Art: Amateur Artists and Drawing Masters 1600–1800*

Cecil Higgins Art Gallery, *Catalogue of Watercolours in the Collection of the Cecil Higgins Gallery*

Curzon Press, *The Artificial Empire: Orientalism and the Picturesque in the Indian Landscapes of William Hodges*

Gandon Editions, *Catalogue of the Ormonde Collection of Paintings at Kilkenny Castle*

Geffrye Museum, *Mary Beale 1632–1699*

Harewood House Trust, *Thomas Girtin in the North*

Harris Museum and Art Gallery, *Arthur William Devis 1762–1822*

Laing Art Gallery, *Art Treasures in the North: Northern Families on the Grand Tour*

Liverpool University Press, *Gainsborough's Vision*

London Borough of Hammersmith and Fulham, *Victorian Artists and Craftsmen in Hammersmith and Fulham*

National Museums Liverpool, *Constable's Clouds*

Oblong Creative Ltd, *John Carr: Architect*

Public Monuments and Sculpture Association, *Public Sculpture of North-East England*

Royal Collection Trust, *The Decoration and Furnishing of the Private Apartments of Windsor Castle 1827–30*

Serpentine Gallery, *Bridget Riley Paintings from the 1960s and 70s*

Temple Newsam House, Leeds Museums and Galleries, *Catalogue of the Warner Collection of Textiles at Temple Newsam*

Whitechapel Art Gallery, *Live in your Head: British Conceptual and Experimental Work of the Sixties and Seventies*

Whitworth Art Gallery, *Catalogue of the Historic Drawings in the Whitworth Art Gallery Collection*

2000

Antique Collectors' Club, *Frederick Sandys 1829–1904: A Catalogue Raisonné and Biography*

Archaeopress, *The History of Gem-Engraving in Britain from Roman Times to the Present*

Ashgate Publishing Ltd, *The Development of the Law Court as a Building Type before 1914*

Ashgate Publishing Ltd, *Building on Ruins: The Roman Monument in English Architecture*

Association for Cultural Exchange, *English Medieval Alabasters*

Barber Institute of Fine Arts, *The Blue Bower: Rossetti in the 1860s*

Ben Uri Gallery, London Jewish Museum of Art, *The Ben Uri Story from Art Society to Museum and the Contribution of Jewish Artists to the Modern British Movement*

British School at Rome, *Lutyens Abroad*

Chapels Society, *The Contexting of a Chapel Architect: James Cubitt 1836–1912*

English Heritage, *Catalogue of Oil Paintings at Kenwood House*

Ferens Art Gallery, *From Medieval to Regency: A Catalogue of Old Masters in the Collection of the Ferens Art Gallery*

Gainsborough's House, *Gainsborough's House Review 1999/2000*

Holburne Museum of Art, *'Love's Prospect': Gainsborough's Byam Family and the 18th-century Marriage Portrait*

Huntington Library, Art Collections and Botanical Gardens, *Catalogue of British Paintings in the Huntington Art Collections*

Leighton House Museum, *Public Artist, Private Passions: The Work of Edward Linley Sambourne*

National Galleries of Scotland, *Andrew Geddes, Painter-Printmaker*

National Gallery of Ireland, *Irish Paintings in the National Gallery of Ireland*

National Museum of Women in the Arts, *Intrepid Women: Victorian Artists' Travel*

Public Monuments and Sculpture Association, *Public Sculpture in Glasgow*

RIBA Publications, *Serge Chermayeff*

The National Trust, *Miniatures in National Trust Houses*

UCL Art Collections/The College Art Collections, *The Graphic Art of Eric Kennington*

University College, Dublin, *Lord Charlemont and his Circle. Essays in Honor of Michael Wynne*

University of Newcastle, *Kenneth Rowntree*

GRANTS 1998–

2001

Archetype Books, *The Pigments of English Medieval Wall Painting*
Art History, *Special issue of Art History, 'Women's Practice and Contemporary Art: Sexuality, Difference and Excess'*
Ashgate Publishing Ltd, *The Emergence of the Professional Watercolourist*
Ashgate Publishing Ltd, *English Accents: Time Present and Time Past*
Association for the Study and Preservation of Roman Mosaics, *The Roman Mosaics of Britain (Vol. 2)*
Black Dog Publishing Ltd, *Ravilious in Public*
British Sporting Art Trust, *Second Supplement to Bibliography of British Sporting Artists*
Dulwich Picture Gallery, *David Wilkie, Genre Painter*
Guildhall Art Gallery, *The Painted Room of Robert Robinson at Sir John Cass's Foundation Primary School*
Heritage Trust for the North West, *Historic Houses in Lancashire: The Douglas Valley 1300–1770*
Holburne Museum of Art, *'Pickpocketing the Rich': Portrait-painting in Bath 1720–1800*
L'Echelle de Jacob, *Dictionary of British Artists who Exhibited in Paris Salons*
National Museums and Galleries of Wales, *Thomas Jones (1792–1803)*
National Museums Liverpool, *'Picture in focus': Exhibition Catalogue of the Walker Art Gallery's Portrait of Henry VIII*
Norfolk Museums and Archaeology Service, *Cedric Morris and his Circle*
Nottingham Castle Museum and Art Gallery, *Richard Parkes Bonington: Young and Romantic*
Public Monuments and Sculpture Association, *Public Sculpture of the City of London*
Reading University, *Catalogue of the Works of Henry Woodyer*
Tate Britain, *Pure as Italian Air: Turner and Claude Lorrain*
The National Trust, *Catalogue of the Silver Collection, Dunham Massey*
Twentieth Century Society, *Twentieth Century Architecture 6: Sixties, Life, Style, Architecture*
Ulster Architectural Heritage Society, *Buildings of North County Down (Vol. 3)*
University of London, School of Advanced Study, *The Reception of William Beckford in Europe: Literature and the Visual Arts*
Victoria and Albert Museum, *Concise Catalogue of British Sculpture at the V&A*
Walpole Society, *Society Volume LXIV*

2002

Ashgate Publishing Ltd, *Modern Architecture and the End of Empire*
Ashgate Publishing Ltd, *Purchasing Power: Representing Prostitution in 18th-century English Popular Print Culture*
Ashgate Publishing Ltd, *Visions of G. F. Watts: Cultural Enchantment in Victorian Art*
British Library, *The Indian Journals of William Daniell 1788–1792*
British Library, *Thomas Bewick: The Complete Works*
Burlington Magazine, *A New Soane Album Discovered*
Chetham's Hospital and Library, *Chetham's: An Architectural History*
Dulwich Picture Gallery, *John Piper in the Thirties*
Edinburgh University Press, *Painting the Nation: Identity and Nationalism in Scottish Painting 1800–1920*
Gallery Oldham, *William Stott of Oldham (1857–1900)*
Hatton Gallery, *William Roberts: A Retrospective*
Holburne Museum of Art, *'Every Look Speaks': Portraits of David Garrick*
Kingston Museum, *Eadweard Muybridge: Projecting the Living Image*
Manchester University Press, *Models and Supermodels: The Artist's Model in British Art and Culture*
Millstream Books, *Thomas Barker of Bath: A Study in Patronage*
Public Monuments and Sculpture Association, *Public Sculpture of Greater Manchester*
Reaktion Books, *Ape to Apollo: Aesthetics and the Idea of Race, c.1700–1800*
Royal Academy of Fine Arts, Stockholm, *Fredrik Magnus Piper and his English Landscape Records*
Royal Watercolour Society, *History of the Royal Watercolour Society 1804–2004*
Scottish National Portrait Gallery, *Sir Francis Grant*
Sir John Soane's Museum, *The George Dance Catalogue*
Tasmanian Museum and Art Gallery, *John Glover (1767–1849) and the Colonial Picturesque*
University of York, The Borthwick Institute, *Eighteenth-century York: Culture, Space and Society*

2003

Ashgate Publishing Ltd, *Extending the Boundaries: Essays on Irish and Scottish Art and Visual Culture*
Ashgate Publishing Ltd, *Indian Renaissance: British Romantic Art and the Prospect of India*
Ashmolean Museum, Oxford, *A Treasured Inheritance: Silver from the Oxford Colleges*
Boydell and Brewer, *The Correspondence of Dante Gabriel Rossetti Vols. IV and V*
C. Hurst and Co. Ltd, *Palace of the People: The Crystal Palace at Sydenham, 1854–1936*
Corpus Vitrearum Medii Aevi, *The Medieval Stained Glass of St Peter Mancroft, Norwich*
Ernst Museum, *Counterparts: James Pitcairn-Knowles with József Rippl-Rónai. Art and Relations beyond the Nabis*
Estorick Collection, *Blasting the Future! Vorticism in Britain 1910–1920*
Guildhall Art Gallery, *City Merchants and the Arts 1670–1720*

Harris Museum and Art Gallery, *Robert Pateson (1827–1910)*
Heritage Trust for the North West, *Architectural History of Towneley Hall*
Leeds Art Collections Fund, *The Leeds Pottery 1770–1881*
Leeds City Art Gallery, *Newby Hall Archive*
Musées de l'Institut de France, *L'art anglais dans les collections de l'Institut de France*
Norfolk Museums and Archaeology Service, *John Sell Cotman: The James Reeve Collection*
Pinakotheke 'Art Magazine', *Special Russian–British issue 'Anglomania in Russia'*
Princeton University, The Drawing Center, *Ocean Flowers and Ferns*
Public Monuments and Sculpture Association, *Public Sculpture of Staffordshire and the Black Country*
Spire Books, *Six Hundred New Churches*
Tate Britain, *Gwen John: Selections from her Letters and Notebooks*
UCL Art Collections/The College Art Collections, *Student Stars at the Slade 1894–1899: Augustus John and William Orpen*
University of Liverpool, *Earthly Delights: Mural Paintings and Other Work by Mary Adshead*
Walpole Society, *Society Volumes LXVI and LXVII*
Watts Gallery Trust, *The Vision of G.F. Watts*
White Cockade Publishing, *Is Mr Ruskin Living too Long? Selected writings of E.W. Godwin on Victorian Architecture, Design and Culture*

2004

Bowes Museum, *The Lady Ludlow Collection of English Porcelain*
British Society of Master Glass Painters, *The Stained Glass Collection of Sir John Soane's Museum*
Buildings Book Trust, *The Buildings of England series* (3 years)
Chippendale Society, *Facsimile Reprint of Thomas Chippendale's 'Director'*
Decorative Arts Society, *Decorative Arts Society Journal (Arts and Crafts Issue No. 28)*
Dulwich Picture Gallery, *The Triumph of Watercolour: The Early Years of the Royal Watercolour Society 1805–1850*
Frances Lincoln Ltd, *The Architecture of Connell, Ward and Lucas*
Gallery Oldham, *Creative Tension: British Art 1900–1950*
London Historic Parks and Gardens Trust, *The London Gardener Vol. 10*
McGill-Queen's University Press, *Monuments and the 18th-century British Empire: Persuasion and Propaganda*
Nottingham Castle Museum and Art Gallery, *Nottingham's Medieval Alabaster Carvings*
Paul Watkins Publishing/Shaun Tyas, *Imported Images: Netherlandish late Gothic sculpture in England c. 1400–1550*
Paul Watkins Publishing/Shaun Tyas, *Towers of Crim Tartary*
Public Monuments and Sculpture Association, *Public Sculpture of Outer South and West London*
Reaktion Books, *Designing the Seaside: Architecture, Culture and the Seaside Resort*
Royal Collection Trust, *The Wisdom of George III*
Society of Antiquaries of London, *Antiquarian Gleanings in the North of England*
Southampton City Art Gallery, *Elements of Abstraction: Space, Line and Interval in Modern British Art*
Spire Books, *The Evolution of Country House Chapels*
University of Oklahoma Press, *American Indians in British Art, 1700–1840*
Wiltshire Heritage Museum, *Art in Wiltshire*

2005

Ashgate Publishing Ltd, *The Look of Van Dyck: The 'Self-Portrait with a Sunflower' and the Vision of the Painter*
Ben Uri Gallery, London Jewish Museum of Art, *Embracing the Exotic: Jacob Epstein and Dora Gordine*
Corpus Vitrearum Medii Aevi, *The Medieval Stained Glass of Cheshire and Lancashire*
Djanogly Gallery, University of Nottingham, *From Victorian to Modern: Laura Knight, Vanessa Bell, Gwen John 1890–1920*
Guildhall Art Gallery, *William Powell Frith*
Public Monuments and Sculpture Association, *Public Sculpture of South London*
Reaktion Books, *Britain (Modern Architectures in History series)*
Reaktion Books, *Peter Lanyon*
RIBA Enterprises Ltd, *Eric Lyons and Span*
Royal Pavilion and Museums, *Rex Whistler: The Triumph of Fancy*
The Buildings of Scotland Trust, *Buildings of Scotland: Borders*
The National Trust, *The Hardwick Hall Embroideries*
The Wordsworth Trust, *Constable and the Lake District, 1806*
Trefoil Press/Trilistnik, Moscow, *George Dawe (1781–1829)*
York Museums Trust, *Constantine the Great: York's Roman Emperor*
Yorkshire Archaeological Society, *Lady Anne Clifford: Culture, Patronage and Gender in 17th-century Britain*

2006

Black Dog Publishing Ltd, *Ellis Woodman: 'A conversation with James Gowan'*
Dulwich Picture Gallery, *Catalogue of British Paintings*
Ferens Art Gallery, *Victorian and Edwardian Art in the Collection of the Ferens Art Gallery*
Geffrye Museum, *Home and Garden: Paintings and Drawings of English Middle-class, Urban, Domestic Spaces, 1914–2006*
John Benjamins Publishing Company, *The Auction of King William III's Paintings: International Art Trade and Diplomacy*
Northwestern University, Mary and Leigh Block Museum of Art, *The Art and Craft of the Machine: British and American Design in the Age of Industry*
Nottingham Castle Museum and Art Gallery, *Wedgwood at Nottingham*
Pallant House Gallery, *Poets in the Landscape: The Romantic Spirit in British Art*

Paul Holberton Publishing, *My Highest Pleasures: The Fine Arts in Dr Hunter's Museum*
Paul Holberton Publishing, *William Orpen: An Onlooker in France, A critical edition*
Public Monuments and Sculpture Association / Liverpool University Press, *Public Sculpture of Bristol*
Reaktion Books, *Designing Modern Britain*
Routledge/Taylor and Francis Books, *Landscapes of Taste: The Art of Humphry Repton's Red Books*
Sir John Soane's Museum, *Cork Models in Sir John Soane's Museum*
Surrey Gardens Trust, *A Celebration of John Evelyn*
Tate Britain, *Neoclassical Sculpture in Britain*
The Buildings of Scotland Trust, *The Buildings of Scotland: Perth and Kinross*

2007

Ben Uri Gallery, London Jewish Museum of Art, *Whitechapel at War: Isaac Rosenberg and his Circle 1911–1918*
Berg Books, *Inventing Van Eyck: The Remaking of an Artist for the Modern Age*
Four Courts Press, *Studies in the Gothic Revival*
Gallery Oldham, *Creative Tension: British Art 1950–2000*
National Galleries of Scotland, *Henry Raeburn: Critical Reception and International Reputation*
National Gallery of Victoria, Melbourne, *Modern Britain: 1900–1960. Master Works from Australian and New Zealand Collections*
National Museums Liverpool, *British Drawings and Watercolours in the Lady Lever Art Gallery*
Public Monuments and Sculpture Association, *Public Sculpture of Herefordshire, Shropshire and Worcestershire*
Royal Pavilion and Museums, *Chinese Whispers: Chinoiserie in Britain 1650–1930*
Southampton City Art Gallery, *Robert Bevan and the Cumberland Market Group*
Sussex Academic Press, *Beyond the Border: Huguenot Goldsmiths in Northern Europe and North America*
Unicorn Press, *Laura Knight: Paintings and Drawings of the Ballet and the Stage*
University of Cambridge, Hamilton Kerr Institute, *The Westminster Retable: History, Technique, Conservation*
University of Chicago Press, *Treasuring the Gaze: Intimacy and Extremity of Vision in Eye Miniature Portraits*
Walpole Society, *Society Volume LXX*

2008

Beazley Archive, University of Oxford, *The History of Gem Engraving in Britain from Antiquity to the Present*
Ben Uri Gallery, London Jewish Museum of Art, *The Forced Journey: Artists in Exile in Britain, c.1933–45*
Birmingham Museums and Art Gallery, *Matthew Boulton: Selling What all the World Desires*
British School at Rome, *Images from the Past: Rome in the Photographs of Peter Paul Mackey 1890–1901*
British School at Rome, *Roma Britannica: Art Patronage and Cultural Exchange in 18th-century Rome*
Buildings Book Trust, *The Buildings of England series* (3 years)
Cheltenham Art Gallery and Museum, *Hugh Willoughby: The Man who loved Picassos*
Corcoran Gallery of Art, Washington, *Helios: The Art of Eadweard Muybridge*
Dorset Natural History and Archaeological Society, *Georgian Faces*
Editions Nicolas Chaudin, *Face à la Révolution et l'Empire: Caricatures anglaises (1789–1815)*
Francis Boutle Publishers, *Silvanus Trevail: Cornish Architect and Entrepreneur*
Georg Olms Verlag, *Arrangement in Business: The Art Markets and the Career of James McNeill Whistler*
Hogarth Arts Ltd, *Regarding Thomas Rowlandson, 1757–1827: His Life, Work and Acquaintance*
La Providence, The French Hospital, *The French Hospital in England: Its Huguenot History and Collections*
Manchester University Press, *Women Artists in Britain, 1918–1940: A fair field and no favour*
Master Drawings Association, *A second supplement to John Hayes's 'The Drawings of Thomas Gainsborough'*
National Galleries of Scotland, *Catalogue of English Drawings and Watercolours, 1600–1900*
Nottingham Castle Museum and Art Gallery, *Picturing Britain: Paul Sandby 1730–1809*
Oxford University Press (India), *Illustrating India: The Early Colonial Investigations of Colin Mackenzie (1784–1821)*
Public Monuments and Sculpture Association, *Public Sculpture of Westminster*
Sansom and Company Ltd, *Sir Joshua Reynolds: A Life in Art*
Spire Books, *Into the Belly of the Beast: Exploring London's Victorian Sewers*
Tate Britain, *William Blake: The 1809 Descriptive Catalogue*
Walpole Society, *Society Volume LXXI*
Yale University Press, *Representations and Revolutions: Images of Kings and Commonwealths, 1603–1660*

2009

Agnes Etherington Art Centre, *View of Gibraltar: Wrong or Wright?*
Antiquarian Horological Society, *English Clockmakers Trading in the Chinese and Ottoman Markets, 1580–1815*
Ashgate Publishing Ltd, *Reframing the Baroque*
Ashgate Publishing Ltd, *Walter Pater and the Language of Sculpture*
Barber Institute of Fine Arts, *Objects of Affection: Pre-Raphaelite Portraits by John Brett*
Birmingham Museum and Art Gallery, *The Poetry of Drawing: Pre-Raphaelite Designs, Studies and Watercolours*
British Art Journal, *The British Art Journal, 10th Anniversary Special Issue*
Church Monuments Society, *A painted canvas funeral monument of 1615 in the Society of Antiquaries of London and its comparators*
Corpus Vitrearum Medii Aevi, *The Medieval Stained Glass of Merton College, Oxford*

Frontier Publishing, *The Glorious Dead: Figurative Sculpture of the British First World War Memorials*
IHS BRE Press, *Edward Prior (1852–1932): Architect, Scholar and Gentleman*
Lund Humphries, *The Art of Prunella Clough: Regions Unmapped*
Mercer Art Gallery, Harrogate Borough Council, *John Atkinson Grimshaw (1836–1893): Painter of Moonlight*
Nottingham City Museums and Galleries, *Nottingham Brown Salt-glazed Stoneware 1690–1800*
Oxford University Press, *Passport to Peking: A Very British Mission to Mao's China*
Paul Holberton Publishing, *Linley Sambourne*
Public Catalogue Foundation, *Oil Paintings in Public Ownership Series*
RIBA Enterprises Ltd, *Sir Basil Spence: Buildings and Projects*
Spire Books Ltd, *R.D. Chantrell (1793–1872) and the Architecture of a Lost Generation*
Stanford University Press, *Britain's Chinese Eye: Literature, Empire and Aesthetics in the 19th Century*
University of Cambridge, Kettle's Yard, *Savage Messiah: A Biography of the Sculptor Henri Gaudier-Brzeska*
University of Pennsylvania Press, *Allegiance and Autonomy: British Art and the Seven Years' War*
V & A Publishing, *Artistic Circles: Design and Decoration in the Aesthetic Movement*
Walpole Society, *Society Volume LXXII*
Wolverhampton Art Gallery, *Cranbrook Colony of Artists: A Fresh Perspective*

2010

Ashmolean Museum, *Entente Cordiale: Lucien Pissarro's Eragny Press 1895–1914*
Australian Scholarly Publishing, *Making Melbourne's Monuments: The Sculpture of Paul Montford*
Berghahn Books Ltd, *Ernst L. Freud, Architect, and the Case for the Modern Bourgeois Home*
Boydell and Brewer, *The Medieval Art and Architecture of Bristol Cathedral*
Brepols Publishers, *Rubens in London: Art and Diplomacy*
British Museum, *Anglo-Saxon Art*
Burlington Magazine, *Postscript to Paul Nash's 'Landscape at Iden': From Millet's 'Angelus' to 'Objects in Relation'*
Compton Verney, *Stanley Spencer and the English Garden*
Frances Lincoln Ltd, *As They Really Were: Citizens of Alnwick 1831*
Henry Moore Institute, *A Biographical Dictionary of Sculptors in Britain*
Holburne Museum of Art, *Gainsborough's Landscapes: Themes and Variations*
Liverpool University Press, *Visions of Blake: William Blake in the Art World 1830–1930*
Modern Art Press, *William Nicholson: A Catalogue Raisonné of the Oil Paintings*
Moggerhanger House Preservation Trust, *Moggerhanger Park: An Architectural and Social History*
Philip Wilson Publishers, *The Face of Courage: Eric Kennington, Portraiture and the Second World War*
Public Monuments and Sculpture Association, *Public Sculpture of Cheshire and Merseyside (except Liverpool)*
Reaktion Books, *Animal Encounters: Episodes in a Millennium of Interaction with the Animal Kingdom*
Royal Pavilion & Museums, *Radical Bloomsbury: Vanessa Bell and Duncan Grant, 1905–1925*
V & A Publishing, *Alastair Morton and Edinburgh Weavers: Textiles and Modern Art*
Victorian Society West Yorkshire Group, *Building a Great Victorian City: Leeds Architects and Architecture 1800–1914*
Watts Gallery, *Compton: An Artists' Village*
Yale University Press, *Rebranding Rule: Images of Restoration and Revolution Monarchy, 1660–1714*
York Museums Trust, *William Etty: Art and Controversy*
Handel House Museum, *The Music Party: Works by Marcellus Laroon (1700–1760)*

RESEARCH SUPPORT GRANTS

2000

Katherine Allocco, *Edward II and Queen Isabella*
Charlotte Chastel-Rousseau, *Royal Monuments and Public Spaces in Great Britain 1714–1820*
Stefanie Knoll, *Funerary Monuments Erected between 1580 and 1680 to Commemorate Professors ... [at] Oxford, Tubingen and Leiden*
Amanda Luyster, *Image, Text, Context: 'Tristan and Isolde' in Medieval Architecture*
Angela Thirlwell, *William Michael Rossetti and Lucy Madox Brown Rossetti*
Catherine Tite, *The Elite Family: Representation and English Visual Culture 1750–1789*
Penelope Treadwell, *Biography of Johan Zoffany*

2001

Mary Bennett, *A Catalogue of the Works of Ford Madox Brown*
Hugh Brigstocke, *William Young Ottley's Collection*
Christina Carlson, *From Conflict to Catholicism: Anti-Popery as 'Social Contract' in Political Cartoons and Political Drama in England 1603–88*
Rebecca Daniels, *Walter Sickert and Popular Art*
Bianca de Divitiis, *Sir John Soane at Pitzhanger Manor*
Jennifer Edes-Pierotti, *Picture Perfect: Behavioral Modification in Late Medieval English Wall Painting*
Karen Go, *Early 20th-century Modernism*
Ruth Harland, *Sir Frank Dicksee*
Anne Helmreich, *Landscape Painting in Britain 1880–1920*
Jennifer Holmes, *The City and Gender in Vorticism and Italian Futurism c.1909–18*
Lynn Knight, *Biography of Clarice Cliff*
Deborah Lewittes, *Architecture in the Diaspora: England 1927–57*
Melinda McCurdy, *English History Painting c.1820–1837*
Maria Grazia Messina, *Shakespeare in European Painting 1750–1850*

GRANTS 1998–

Richard Plant, *The Architecture of the Anglo-Saxons*
Jenny Ramirez, *Clementina Hawarden (1822–1865)*
Michael Rosenthal, *The Artless Landscape: Colonial Imagery of Australia 1788–1840*
Deborah Shaffer, *Fashioning an Ideal of Intimacy: British Family Portraits 1730–90*
Dimitry Shvidkovsky, *British Architecture and Gardens XVI–XVIII Century*
Matthew Sturgis, *Biography of Walter Sickert*
Nicholas Tracy, *Britannia's Palette: The Arts of Naval Victory*

2002

Alissa Ardito, *The English Garden City Movement and the American City Beautiful Movement*
Oliver Bradbury, *Lord Northwick's Patronage of the British School of Painting, 1795–1859*
Anna Bronovitskaia, *A Pictorial Taste for History: Burne-Jones's Interpretation of Art History Ideas*
Gill Clarke, *Evelyn Dunbar (1906–1960)*
Howard Colvin, *Biographical Dictionary of British Architects 1600–1840*
Bianca de Divitiis, *Sir John Soane at Pitzhanger Manor*
Denine Lynette Dudley, *Art, Taste and Self-fashioning: Henrietta Louisa Jeffreys, Countess of Pomfret (1698–1761)*
Nicholas Eastaugh, *George Field's Pigments for 'Pigmentum Project'*
Mark Girouard, *Elizabethan and Jacobean Architecture*
Eileen Harris, *The Life and Works of Thomas Wright of Durham*
Barrett Kalter, *The Material Cultures of Gothicism, 1750–1825*
Catherine Lampert, *Euan Uglow 1932–2000*
Thomas McGeary, *Music Opera and Travellers on the Grand Tour*
Julie Park, *Beautiful Mischief: Dollship and the Birth of Pandora in 18th-century England*
Jennifer Ramkalawon, *The History of the Institute of Contemporary Arts*
Kent A.C. Rawlinson, *The Household Chapel and Chaplain in Medieval England c.1250–c.1500*
Dennis Sharp, *Connell, Ward and Lucas*
Jason Shron, *Modernity and the British Railway Landscape 1825–1860*
Ekaterina Vyazova, *'England' and 'Englishness' in Russian Artistic Culture of the late 19th Century*
Michael Walsh, *Biography of C.R.W. Nevinson*

2003

Anthony Bailey, *A Life of John Constable*
Wendy Baron, *Walter Sickert*
Alixe Bovey, *The Smithfield Decretals*
Michael Charlesworth, *The History of the Landscape Garden at Wentworth Castle*
Ian Christie-Miller, *The Grete Herball, 1526*
Linda Cabe Halpern, *The Durham Garden Designs of Joseph Spence*
Caroline Dakers, *Mercantile Taste in the Victorian Period: James and Charles Morrison at Basildon 1838–1909*
Carole Fry, *The Dissemination of Palladian Architecture throughout England 1700–1775*
Paul Goldman, *John Everett Millais and the Art of Illustration*
Melanie Hall, *Shakespeare's Birthplace and Carlyle's House*
Maria Hayward, *Catherine of Aragon*
John Kenworthy-Browne, *Joseph Nollekens*
Michael Lobel, *Paolozzi's Sources: Time and History in Postwar Britain*
Todd Longstaffe-Gowan, *Late 18th-century drawings by John Spiers of Hampton Court Palace*
Joanne Lukitsh, *Julia Margaret Cameron and Sir Coutts Lindsay*
Christopher Newall, *Alfred William Hunt*
Alison F. O'Byrne, *Walking, Rambling and Promenading in 18th-century London*
Jill Pearlman, *The Isokon Flats: The Biography of a British Modernist Icon*
Vyacheslav P. Shestakov, *Pre-Raphaelite Art: Its History and World Influence*
Stephane Roy, *Another Tale of Two Cities: Prints and Printmaking in 18th-century London and Paris*
Julie Sheldon, *Elizabeth Eastlake*
Mei-Ying Sung, *William Blake's Engravings of the Book of Job*
Nicholas Tromans, *David Wilkie*
Katharina Wippermann, *Frederic Leighton's Education at the Städelschule in Frankfurt am Main*

2004

Vanessa Alayrac, *Chinoiserie in 18th-century England*
Julia Armstrong-Totten, *The Career of Picture Dealer Extraordinaire, Michael Bryan (1757–1821)*
Christopher Augerson, *The Artistry and Technology of Carriage Painting and Decoration*
Ross Balzaretti, *British Travellers in Liguria*
Claire Bowen, *Iconographic Narratives of World War I*
Alex Bremner, *Ecclesiology and the Colonial Church: Architecture, Empire and Identity in the mid-Victorian Imagination 1840–70*
Edward Chaney, *The English College Pilgrim Record Book*
Luciano Cheles, *The Impact of Piero della Francesca on Artists of the British School 1913–38*
John Cherry, *Catalogue of the Rawlinson Seals in the Ashmolean Museum, Oxford, Italian section*
Alan Crawford, *The Arts and Crafts Movement in England*
Katia Dabdoub, *The Furniture Trade of Gillows of Lancaster to the Caribbean*
Pamela M. Fletcher, *'Let me be your banker': The Rise of the Commercial Art Gallery in mid-Victorian London*
Elizabeth Goldring, *Painting at the Elizabethan Court: Robert Dudley, Earl of Leicester and Early English Patronage and Collecting*
Tamara Griggs, *Drawn from Nature: Text and Image in 'The Antiquities of Athens', 1762–1816*

David Hansen, *John Dempsey's 1820s Portraits of the British Urban Poor*
Tanya Harrod, *The Potter Michael Cardew*
Vaughan Hart, *John Vanburgh: Storyteller in Stone*
Robert Hewison, *Ruskin's Venetian Drawings and Notebooks in the Ruskin Library, Lancaster*
Gill Hunter, *William White*
Noah Hysler-Rubin, *Patrick Geddes, Town Planner in the British Colonies*
Joseph James, *The Designs and Fine Bindings of Talwin Morris (1865–1911)*
Richard Johns, *Sir James Thornhill*
Steven R. Kendall, *Classicism and Modernity: Frederic Leighton, the French Academy, and the Anglicised Nude*
Evgeny Khodakovsky, *Alexander Cozens and his 'Encyclopedia of Landscape'*
Jordana Mendelson, *Roland Penrose's Collages: Postcards, Color, and Camouflage*
Christiana Payne, *John Brett (1831–1902)*
Amy Sargeant, *Alexander MacKendrick's Film 'The Man in the White Suit'*
Paul Michael Snell, *'The Priest of Form': John Dando Sedding and the Languages of Late Victorian Architecture*
William Vaughan, *Samuel Palmer*
Jon Wood, *The Sculptor's Studio in Britain: Place, Representation and Reconstruction*

2005

Hugh Belsey, *Thomas Gainsborough*
Peter Black, *Dr William Hunter's Art Collection*
Ruth Brimacombe, *A Grand Tour in the Greater Britain: Art and the Prince of Wales's Royal Progress to India in 1875–6*
Lisa Brocklebank, *Eveleen Myers: 'Spirit' Photographer*
Anne Bush, *Leading the Witness: 19th-century Images of Rome*
Mercedes Ceron, *Defective Perceptions: Marketing Visual Culture in late 18th-century Spain*
Ingrid Ciulisova, *British Portraits in Slovak Art Collections*
David P. Connell, *William Dugood's Collection of Casts at Burton Constable Hall*
Diana Dethloff, *Peter Lely Catalogue Raisonné*
Anne Dulau, *Dr William Hunter's Art Collection*
Celina Fox, *The Art of Industry in the Age of Enlightenment*
Nancy E. Green, *Bloomsbury: A Sense of Place, from Holland Park to Charleston*
Sarah Louise Hoglund, *The Birth of the Cemetery: Death and the Construction of Britishness*
Helen McCormack, *Dr William Hunter's House in Great Windmill Street c.1768–1789*
Diana Maltz, *Bohemia's Bo(a)rders: Queer Space in the Fin de Siècle*
Hiram Morgan, *Renaissance Images of the Irish, 1521–1690*
John Potvin, *Vale(d) Pleasures: Charles Shannon and Charles Ricketts and the Art of Domesticity*
Amanda Reeser Lawrence, *Rewriting Modernism: The Architecture of James Stirling from 1955 to 1983*
Elizaveta Renne, *Preparation for a full catalogue of British Paintings in the Hermitage*
Nicolas Roquet, *William Burges (1827–1881): A Life in Costume*
Jonathan Sachs, *Picturing Palmyra, Reading Homer: Robert Wood's Travels, Copperplate Engraving and Classical Scholarship*
Kimberley Skelton, *Planning Anew: The English Country House and Social Identity in the 1650s*
Abbie N. Sprague, *Edward Wadsworth (1889–1947): The Queen Mary Commission*
Rosemary Sweet, *The Grand Tour in Italy in the 18th Century*
Ulrike Tomalla, *Fashionable Images: 18th-century English Pocket Book Illustrations*
Michael Walsh, *The Life and Work of C.R.W. Nevinson*
Susan Wilson, *The 19th-century English Swiss Cottage*

2006

Prudence Ahrens, *Arthur Haythorne Studd (1863–1919)*
Geoffrey Brandwood, *The Architecture of Paley and Austin*
Alex Bremner, *The History of Anglican Architecture in the Antipodes*
Jessica Buskirk, *Intimacy and Anticipation: The Male Subject in 15th-century Personal Devotional Portraits*
Alan Crawford, *British Elements and Influence in the Work of the Architects Charles and Henry Greene*
William Eisler, *The British Medals of the Dassiers, 1725–1751*
Richard Garnier, *Life and Work of Alexander Roos*
Cristiano Giometti, *Giovanni Battista Guelfi (1690–1736): The Career of a Roman Sculptor in Georgian London*
Jason Kelly, *Archaeology and Identity in the British Enlightenment: The Society of Dilettanti, 1732–1816*
Stephen Kite, *Ruskin and Stokes and the Architectonic Surface: Venice and Verona*
Julian Luxford, *The West Front of Peterborough Cathedral: its Architectural and Sculptural Iconography*
Brenda Martin, *Dora Gordine (1898–1991)*
Alla Myzelev, *Russia in Bloomsbury: Influences of the Russian Arts and Crafts Movement in England 1890–1930*
Patrick Noon, *A Complete Catalogue of the Oil and Watercolour Paintings of Richard Parkes Bonington*
John Plunkett, *Optical Recreations: A History of Screen Practice 1780–1900*
Dominic Rahtz, *T.E. Hulme's Anti-Humanist Theory of Art*
Mary Roberts, *Refashioning the Empire: British Artists/Ottoman Patrons*
Urmila Seshagiri, *Race and the Modernist Imagination: The Politics of Form, 1890–1930*
Yuthika Sharma, *At the Margins of Empire: The Art and Architecture of Estates in the Delhi Suburbs (1803–1857)*
Paul Michael Snell, *Sedding in America*
Fabrizia Spirito, *View Painting and Grand Tour: Lusieri's Unpublished Views and Drawings*

GRANTS 1998–

Pamela Trimpe, *Bovine Portraits: Victorian Big Beasts*
Catherine Wallace, *The Paintings of Henry Scott Tuke RA (1858–1929)*
Dana Wheeles, *Imagining the Renaissance: Art, Historiography and the 19th Century*
Amelia Yeates, *The Artist and Masculinity in Burne-Jones's 'Pygmalion and the Image'*

2007

Katherine Acheson, *Visual Rhetoric and 17th-century English Print Culture*
Adriano Aymonino, *The First Duke and Duchess of Northumberland: Political Strategies, Patronage and Collecting in the Age of the Grand Tour*
Elizabeth Bishop, *The Architectural Infrastructure of Empire: The British Mitigation of Imports via the Warehouses of London's Docklands*
Olga Borodkina, *Aesthetic Movement: Literature and Art Criticism to Visual Arts*
Hugh Brigstocke, *A Catalogue of Drawings assembled by William Ottley*
Antonio Brucculeri, *The Urban Approach of Edwin Lutyens: A Study in the War Years, 1938–1943*
Patricia Crown, *Edward Frances Burney (1760–1848)*
Elizabeth Darling, *The Work and Life of Wells Coates, Architect–Engineer*
Bianca de Divitiis, *Eighteenth-century British Collectors in Naples: A New Source for the Acquisition of Antique Sculpture*
Sigrid Dagmar De Jong, *Rediscovering Architecture; Paestum in 18th-century Architectural Thought*
Anne Dulau, *Boucher and Chardin in 18th-century Britain*
Robert Folkenflik, *Portraits of Samuel Johnson*
Amy Frost, *Commissions by Henry Edmund Goodridge (1797–1864) for the 10th Duke of Hamilton*
Helen Gyger, *John F.C. Turner and Christopher Alexander*
Richard Hayes, *John Ruskin and the Road to Ferry Hinksey: Secular Volunteerism in 19th-century England*
Alistair Kwan, *Building Science: Architecture and the Early Modern Study of Nature*
Ann Smart Martin, *'Banish the Night': Illumination and Reflection in Early Modern England and America*
Susan Morrison, *Images of Excrement in Late Medieval England*
John Munns, *The Crucified Body of Christ: Cross, Passion, Image and Devotion in England 1066–1215*
Richard James Nieman, *The Minor Cruciform Churches of Anglo-Norman Sussex and the New Norman Aristocracy*
John Potvin, *Domesticating Passion: Sir Cedric Morris and Arthur Lett-Haines and the Art of Modern Living*
Tania Sengupta, *Architecture of Governmental and Civic Domains: Colonial Encounter in District Towns, Bengal, British India*
Robert Tittler, *Portraits, Painters and Publics in Post-Reformation England: The Canterbury Experience*
Catherine Walden, *Redemption and Remembrance: The English Episcopal Tomb in the 12th and 13th Century*
Kaylin Weber, *Benjamin West and his Aesthetic Environment*
Matthew Woodworth, *The 13th-century Choir and Transepts of Beverley Minster*

2008

Alison Brisby, *The Painted Works of George Howard, 9th Earl of Carlisle*
Samantha Burton, *Tourism and Identity in the Work of Elizabeth Armstrong Forbes, Harriet Ford, Mary Alexandra Bell Eastlake and Helen McNicholl*
Georgina Cole, *The Paintings of Joseph Highmore and Thomas Gainsborough in British Institutions*
Viccy Coltman, *Marble Mania: The Art History and Historiography of Sculpture in Britain since 1760*
Ruth Cribb, *Eric Gill and Transformative Practices in British Sculpture 1909–1940*
Andrea De Meo, *Features and Functions of Court Catholic Chapels between the 16th and 17th Century*
Susanna Falabella, *Thomas Martyn (1735–1825): The Analysis of the Unpublished Correspondence for the Definition of the Historic–Artistic Interests of a Traveller through Italy*
Amy Hale, *The Work of Ithell Colquhoun*
Elizabeth Lebas, *Forgotten Futures: British Municipal Cinema, 1920–1978*
Marina Lopato, *Catalogue of British Silver in the Hermitage Museum*
Helen McCormack, *Dr William Hunter and the British School of Artists*
Lucinda Middleton, *Henry Bone, his Workshop and Family*
Paola Modesti, *Architectural Exempla between Venice and England in the 18th Century: Travels, Drawings, and Books*
Edward Nygren, *The Letters of James Ward, RA (1769–1859)*
Temi-Tope Odumosu, *The Black Joke: Iconographies of African People in 18th- and 19th-century English Satirical Prints*
John Potvin, *Lord Ronald Sutherland-Gower: Artist, Dilettante Art Historian, Collector, Decorator*
Robert Proctor, *Roman Catholic Church Architecture in Britain, 1955–1975*
Patricia Reed, *Catalogue Raisonné of the Oil Paintings of William Nicholson (1872–1949)*
Kate Retford, *David Allan and the Conversation Piece in Britain, c.1720–1790*
Salisbury and South Wiltshire Museum Trust, *Constable and Salisbury*
Giovanni Santucci, *The Largest Talman Album: A Nexus between Catholic and Anglican Ecclesiastical Architecture*
Evelyn Silber, *Selling the Moderns in Britain: The Leicester Galleries and the Changing Face of Dealing and Collecting in London 1900–1960*

Amy Sargeant, *Port Sunlight: Art, Advertising and Industry*
Abbie N. Sprague, *The Birmingham School of Art: Arts and Crafts Painting in Birmingham*
Glenn Sujo, *Jankel Adler in Britain*
Francois Tainturier, *Rangoon and Mandalay in mid-19th-century Burma*
Chiara Teolato, *Roman Decorative Bronzes and the Taste for the Antique in the British Country House (1750–1820)*
Gwen Yarker, *Georgian Faces*
Carolyn Yerkes, *Sir Thomas Browne and 17th-century Diagrams*

2009
John Barrell, *Edward Pugh's 'Denbighshire'*
Jessica Berenbeim, *English Gothic Manuscript Illumination*
Stephen Bottomore, *The Art of Painting Films*
George Breeze, *The Craftsman Painter: Joseph Southall and the Tempera Revival*
Luca Caddia, *'Sub Rosa Aeternitatis': Alma-Tadema and the Collection of Identity*
Viccy Coltman, *Scots in India*
Renate Dohmen, *Painting with Colour and Light: The Art of the Amateur Artist in British India*
Sonja Drimmer, *The Visual Language of Vernacular Manuscript Illumination: John Gower's 'Confessio Amantis'*
Katharine Eustace, *Hew Lorimer (1907–1993): A Sculptor's Life in Context*
Kristen Fairey, *'Tres testimonium dant': The Architecture and Rhetoric of Sir Thomas Tresham's Three Lodges of the 1590s*
Jennifer Ferng, *Rococo Interior Designs of John Vardy and Use of Colour ... in the Architecture of William Butterfield*
Michael Gaudio, *'Prosper Thou Our Handyworks': Prints and Protestant Devotion at Little Gidding, 1625–1642*
Ivelin Ivanov, *Between Imagination and Reality: War in 13th- to 15th-century English Gothic Manuscripts*
Catherine Jolivette, *Art and the Atom: British Art in the Nuclear Age*
Dipti Khera, *Urban Imaginings Between Empires: Picturing British India's 'Land of Princes'*
Roy Kozlovsky, *The Architecture of Childhood: English Modernism and the Welfare State*
Jason LaFountain, *The Puritan Art World*
David Mackie, *The Complete Catalogue of the Works of Sir Henry Raeburn (1756–1823)*
Caroline Malloy, *A Bit of Irish for Everyone: Visual and Material Fragments of Irishness at International Exhibitions, 1851–1939*
Jeffrey Miller, *The Building Program of Walter de Gray*
Bénédicte Miyamoto, *The Value of Art in 18th-century Britain: Moral, Aesthetic and Economic Perspectives*
Anne-Françoise Morel, *The Construction of Meaning in 17th- and 18th-century Church Architecture in England*
David Raizman, *Presentation Furniture in England, 1851–1889*
Chitra Ramalingam, *Henry Fox Talbot and the art of fixing transience*
Romita Ray, *Under the Banyan Tree: Relocating the Picturesque in British India, 1700–1947*
Sarah Thomas, V*isual Encounters in the New World: Race and Slavery through British Eyes, 1800–1850*
Maria Toscano, *John Strange and John Hawkins Italian Correspondences*
David Taylor, *Theatre and Graphic Satire, 1737–1837*

2010
Alena Artamonova, *Sir Thomas Lawrence and the British Portrait Tradition*
Piers Baker-Bates, *'The dullest country in Europe': Exploring Relations between British Artists and Collectors and Spain in the 18th Century*
Jan Blanc, *The writings of Sir Joshua Reynolds*
Mark Broughton, *Art and Architecture in 'Brideshead Revisited'*
Michelle Carriger, *He, She, or It: Contested Performances of Victorian Femininity in Britain and Japan*
Gill Clarke, *Randolph Schwabe: Artist and Teacher*
Zirwat Chowdhury, *Anglo-Indian Encounters: British Art and Architecture, 1780–1836*
Carly Collier, *The Re-evaluation of Medieval and Early Renaissance Italian Art in British Taste during the Long 18th Century*
Renate Dohmen, *Painting with Colour and Light: The Art of the Amateur Artist in British India: Madras, Bombay and the 'Hindoo Patriot'*
Alexis Drahos, *The Influence of Hutton's Theories on British Landscape Painting during the First Half of the 19th Century*
Sibylle Erle, *Seeing the Face Read: The Role of the Silhouette in Johann Caspar Lavater's 'hysiognomy'*
Polina Ermakova, *Laurence Sterne's 'A Sentimental Journey through France and Italy': Poetics of the Novel and the Visual Culture of the Enlightenment*
Meredith Gamer, *Criminal and Martyr: Art and Religion in Britain's Early Modern 18th Century*
Yvonne Gaspar, *Richard Bradley (1688?–1732): English Botany in Transition*
Gabriel Gee, *The John Moores Painting Prize: A History of British Painting in the Second Half of the 20th Century*
Pamela Gerrish-Nunn, *Eleanor Fortescue Brickdale and the Survival of Pre-Raphaelitism*
Albert Grimstone, *Edward Pearce senior: Drawings, Engravings, Paintings and Interior Design*
Ann Gunn, *The Prints of Paul Sandby (1731–1809): A Catalogue Raisonné*
David Hansen, *Poor People: John Dempsey and his 'remarkable character' Portraits*
Clare Haynes, *Idol or Ornament? Art in the Church of England 1660–1830*

GRANTS 1998–

Gordon Higgott, *Edward Pearce senior: Drawings, Engravings, Paintings and Interior Design*
Alba Irollo, *The Lure of the Antique from Pompeii to Victorian London: The Diffusion of Small Casts in Bronze and the Beginnings of the 'New Sculpture'*
Katherine Isard, *Architectural Commonplaces; Books, Reading and Building Practice in the Early Modern Period*
Iain Jackson, *Maxwell Fry and Jane Drew: Architecture, Collaborations and Postcolonial Settlements*
Maija Jansson, *Art and Diplomacy: Document Design in 17th-century Great Britain*
Chloe Kroeter, *Silent Protest: Art, Activism, and Deaf Periodicals in Victorian Britain*
Sarah MacDougall, *Mark Gertler: A Complete Catalogue of Paintings and Drawings*
David Mackie, *The Complete Catalogue of the Works of Sir Henry Raeburn (1756–1823)*
Kristin Mahoney, *The Politics of Post-Victorian Aestheticism: Caricatures by Max Beerbohn and Beresford Egan*
Lucinda Middleton, *Henry Bone, his Workshop and Family*
Catriona Murray, *The Cult of the Deceased Prince under the Stuart Monarchy*
Darren Newbury, *Windows on South Africa and the Caribbean: The Bryan Heseltine Photographic Collection*
Lauren Pepitone, *Church and Hall: Historicism and Homosociability at the Temple*
Eleonora Pistis, *Architectural Culture in early 18th-century Oxford*
Robert Proctor, *Roman Catholic Church Architecture in Britain, 1955–1975*
Kate Robertson, *The Expatriate Experience: Australian Artists Abroad 1890–1914*
Henrietta McBurney Ryan, *The Drawings for Mark Catesby's 'Natural History of Carolina, Florida and the Bahama Islands'*
Larry J Schaaf, *British Photographic History Sources in Australia*
Ekaterina Skvortsova, *The Art of J.A. Atkinson and J. Walker as an Example of English–Russian Artistic Links*
Banmali Tandan, *British Architecture in Calcutta during the Georgian Age*
Carl Thompson, *Maria Graham's Contribution to Art History, and her Participation in the 'Callcott Circle' of the 1830s*
Amy Todman, *Contours of Celestial and Terrestrial Topographies: Pictorial Representations and Constructions of Place in Britain c.1600–1820*
Tatyana Tyutvinova, *British Drawings of the 18th to early 20th Century from the Pushkin State Fine Arts Museum Collection*
Ahenk Yilmaz, *Sir John Burnet and the Memorializaton of Gallipoli Battles*

Barns-Graham Research Support Grant
(administered on behalf of the
Wilhelmina Barns-Graham Trust)

2009

John Curley, *The Art that Came in from the Cold: Painting, Photography, and Cold War Visuality*

2010

Emma Acker, *A Sense of Place: The Aerial Abstractions of Richard Diebenkorn and Peter Lanyon*

GRANT AND FELLOWSHIP AWARDS

Total sum awarded 1970–1997: £413,719

Note: grants and fellowships were not differentiated during this period.

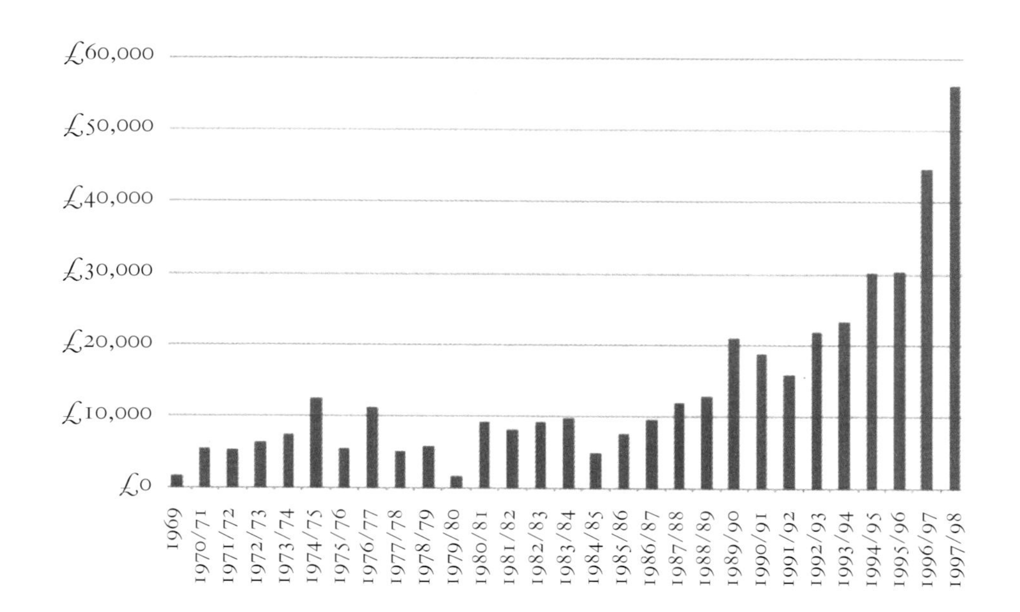

Total sum awarded 1998–2010: £5,706,703

Note: after 1998 grants and fellowships were differentiated; fellowship totals per year are in blue, grants in red.

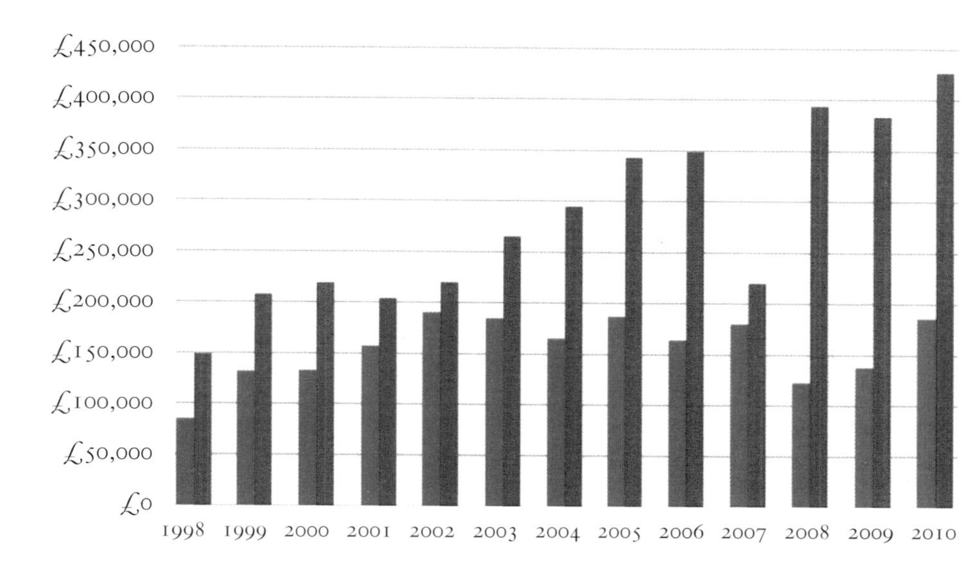

FELLOWSHIPS

THE Paul Mellon Foundation did not operate a Fellowship programme. The first formal fellowships were awarded by the Paul Mellon Centre to Yale graduate students in 1977.

YALE GRADUATE FELLOWSHIPS 1977–80

The first fellowships were inaugurated in 1977–78 for Yale graduate students whose PhD dissertations were wholly or largely concerned with British art. Two fellowships were awarded in that year and one the following year but the Centre was under financial pressure at the beginning of the 1980s and the programme was discontinued.

1978–79
Elizabeth Black, *Manuscripts of the Linsey Psalter Group: Early Gothic Illumination*
Matthew Lalumia, *The English Art Scene and the Crimean War*

1979–80
Hilarie Faberman, *The Work of Augustus Egg*

ANDREW W. MELLON FOUNDATION FELLOWSHIP

This fellowship was established in 1977 following a review of the long-standing exchange fellowship which existed between Yale University and Clare College, Cambridge, established by Paul Mellon in 1932 after he graduated from Cambridge. The Mellon Fellowship was created to promote friendship and understanding between England and the United States, to encourage a mutual expression of interest in the life and thought of both nations, to advance the cause of education by the exchange of ideas of educational methods, and to create a special tie between Cambridge and Yale.

In the light of the review it was agreed that the Andrew W. Mellon Foundation would fund four fellowships annually, one of which was to be administered via the Advisory Council of the Paul Mellon Centre. Candidates were chosen by a competition open to applications from the entire United Kingdom in the field of the history of British art. Candidates were normally under twenty-five years of age and generally, though not necessarily, enrolled for a higher degree. The successful candidate was expected to take up residency at Yale and be affiliated with the Yale Center for British Art for one year, with the possibility in exceptional circumstances of an additional year's extension. Applications for the fellowship were first invited in 1978 and the first successful candidate took tenure in the academic year 1978–79. The Andrew W. Mellon Foundation renewed their support of the fellowship for further six-year periods in 1980, 1987 and 1993. As a result of changes in graduate studies at British universities from the mid-1980s doctoral candidates were under pressure to complete their dissertations in three years so the prospect of a year's overseas fellowship became less enticing and from that time the number of applicants for the fellowship diminished.

1979–80
Nicola Shilliam, *Foreign Influences on and Innovation in English Tomb Sculpture in the first half of the 16th Century*

1980–81
Duncan Bull, *British Landscape Artists in Italy in the 18th Century*

1981–82
Stephen Deuchar, *British Sporting Art*

1983–83
Peter Funnell, *Richard Payne Knight (1751–1824)*

1984–85
Susan Morris, *Thomas Girtin*

1985–86
Sheila O'Connell, *William Hogarth and Popular Imagery*

1986–87
John Morrison, *Scottish Genre Painting in the 19th Century*

1987–88
David Mackie, *Catalogue of the Paintings of Sir Henry Raeburn*

1988–89
Harry Mount, *The History of Changing Attitudes to 17th-century Dutch Genre Painting in 18th- and early 19th-century Britain*

1990–91
Mark Hallett, *The Political Dimension to British Satirical Prints in the first half of the 18th Century*
Jessica Morgan, *British Artists in America from the 1950s to the Present Day*

1995–96
Kevin Ottley, *William Dyce and Early Italian Painting*
Pascal du Puy, *Graphic Satire in late 18th-century England*

1996–97
Sophie Carter, *The Image of the Prostitute in 18th-century British Art*

1997–98
Susan Jenkins, *The Career of James Brydges, 1st Duke of Chandos, as a Patron of the Arts in the early 18th Century*

1998–99
Richard Pound, *Victorian Comic Periodicals*
Nicola Tyson, *Caricature and Social Practice 1725–97*

PAUL MELLON CENTRE FELLOWSHIPS 1987–1998

The Paul Mellon Centre Fellowship was established in 1987 with the aim of providing support for (primarily American or Canadian) doctoral candidates specialising in any area of the history of British art before 1960. In particular the fellowship was conceived to enable students to spend time in the UK using academic research resources, libraries, archives, galleries and museums undertaking primary research for their dissertations. During the period of tenure fellows were attached to the Centre and in some years the fellowship was split between candidates if a full academic year in London was not required. The fellowship ran from 1987 until the introduction in 1998 of the Centre's new fellowship programme.

1987/88
Mark Crinson, *Nineteenth-century British-designed Consulates and Churches in the Near East*

1988/89
Dian Kriz, *Turner in the Context of early 19th-century British History*

1989/90
David Nolta, *British Artists and Travellers in Naples in the 18th Century*

1990/91
Daniel Abramson, *The Architectural, Economic and Political History of the Bank of England in the 18th Century*
Robyn Asleson, *The Significance and Meaning of the Classical Revival in late 19th-century British Painting*

1991/92
Melissa Hall, *Modernism, Militarism and Masculinity: Modern Art Discourse and British Official War Art during the First World War*
Joel M. Hoffman, *Imagining the Industrial Village: Visual Arts in the Utopian Community of Bournville, England*

1992/93
Stephen Gleissner, *The Art of Patronage of Charles II*
Kathryn Smith, *Fourteenth-century Book of Hours* (turned down in favour of Fulbright scholarship)

1993/94
Alexander Curtis, *The City of London churches designed by Sir Christopher Wren*
James Sutton, *The Patronage of the Cecil family, with special reference to Theobalds and Hatfield House*

1994/95
Elizabeth Mansfield, *Art Criticism of the 19th-century Writer Emilia Frances Dilke*

1995/96
James Ganz, *Development of the Mezzotint Engraving in later 17th-century England*
Britt Salvesen, *Stereoscopy in Victorian Art*

1996/97
Karen Olsen, *Creations of Empire: Liberty and Company and the Commodification of Britishness*
Romita Ray, *Representing India: The Picturesque and the Art of the British Raj, 1757–1900*

1997/98
Elizabeth Barker, *The Candlelight Pictures of the 18th-century Painter, Joseph Wright of Derby*
Elizabeth Chew, *Female Art Collecting and Patronage in 17th-century Britain*
Helene Furjan, *The architecture of Sir John Soane's House in Lincoln's Inn Fields in London*

1998/99
Lynn Schibeci, *The London Auction House and the Commodification of English Taste, 1780–1820*
Eleanor Hughes, *Vessels of Empire: 18th-century British Marine Painting*
Diane Waggoner, *Picturing the Child: Desire, Nostalgia and National Identity in Victorian Visual Culture*

DOCTORAL FELLOWSHIPS 1998–2002

1998–2002
Morna O'Neil (Yale University) PhD dissertation, *Art is Born Again: The Allegorical Paintings of Walter Crane*

1998–2002
Douglas Kibbey (Yale University) PhD dissertation *The Aggregate Object: Small-Scale Spoliation in the Middle Ages*

1998–2001
Jonathan Shirland (University College London) PhD dissertation, *Popular Culture and the Art of Wyndham Lewis*

1998–2001
Sarah Monks (Courtauld Institute of Art) PhD dissertation, *Marine Art and the Public Sphere in England 1739–1795*

1999–2001
Tara Hamling (University of Sussex) PhD dissertation, *The English Interior 1558–1660: Iconography and the role of imagery*

FELLOWSHIPS

THE NEW FELLOWSHIPS PROGRAMME

After 1997 a new fellowship programme was introduced: Senior, Rome, Postdoctoral, Junior and Conservation Fellowships.

Senior Fellowships

The Senior Fellowship was created to support established scholars to complete a manuscript for immediate publication. The awards are made for the writing period and not for primary research. Fellowships are offered either as a stipend to the Fellow (if an independent scholar) or to their institution or university to fund a temporary replacement.

1999

Edward McParland, *Building Anglo-Ireland: Public Architecture 1680–1760*
Christopher Wilson, *The Medieval Cathedral of St Paul's*

2000

Frances Spalding, *John and Myfanwy Piper*

2001

Andrew Causey, *English Landscape and National Identity*
Diana Donald, *Animal Imagery in British Art c.1750–1850*
Peter Draper, *Architecture and Identity: The Formation of English Gothic*

2002

David Alexander, *Dictionary of British & Irish Engravers 1714–1830*
Ian Christie, *The Time Traveller: Robert Paul and the Early Moving Picture Business in Britain*
Celina Fox, *The Art of Industry: Art, Science and Technology in 18th-century Europe*
John Peacock, *The Look of Van Dyck: the 'Self-Portrait with a Sunflower' and the Painter's Vision*

2003

Megan Aldrich, *A Nonconformist Vision: Thomas Rickman and the Gothic Revival*
Anthea Callen, *Dangerous Liaisons: Art and Anatomy from Albinus to Freud*
Michael Hatt, *Mirrors and Shadows: The Visual Culture of Male Homoeroticism in Late Victorian Britain*
Kay Dian Kriz, *Slavery, Sugar and the Culture of Refinement: Picturing the British West Indies, c. 1700–1840*
Gavin Stamp, *British Architecture between the Wars*

2004

Nigel Aston, *Religion, Enlightenment and Art in 18th-century Britain and Europe*
Valentine Gatrell, *Satirical Print and Cultural Change in London, c.1770–1830*
William Pressly, *Writing the Vision for a New Public Art: James Barry's Murals at the Royal Society of Arts*
Elizabeth Prettejohn, *Art for Art's Sake: Aestheticism in Victorian Art*

2005

Vaughan Hart, *John Vanbrugh: Storyteller in Stone*
Angela Rosenthal, *The White of Enlightenment: Racializing Bodies in 18th-century Britain*
Amy Sargeant, *'The Man in the White Suit': New Textiles and the Social Fabric*
Frances Spalding, *John and Myfanwy Piper*

2006

Mark Hallett, *Sir Joshua Reynolds: Portraiture and Display in 18th-century England*
Marcia Pointon, *Brilliant Effects: Jewels, Jewellery and their Imagery*
Nigel Thorp, *The Correspondence of James McNeill Whistler*

2007

Daniel Abramson, *Architecture in the Age of Obsolescence*
Lene Østermark-Johansen, *From Front to Back: Walter Pater and the Language of Sculpture*
Banmali Tandan, *British Architecture in Calcutta in the Georgian Age*
Volker Welter, *Architecture without Quality? Ernst L. Freud and Bourgeois Modernism in Architecture*

2008

Mark Crinson, *Stirling and Gowan: Post-Industrial Architecture*
William Vaughan, *'Mysterious Wisdom': The Art and Career of Samuel Palmer*

2009

Timothy Ayers, *The Medieval Stained Glass of Merton College, Oxford*
Anna Gruetzner Robins, *The Artists of the 1890s*

2010

Tarnya Cooper, *Portrait Painting and the Urban Elites of Tudor and Jacobean England and Wales*
Martin Hammer, *Francis Bacon: Images of Power*
Mark Laird, *The Environment of English Gardening, 1650–1800*
Sam Smiles, *Turner's Last Paintings: The Artist in Old Age and the Idea of Late Style*
David Solkin, *Art in Britain 1660–1837*

Rome Fellowships

1999

Helen Langdon, *The Idea of Naples: English Artist Travellers and Writers in Romantic Naples*

2000

Ilaria Bignamini, *Digging and Dealing in 18th-Century Rome*
Hugh Brigstocke, *The Rediscovery of the Italian Primitives and the Concept of Christian Art in 19th-century Britain*

2001
Richard Read, *Adrian Stokes, The Early Career: Art Criticism, Literature and Psychoanalysis*

2002
Richard Wrigley, *Images of Rome in British Romantic Art*

2003
Elizabeth Sears, *Art Historians in Rome in the 1920s and 1930s*

2004
Edward Corp, *The Stuart Court in Italy, 1717–1766*

2005
Chloe Chard, *Laughter and the Imaginative Geography of Italy c.1750–1830*
John Wilton-Ely, *The Adam Style: A Revolution in Design*

2006
Andrew Moore, *Thomas Coke's Grand Tour*
Carol Richardson, *The Venerable English College: A Study in Anglo-Roman Cultural Relations 1361–1920*

2007
Viccy Coltman, *Marble Mania: The Art History and Historiography of Sculpture in Britain since 1760*

2008
William Eisler, *The Medals of Martin Folkes: Art, Newtonian Science and Masonic Sociability in the Age of the Grand Tour*

2009
Ana Maria Suarez Huerta, *Travels Across Europe in the 18th Century: The Unique Case of Spain*

2010
David Rundle, *The English Hand in Rome: Barbarous Britons and the Renaissance Arts of the Humanist Book, 1400–1520*

Postdoctoral Fellowships

The Postdoctoral Fellowship offers support to candidates who require time to convert their PhD dissertations into a publishable manuscript, a series of articles or an exhibition catalogue. Alternatively, the fellowship supports new research arising out of a successfully submitted doctoral dissertation where that research may readily lead to publication. Candidates' dissertations must have been completed within the previous four years. Fellowships are awarded for a period of up to six months and funds can, if appropriate, be used to fund a temporary replacement at a fellow's institution. Fellows may chose to be affiliated with either the Paul Mellon Centre or the Yale Center for British Art.

1998
Christina Baird, *The Liverpool China Trade 1834–1880*
Andrea Fredericksen, *The Metropolitan Picturesque: Associating Ideas in Modern London*
Lucy Peltz, *The Extra-Illustration of London: Status, Sociability and the Urban Imagination*
Greg Smith, *Watercolour and the Public Domain 1760–1824*

1999
Timothy Ayers, *The Medieval Stained Glass of Wells Cathedral*
Jordana Pomeroy, *Collecting the Past to Create a Future: Old Masters, Artists and Patrons in 19th-century England*

2000
Vittoria Di Palma, *The School in the Garden: Aesthetics and Perceptions of Landscape in Britain 1640–1740*
Diana Maltz, *Beauty for the People: Aestheticism and the Urban Working Class 1870–1914*
Cindy McCreery, *Satirical Prints of Women in late 18th-century England*
Jason Rosenfeld, *New Languages of Nature in Victorian England: The Pre-Raphaelite Landscape, Natural History and Modern Architecture in the 1850s*

2001
Carol Davidson Cragoe, *Written in Stone: Architecture, Liturgy and the Laity in English Parish Churches c.1125–1250*
Helene Furjan, *Sir John Soane and the House-museum*
Michaela Giebelhausen, *Representation, Belief and the Pre-Raphaelite Project*
Holger Hoock, *The Royal Academy as a 'National Institution' 1768–1820*
Frederica Law-Turner, *The Ormesby Psalter*
Martin Myrone, *Body-building: British Historical Artists in London and Rome and the Remaking of the Heroic Ideal c. 1760–1800*
Valerie Scott, *The Classical Orders in 16th-century English Architecture*

2002
Robert Burstow, *Sculpture for Democracy: Modern Public Sculpture in 'New Britain' 1945–1953*
Viccy Coltman, *Fabricating the Antique: Neoclassicism in England, c.1763–1796*
David Getsy, *Corporeal Engagement Figuration and Materiality in the Formulations of Modern Sculpture in Britain, from the late Victorians to the English Modernists*
Elizabeth Goldring, *'The Painted gloss of Pleasure': Sir Philip Sidney and the Visual Arts in Renaissance England*
Denise Blake Oleksijczuk, *The Dynamics of Spectatorship in the First Panoramas: Vision, the Body and British Imperialism 1787–1820*
Lara Perry, *Beauties: Women, History and the 19th-century National Portrait Gallery*
Simon Sadler, *Archigram*
Tatiana String, *Holbein and Beyond: Henry VIII and Art*

FELLOWSHIPS

2003

Sonia Ashmore, *Liberty's Orient*

Asia Haut, *Visions Bred on Sense by Fancy: The Transvaluation of Science, Sexuality and Polemics in the Work of Henry Fuseli and his Contemporaries*

Eleanor Hughes, *Vessels of Empire: 18th-century British Marine Paintings*

Matthew Plampin, *From Rio to Romola: Morality and Didacticism in the English Appreciation of Early Italian Art 1836–63*

Aris Sarafianos, *Art Practices and the History of Medical Knowledge in Britain: Reciprocal Transformations, 1757–1846*

Rachel Stewart, *Choice and Reasoning in the West End House*

2004

Alex Bremner, *Ecclesiology and the Colonial Church: Architecture, Empire, and High Victorian Theory 1841–68*

Rosemarie Dias, *John Boydell's Shakespeare Gallery and the Promotion of a National Aesthetic*

Nicholas Grindle, *Experiment and Experience in British art, 1600–1800*

Matthew Hargraves, *Candidates for Fame: The Society of Artists of Great Britain, c.1760–1791*

Sarah Monks, *Making Waves: The Seascape in British Visual Culture 1672–1824*

Joseph Monteyne, *Marking the Boundaries of Self and City: Print Culture and Spatial Practice in Early Modern London*

Rebecca Virag, *Images of Inheritance: The Influence of Eugenic Ideas and Socio-Biological Theory in British Art c.1890–1918*

2005

Richard Checketts, *The Visible and the Invisible in Shaftesbury's Theory of Art*

Hanneke Grootenboer, *Treasuring the Gaze: British Eye Miniature Portraits*

Lucy Jessop, *Architecture and the Government Minister 1688–1714*

Richard Johns, *James Thornhill and Decorative Painting in England*

Helen Pierce, *Unseemly Pictures: Political Graphic Satire in Early Modern England*

Geraldine Robinson, *Politics, Design and the Post-War 'Prefab'*

2006

Riann Coulter, *The Cultural Identity of the Northern Irish Artists Gerard Dillon and Colin Middleton and the Dublin-born artist Louis le Brocquy*

Davide Deriu, *'London from Aloft': The Image of the City in the Photographs of Aerofilms, 1919–1939*

Hannah Greig, *The Fashionables: London's Beau Monde in the 18th Century*

2007

Tracy Anderson, *The Crown and the Jewel: Images of Royalty and Viceroyalty in the Spectacle of Imperial Britain and India*

Anne Bordeleau, *Charles Robert Cockerell (1788–1863)*

Eleanor Fraser Stansbie, *Richard Dadd: Art and the 19th-century Asylum*

Alla Myzelev, *Peasant Arts' Revitalization in England: Histories and Meanings*

Morna O'Neill, *Walter Crane: The Arts and Crafts, Painting, and Politics*

Richard Williams, *The Reformation of an Icon: Images of Christ in Early Modern England*

2008

Altino Rocha, *War, Science and Architecture: From Crystallography to Architecture Computing*

Rebecca Scragg, *Consuming Contemporary Art: London 1914–23*

Hester Westley, *Traditions and Transitions: St Martin's Sculpture Department, 1960–1969*

Mimi Yiu, *Building Platforms: Staging the Architecture of Early Modern Subjectivity*

2009

Ann-Marie Akehurst, *Architecture and Philanthropy in 18th-century York*

Christina Bradstreet, *Scented Visions: Picturing Perfume in Victorian Art*

Ruth Brimacombe, *Imperial Avatars: Art, India and the Prince of Wales in 1875–6*

Juliana Dresvina, *The Cult of St Margaret of Antioch in Medieval Europe*

Manolo Guerci, *An Architectural and Social History of Northumberland House in the Strand, London, 1605–1874*

Emily Weeks, *Cultures Crossed: John Frederick Lewis (1804–1876) and the Art of Orientalist Painting*

2010

Adriano Aymonino, *A Mirror of the Enlightenment: The Patronage, Collections and Cultural World of the 1st Duke and Duchess of Northumberland in Georgian Britain*

Madhuri Desai, *Resurrecting Banaras: Urban Space, Architecture and Colonial Mediation (1781–1936)*

Kate Grandjouan, *Close Encounters: French Identities in English Graphic Satire c.1730–1799*

Helen McCormack, *A Collector of the Fine Arts in 18th-century Britain: Dr William Hunter (1718–1783)*

Mellie Naydenova-Slade, *Images of the Holy Kinship: The Iconography of the Extended Family of Christ, c.1170 to c.1525*

Junior Fellowships

The Junior Fellowship was established in 1998. Its aim was to provide support for scholars in the advanced stages of research for doctoral dissertations to undertake research in the UK (based at the Paul Mellon Centre) or in the United States (based at the Yale Center for British Art). Fellowships are awarded for a period of up to three months.

1999

Michael Gaudio, *'Counterfeited According to the Truth': Producing Knowledge of Native America 1585–90*

David Getsy, *Corporeality and Eroticism in the Formulations of Modern British Sculpture from the Late Victorians to the English Modernists*

Thomas Schmutz, *The Materials of Painting: Colour Manufacturing, Colour Theory and Artists' Techniques as Conditions of Artistic Production in England 1780–1880*

2000

Jennifer Edes-Pierotti, *Medieval English Parish Art*

Douglas Fordham, *Imperial Rivalry: British and French Art during the Seven Years' War*

Anne Nellis, *The English Landscape Painter Abroad: Tourism, Genre and Modernity in the Post-Napoleonic Period*

Elizabeth Pergam, *Facing the Past: The Manchester Art Treasures Exhibition of 1857 and the State of Art in mid-Victorian Britain*

2001

Cassandra Albinson, *Modernity and the Noblewoman: Aristocratic Portraiture in Britain 1832–1885*

Rosemarie Dias, *Boydell's Shakespeare Gallery: Exhibition Culture and Spectatorship in the late 18th Century*

Jennifer Hallam, *Re-Presenting Women in Early Stuart England: Gender Ideology, Personal Politics and the Portrait Arts*

Morna O'Neill, *'Art is Born Again' : The Allegorical Paintings of Walter Crane*

Catherine Reed, *Exhibiting National Character at the 1951 Festival of Britain*

Maria-Dolores Sánchez Jáuregui Alpañés, *Eighteenth-century Anglo-Italian Relationships*

2002

Jonathan Canning, *The Stone-Cage Chantry Chapel and the Architecture of Perpetual Commemoration in Late Medieval England*

Emma Winter, *The Transformation of Taste in Germany and England 1797–1858*

2003

Byron E. Bronston, *For the Good of the Realm: Architecture, Urban Form, and Early Capitalist Enterprise*

Karen Junod, *Writing the Lives of Artists: The Role of Biography in the Construction of Artistic Identity in late 18th-and early 19th-century Britain*

Thomas Latham, *The American War of Independence, Metaphor and Visual Imagery in Britain*

Lindsey Pedersen, *Gender, Race and Imperial Crisis in Visual Representations of the Indian Mutiny 1857–58*

Simone von der Geest, *'Know then thyself': Jonathan Richardson's Portrait Theory and Portrait Painting*

2004

Catherine Anderson, *Embodiments of Empire: Figuring Race in Late Victorian Painting*

Colette Crossman, *Art as Salvation: Reconsidering Religion in the Work of Edward Burne-Jones*

Joanna Guldi, *Privacy Revolution: Looking for Retreat in an Insecure World 1780–1832*

Katherine Wheeler, *Renaissance Architectural History at the Rise of Modernism in Britain*

Chloe Wigston Smith, *Clothing the Self: Dress, Identity, and the Everyday in 18th-century Britain*

2005

Tracey Avery, *Comfort and Identity: Furnishing Greater Britain in Australia, 1880–1920*

Jo Briggs, *Media Empires: Artistic Reactions to the Boer War in the Visual Culture of Munich, Paris and London*

Ruth Brimacombe, *A Grand Tour in the Greater Britain: Art and the Prince of Wales's Royal Progress to India in 1875–6*

Alexis Goodin, *British Artists and the Representation of Egypt, 1838–1902*

Ryan Johnston, *Bunk! Eduardo Paolozzi's Collage and Post-War Modernism in Britain 1944–1956*

Alla Vronskaya, *Sir Reginald Blomfield as a Garden Designer: A British and European Perspective*

2006

Jongwoo Jeremy Kim, *Royal Academicians and the Crisis of Masculinity in Modern England*

Cory Korkow, *Queenship and the Construction of National Identity in 19th-century British Visual Culture*

Alistair Kwan, *Architecture for the Pursuit of Knowledge: The Modernisation of Sciences as Told by its Built Spaces*

Shalini Le Gall, *Evangelical Imperialism: Holman Hunt and Religious Painting in the Middle East*

Andrea Wolk, *A Material Empire: Art as Secular Ministry in the Work of Edward Burne-Jones*

2007

Jeremy Melius, *Art History and the Invention of Botticelli*

Nathaniel Stein, *London in the Viewer: British Stereoscopy and Urban Embodiments, 1830–1880*

Katharine Williams, *A Study of Themes in the Architecture, Symbolism and Experience of Great War Memorials of the 1920s*

Shundana Yusaf, *Wireless Sites: Radio and Architecture in Britain (1927–1945)*

FELLOWSHIPS

2008

Laurel Flinn, *Elegant Buildings and Pestilential Alleys: Regulation and Resistance in the Transformation of London's West End, 1750–1830*

Caroline Fuchs, *Colour Value: The Autochrome in Great Britain*

Matthew Woodworth, *The 13th-century Choir and Transepts of Beverley Minster*

2009

Christina Smylitopoulos, *A Nabob's Progress: Graphic Satire, 'The Grand Master' and the Source of Indian Excess, 1770–1830*

2010

Irene Sunwoo, *Alvin Boyarsky's 'Well-Laid Table': Experiments in Architectural Pedagogy*

Conservation Fellowships

The Conservation Fellowship was established in 1998 to support academic research relating to conservation rather than the physical task of conservation and restoration. The Centre has worked with the Hamilton Kerr Institute at the University of Cambridge and the Courtauld Institute of Art and awards the Fellowship for periods of three years.

1998/9–2001

Alison Norton (at Yale Center for British Art), *Research in the YCBA conservation studio*

1999–2001

Jenny Rose (at Hamilton Kerr Institute), *Research on 17th-century Portraits from the Royal Collection and Helmingham Hall*

2001–4

Helen Brett (at Hamilton Kerr Institute), *Research on Paintings at Parham Park, Weston Park and the Foundling Museum collections*

2004–7

Helen Howard (at Courtauld Institute of Art), *Research on Polychromy on Tombs in Westminster Abbey Sanctuary*

Clare Richardson (at Courtauld Institute of Art), *Research on Paintings by Rebecca Dulcibella Orpen at Baddesley Clinton*

2007–9

Ian Perrins (at Hamilton Kerr Institute), *Six Paintings by William Ashford of Mount Merrion Park from the Fitzwilliam Museum*

2010–13

Christoph Vogtherr (Wallace Collection), *Wallace Collection Paintings by Sir Joshua Reynolds*

Yale Traveling Scholarships

As support for research within the Yale graduate student community the Centre introduced in 2001 Travelling Scholarships to provide support for students to conduct a short research trip (often to the UK or Europe) relating to their doctoral research.

2001

Dennis Carr
Douglas R. Fordham
Maya Jasanoff
D. Marshall Kibbey
Mary Pollard Murray
Ravit Reichman
Karin Roffman
George Shuffleton
Timothy Sullivan
Stephen C. Vella
Emily Weeks
Emily Wilson

2002

John Curley
Earle Havens
Roger Levine
Seth Lobis
Todd Porter
Catherine Rockwood
Eric Stryker
Stephen C. Vella
Juliette Wells
Catherine Louise Whalen

2003

Emily Anderson
Jo Briggs
Brett Foster
Paul Grant-Costa
Jennifer Ann Greenhill
Benjamin Madley
Megan Mathis Quigley
Aaron Matz
Jennifer Raab
Vanessa Lyndal Ryan
Olivia Horsfall Turner
Vanessa Wolf
Andrea Wolk

2004

Charles Nicholas Baldock
Julie Bowring
Brooke Conti
Sarah Cree
Kristin Henry
Ethan W. Lasser
Courtney Martin
Rachel Oberter
Jose Emmanuel Raymundo
Angela Sagues
Randi Saloman
Camilla Schofield

2005

Joshua Guild
Alistair Kwan
Lindsay O'Neill
Jean Nahoko Otsuki
Irene Violet Small

2006

Prajna Desai
Crawford Alexander Mann II
Laura Miles
Randi Saloman
Bernard Zirnheld

2007

Karilyn Crockett
Philipp Ekardt
Ashley Jones
Gustav Percivall
Lynn W. Saltonstall

2008

Dana Byrd
Christine Delucia
Hans Gustav Percivall
Emily Setina

2009

Nathan Bright
Meredith Jane Gamer
Daniel Mark Greenberg
Sylvia Waisbren Houghteling
Anna Evangeline Kesson
Alexandra Dika Seggerman
Allison Nicole Stielau
Maria Taroutina

2010

Kathryn Joan Everett
Jorge Ricardo Gomez Tejada
Stephanie Lynn Luther
Christine A. Schorfheide
Luke Smythe
Mary Danielle Ward Griffin

Paul Mellon Centre/Yale Center for British Art/World Monuments Fund

In 2010 a collaboration between the Paul Mellon Centre, the Yale Center for British Art and the World Monuments Fund led to the establishment of what is intended to be an annual award for a Yale graduate student

2010

Laurel Bradley, *Research in London, at Stowe and at the Huntington Library in California, on the architectural history of Stowe House*

RESEARCH SEMINARS

In its early years the Centre's involvement with 'public' activities was minimal and although occasional advice was given to various institutions the Centre did not operate its own programme of events, largely because the premises in Bloomsbury Square were unsuitable for anything other than small seminars. In the Autumn of 1980, Professor David Bindman of Westfield College, University of London approached the Assistant Director and Librarian with a proposal to hold a series of evening seminars during university term time for postgraduate students working on historic British art. These occasions provided postgraduate students at various stages of their research (as well as established professionals) with an opportunity to present their work to a small audience of about thirty fellow scholars. There was no funding for these events but they proved to be stimulating occasions and brought together many individuals who subsequently forged firm friendships as well as successful professional academic careers in the field. Also, in 1985–86 the Centre joined forces with the Courtauld Institute's Victorian Art Research Seminar, organised by John House and Hilary Morgan and evening seminars were held at the Paul Mellon Centre. The seminar series survived, more or less without interruption, until the Spring of 1990. From 1992 properly funded lecture series began to be hosted by the Centre in Bloomsbury Square but it was not until the move to 16 Bedford Square in 1996, with its larger public spaces, that a more ambitious programme could be envisaged. In 2002 the Centre revived its Research Seminar series and invited recipients of the Centre's fellowships to present work in progress.

November–December 1980
Eighteenth-century English Art Seminar

Katie Scott — *The Rococo Interior in France*
Brian Allen — *The Rococo in England*
David Bindman — *Roubiliac at Trinity College Cambridge*
Tessa Murdoch — *Roubiliac in his Setting*

January–March 1981
Eighteenth-century English Art Seminar

Stephen Deuchar — *Wootton in his Setting*
B. Robertson — *Paul Sandby*
R. Godfrey — *Stubbs as a Printmaker*
Malcolm Baker — *Roubiliac and his European Background*
J. Sunderland — *John Hamilton Mortimer*
Diana Dethloff — *The Collecting of Drawings in England in the early 18th Century*

May–June 1981
Eighteenth-century English Art Seminar

Kim Sloan — *Alexander Cozens in Russia and Italy*
David Alexander — *Genre Prints in the 18th Century*
Sheila O'Connell — *Arthur Pond*
Robert Folkenflik — *Dr Johnson and Art*
Julius Bryant — *Artists and Revolution*
Susan Morris — *Thomas Girtin*

October–December 1981
Eighteenth-century English Art Seminar

David Bindman — *Roubiliac in Westminster Abbey*
Catherine Gordon — *The Raphael of Domestic Life: Illustrations to the Novels of Samuel Richardson*
Richard Godfrey — *Robert Robinson, Painter and Engraver: Minor Master of the 17th Century*
Aileen Ribeiro — *Costume and English Painting in the 18th Century*
Ann Lyles — *John Varley*

RESEARCH SEMINARS

February–March 1982
British Art Seminar

Tessa Murdoch	*Louis Chéron and the St. Martin's Lane Academy*
David Alexander	*Robert Seymour (1798–1836), Caricaturist and Illustrator*
Alex Kidson	*Political Portraiture in the late 18th Century*
Charles Rhyne	*John Constable*
Kim Rorschach	*Frederick, Prince of Wales as a Patron*
Duncan Bull	*Staffage*

May–June 1982
British Art Seminar

Brian Allen	*The First Exhibition of the Royal Academy in 1769*
Vivien Knight	*Francis Grose and Topographical Landscape*
Andrew Wilton	*Some Thoughts on William Pars*
Kim Sloan	*Alexander Cozens' Systems*
Julius Bryant	*Thomas Banks: A Change of Image*

November–December 1982
British Art Seminar

David Bindman	*Blake and Popular Art*
Barbara Coffey	*Sir George Hayter, Portrait and History Painter to Queen Victoria*
Katie Scott	*Royal Patronage of Painting in France 1700–1730*
Michael Rosenthal	*Constable's 'Salisbury from the Meadows' 1831*
Alastair Laing	*Fischer von Erlach's Mitrowitz Tomb and Pyramid Tombs in England*
Christopher White	*Rembrandt in English Art in the 18th Century*

January–March 1983
British Art Seminar

Nicholas Reese	*Turner and Titian's 'St. Peter Martyr'*
David Harris	*Tintern Abbey in Prints and Photographs 1775–1875*
Philip Ward-Jackson	*The French Presence in English Sculpture from 1840 to 1880*
Katherine Di Giulio	*'Breadth of effect' in British Landscape Photography of the 1850s and 1860s*
Richard Dorment	*Alfred Gilbert vs. George Bernard Shaw: The Artist's Responsibility to his Patron*
Stephen Deuchar	*Samuel Whitbread MP: A Patron of British Art*

May–June 1983
British Art Seminar

John Kenworthy-Browne	*Joseph Nollekens: Art and Industry*
Julius Bryant	*'Bashaw' by M.C. Wyatt: Landseer in Marble*
Sarah Hyde	*Genre Subjects in late 18th-century English Art*
Patrick Conner	*Michael Angelo Rooker*
Sheila O'Connell	*Giles Hussey*
David Bindman and Tom Gretton	*The Industrial Revolution and Art* (joint paper)

October–December 1983
British Art Seminar

Sarah Cullen	*George Morland*
Ilaria Bignamini	*George Vertue, Art Historian*
Jane Roberts	*Thomas Sandby and Windsor Great Park*
Marcia Pointon	*Problems of Identity, Definition and Analysis in early 19th-century Anglo-French Watercolour Painting*
Terry Friedman	*James Gibbs and St. Bartholomew's Hospital: The Relationship between Georgian Philanthropy and the Arts*
Evelyn Newby	*William Hoare: An Introduction*

February–April 1984
British Art Seminar

Geoffrey Ashton	*Thomas Baxter's Theatrical Pattern Book*
David Alexander	*Etching in England 1740–1830*
Ellen Chirelstein	*Sir William Drury: An Elizabethan Memorial Portrait*
Mary Beal	*Richard Symonds: An English Royalist Abroad 1649–51*
Linda Cabe	*Peter Tillemans and the Development of the Gardens at Wrest Park*
David Bindman	*Schinkel's Journey to England, Scotland and Wales in 1826*

May–July 1984
British Art Seminar

David Solkin	*Running Away from Vulgarity: Reynolds and the Revolt against Fashion in 18th-century English Portraiture*
John Dixon Hunt	*Ut Pictura Poesis and the Picturesque*
Richard Godfrey	*'This new wild votaru': James Gillray and the Comic Sublime*

November–December 1984
British Art Seminar

Ilaria Bignamini	*The Search for New Cultural Institutions in Britain 1572–1734*
Michael McCarthy	*Drawings for Strawberry Hill in the Lewis Walpole Collection*
Gertrud Seidmann	*Nathaniel Marchant: Gem Engraver*
Garry Apgar	*Jean Hüber (1721–86): The Anglo-Swiss Connection in the 18th Century*

March 1985
British Art Seminar

Nicola Smith	*Frogmore: A 17th-century House Rediscovered*
Linda Ivell	*Cavaliers and Roundheads: 19th-century Attitudes*
Martin Postle	*Reactions to Reynolds as a History Painter*

May–July 1985
Victorian Art Research Seminar

Clare Willsdon	*Official Art in Britain c.1890–1930 and its Continental Relationships: Aspects of the Mural Revival at the Palace of Westminister*
Paul Barlow	*'The Backside of Nature': The Problems of Hogarthianism in Emma Brownlow's Paintings of the Foundling Hospital*
Lynne Bell	*James McNeil Whistler, Victim or Manipulator of the Press? The Evidence of his 1884 Exhibition*

May–November 1985
British Art Seminar

Megan Aldrich	*The Crace Firm of Decorators and their Work c.1780–1900*
Adam White	*The Jacobean Renaissance in Monumental Sculpture*
Evelyn Newby	*Aspects of Pastel Painting in mid-18th-century England*
David Alexander	*'Noted Faces': The Development of the 18th-century Engraved Portrait*
Timothy Clayton	*Some Thoughts on the Meaning of the 'Lion and Horse' and 'Brood Mares' after George Stubbs*

February–March 1986
Victorian Art Research Seminar

Angela Emanuel	*Julia Cartwright, Art Critic and Historian of the Renaissance, 1851–1924*
Philip Attwood	*Women Medallists and the Arts and Crafts Movement*

March 1986
British Art Seminar

Gerard Vaughan	*Dealing in Antiquities in 18th-century Rome: Thomas Jenkins and Charles Townley*
Ian Jenkins	*The Vogue for Greek Vases and Fashionable Portraiture in the late 18th and early 19th Century*
Fintan Cullen	*Questions of National Identity in late 18th-century Irish and Scottish Art*
J.P. Stephenson	*'And Where Do the Polecats Come in?': An Examination of the Practical Side of Painting during the 17th, 18th and early 19th Century*

October–December 1986
British Art Seminar

John Murdoch	*The Legacy of Puritan Iconoclasm and Attitudes to Portraiture in the Augustan State*
Elizabeth Prettejohn	*Varieties of Classical Subject in the 1860s*
Andrew Hemingway	*The Norwich School Myth*
Penelope Gurland	*Martineau's 'Last Day in the Old House'*
Andrew Graham-Dixon	*'Jeremy O'Blarney versus the Conjurer': James Barry's Quarrels with Sir Joshua Reynolds*
Jan Marsh	*Elizabeth Siddall: An Explanation of the Myth*
Duncan Bull	*John Runciman*

January–March 1987
British Art Seminar

Mark Stocker	*Joseph Edgar Boehm: Royalist and Realist*
Carla Rachman	*Sweet Charity: Victorian Images of Giving*
Michael Pidgley	*British Artists and Drawing Instruments*
Lynn Nead	*Approaching Visual Representation: The Role of the Visual within a Cultural History of Victorian England*
Robin Simon	*Wit in Pope and Hogarth*
Rosemary Treble	*R. W. Macbeth: Painter of Toil*
John Wilson	*John Hoppner's History Paintings and Fancy Pictures*

RESEARCH SEMINARS

October–December 1987
British Art Seminar

Cinzia Sicca	*The Collecting of Architectural Drawings in early 18th-century England and their Use in the Training of Architects*
Todd Longstaffe-Gowan	*Natural Conceit and Rustic Folly in the Decoration of the Georgian London Town House: A Social History of the Re-creation of Nature in Town*
Jonathan Cook	*William Hazlitt and the Decline of Art*
Christina Poulson	*The True and the False: Tennyson's 'Idylls of the King' and the Visual Arts*
Lee M. Edwards	*Hubert von Herkomer*
David Ward	*Manliness and Mediaevalism in Victorian Painting*
Bernard Richards	*Ruskin's Version of Turner*
Shearer West	*William Powell Frith, Tom Taylor and the Idea of Hogarth*
Ronald Paulson	*The Aesthetics of Iconoclasm*

March 1988
British Art Seminar

Philip McEvansoneya	*Luke Fildes' 'The Doctor'*
William Vaughan	*Primitivism and Progress: A Victorian Problem*

October–December 1988
British Art Seminar

David Alexander	*The London Print Market in the Reign of William and Mary*
Mark Crinson	*Levanting: Victorian Architecture and the Colonial Project in Egypt*
Ralph Hyde	*'Panoramania!': Art and Artists in the Service of Showmanship*
William Vaughan	*Primitivism and Progress: A Victorian Problem*

November 1989–March 1990
British Art Seminar

Terry Friedman	*Proud, Stupendous Pile: St Paul's Cathedral in the 18th Century*
Matthew Craske	*The Naval Monument and the Struggle for Patriotic Prestige in British Society, 1738–1760*
Robyn Asleson	*Recasting the Canon: Ancient Marbles and the Transformation of Classicism in High Victorian Painting*
Stephen Wildman	*Some Preliminary Thoughts on David Cox's Carthage*
John Wilton-Ely	*Archaeology and the Imagination: Changing Attitudes to Herculaneum and Pompeii in the 18th-century British Interior*
David Mannings	*Reynolds's Oil Sketches*
David Nolta	*Britons on the Bay of Naples*

November 1992–March 1993
The Paul Mellon Centre Seminars 1992–93: Travel and the Representation of the Foreign

Rosemary Bechler	*Byron's Grander Tour*
Richard Wrigley	*'Something in the Air': The Theory and Practice of Influence in Relation to French Artists in Italy in the 18th and early 19th Century*
Chloe Chard	*Destabilizing Travel and Tourism: Transgression, Liminality and the Sublime*
Richard Hamblyn	*Private Cabinets and Popular Geology: The British Audiences for Volcanoes*
Peter de Bolla	*Cornering the Culture Market: Robert Adam on his Grand Tour*
Ilaria Bignamini	*The Royal Family on the Grand Tour, 1763–1798*
Elinor Schaffer	*William Beckford: Exotic Landscapes*
Jeremy Maule	*Predictable Manners: Inscribing the Climate of Otranto*
Tzvetan Todorov	*The Functions of the Foreign*
Ken Arnold	*Trade, Travel and Treasures: 17th-century Artificial Curiosities*
Roy Porter	*Travellers and Great Cities in the 18th Century*
Stephen Bann	*John Bargrave (1610–1680) and the Genealogy of the Grand Tour*
Isobel Armstrong	*Charlotte Brontë: Travel and Fantasy*

November 1996–February 1997
The Paul Mellon Centre Seminars 1996–97: Emma Hamilton, Naples and Enjoyment

Bice Benvenuto	*I Was Born in a Place which Trembles*
Gill Perry	*Musing on the Muses*
Chloe Chard	*Spectral Souvenirs: Emma, Corinne and the Topography of Effemination*
Lori-Ann Touchette	*Emma Hamilton and her 'Attitudes': Mimesis and Museum in Motion*
Marcia Pointon	*Emma Hamilton as a Bacchante*
Helen Langdon	*'The Magick Land': Sirens and Sibyls*
Ludmilla Jordanova	*Feminine Figures*
Asia Haut	*The Spasmodic Landscape: Naples, the Hamiltons and the Marquis de Sade*

October–December 2002
The Paul Mellon Centre Research Seminars 2002

Andrew Causey	*English Art and National Identity, 1918–1939*
Alissa Ardito	*The Gothic Revival of Urbanism and England: The Foundations of the Garden City*
Morna O'Neill	*Walter Crane: The Decorator as Aesthete and the Artist as Socialist*
Diana Donald	*Landseer's Representation of Animals: A Fractured and Tragic Vision of the Natural World*
Denise Oleksijczuk	*Cityscapes and Battle Scenes: Shifting Conceptions of Time and Space in Early British Panoramas*
Elizabeth Goldring	*The Sidney–Leicester Circle and Elizabethan Patronage and Collecting*
Douglas Fordham	*Between Empire and Liberty: British Art and the Seven Years War*
Peter Draper	*On its Own Terms: Early English Gothic Architecture from a Contemporary Perspective*

October–December 2003
The Paul Mellon Centre Research Seminars 2003

Eleanor Hughes	*Accuracy Issues: Marine Painting and the Glorious First of June*
Ian Christie	*'The Childhood of your Art': Robert Paul and the early Moving-Picture Business in Britain*
Cindy McCreery	*Satirical Prints of Women in late 18th-century England*
David Alexander	*From Single Hand to Workshop: The Evolution of the Engravers' Profession in 18th-century Britain*
Celina Fox	*Drawing 18th-century Industry: Surveying the Scene, Engineering the Machine*
John Peacock	*Van Dyck's 'Self-Portrait with a Sunflower'*
Sonia Ashmore	*Liberty's of Regent Street: Architecture, Trade and Empire*
Jason Rosenfeld	*Modernity in 'May': Charles Allston Collins, the Pre-Raphaelite Landscape and the Parks of London in the 1850s*

October–December 2004
The Paul Mellon Centre Research Seminars 2004

Emily Weeks	*The Reality Effect: The Orientalist Paintings of John Frederick Lewis (1805–76)*
Michael Hatt	*The Book Beautiful: Reading, Vision and the Homosexual Imagination in the 1890s*
Megan Aldrich	*Thomas Rickman's Non-conformist Vision*
Alex Bremner	*'Imperial Peace Memorial': The Second Anglo-Boer War and the Origins of Admiralty Arch, 1900–1905*
Anthea Callen	*Anatomising Masculinity at the Royal Academy: Classicism or Brute Matter?*
Rosie Dias	*The Resurrection of Hogarth at John Boydell's Shakespeare Gallery*
Dian Kriz	*Slavery, Sugar and the Culture of Refinement: Imagining the British West Indies c.1700–1840*
Gavin Stamp	*British Architecture between the Wars*

October–November 2005
The Paul Mellon Centre Research Seminars 2005

David Hansen	*John Glover*
Elizabeth Prettejohn	*Art for Art's Sake*
Richard Johns	*James Thornhill's County Patrons*
Nigel Aston	*Popery, Politics and Painting: The Royal Academy and the St Paul's Cathedral Redecorative Scheme of 1773*
Helen Pierce	*Graphic Satire and the Portrait Print in 17th-century England*
Vic Gatrell	*Men, Sex and Caricature in London, 1770–1830*
Eric Stryker	*Francis Bacon: A Logic of Subculture*
William Pressley	*James Barry's Murals at the Royal Society of Arts*

October–November 2006
The Paul Mellon Centre Research Seminars 2006

Nicholas Grindle	*Landscape, Commercial Modernisation and Political Opposition to the Three Kingdoms, 1660–1714*
Jo Briggs	*Global Doubt: Socialist Visual Culture and the Boer War Protest Movement in Fin-de-Siècle London*
Frances Spalding	*Taking Nothing for Granted: John Piper's Pursuit of National Identities*
Riann Coulter	*Louis le Brocquy's 'Presence' Series, 1956–1966: Irish, British or International?*
Amy Sargeant	*The Man in the White Suit: New Textiles and the Social Fabric*
Rachel Oberter	*Spiritualism and the Visual Imagination in Victorian Britain*
Vaughan Hart	*'A Pretty Impudent Countenance': The Architecture of Sir John Vanbrugh*

CONFERENCES

After the appointment of Professor Michael Kitson as Director of Studies in 1986 the Centre began to play a more active role in funding seminars, conferences and symposia although these were usually organised in collaboration with other organisations with facilities large enough to accommodate an audience of more than thirty (the capacity at Bloomsbury Square). A particularly fruitful series of collaborative events with the Education Department of the Tate Gallery followed, several of which (such as the ambitious international conference *Towards a Modern Art World* held in December 1989) set the tone for future programmes. After the Centre's move to Bedford Square in 1996 it was possible to host events accommodating up to ninety participants in its own premises, although larger conferences required the use of other premises. After 1998, through its new grants programme, the Centre has also supported many events which are listed under 'Educational Programme' grants. Several conferences formed the basis of subsequent Paul Mellon Centre publications.

November–December 1986
A series of lectures on Scottish Painting to coincide with the exhibition *Painting in Scotland: The Golden Age*
(held at the Tate Gallery)

Duncan Macmillan	*Art and the Study of Human Nature*
Brian Allen	*Allan Ramsay: The Italian Connection*
David Irwin	*The Picturesque Landscape: From Jacob More to J.M.W. Turner*
Lindsay Errington	*'The mind in the face': The Paintings of David Wilkie*
Catherine Gordon	*Sir Walter Scott and the Visual Arts*
Alastair Rowan	*Barbarous Civility or Civilised Barbarity: The Scottish Country House to 1843*

10–11 July 1987
Symposium on JMW Turner to mark the opening of the Clore Gallery
(held at the Tate Gallery)

Robert Rosenblum	*Turner's Afterlife, 1851–1987*
Eric Shanes	*Turner and Liberty: The Seminal Poetic Pictures of 1800*
Barry Venning	*Turner's Early Genre Paintings*
Andrew Wilton	*Turner and the Sense of Place*
Maurice Davies	*Turner's Lectures on Perspective: An Introduction*
John Gage	*Turner and John Landseer: Translating the Image*
Jerrold Ziff	*Turner's Perception of Himself as the Defender of the Art, as seen in his Great Pictures of 1810–20*
Evelyn Joll	*Turner at Dunstanborough, 1797–1834*
Luke Herrmann	*Turner's 'Liber Studiorum': Aspects of Purpose and Publication*
Nicholas Alfrey	*Turner and the Idea of Hero*
Kathleen Nicholson	*Style as Meaning: Turner's Late Mythological Paintings*
Norman Bryson	*Turner and the Rhetoric of the Sublime*

November–December 1987
Nothing But Money? British Art and Society 1700–1769
(a series of lectures held at the Tate Gallery)

Linda Colley	*The Search for English Art 1700–1760*
Elizabeth Einberg	*Newton and the Visual Arts in the early 18th Century*
David Dabydeen	*Hogarth's 'Harlot's Progress': Politics, Commerce, Corruption*
John Murdoch	*Portraits and Pindarics: Discourses on Man in the Augustan State*
David Bindman	*Hogarth's Politics*
John Styles	*Enforcing the Law in Hogarth's London*
Charles Saumarez Smith	*Hogarth's Interiors*
Ronald Paulson	*Hogarth's Aesthetics*
Roy Porter	*Thomas Coram, the Foundling Hospital and Hospitals in Hogarth's England*
David Solkin	*The Portraiture of Politeness*

14–16 December 1989
Towards a Modern Art World
(conference held at the Tate Gallery)

John Brewer	*Taste and Cultural Production in London and the Provinces in the 18th Century*
Charles Harrison	*England's Climate*
Ronald Paulson	*Hogarth and the Distribution of Visual Imagery*
Michael Podro	*Hogarth and the Spectator Public*
Michael Rosenthal	*Gainsborough's Spectator Public*
Ann Bermingham	*Techné and Mentalité: The Institutionalisation of Amateur Drawing in Britain*
Marilyn Butler	*The Arts and National Identity on the Eve of the French Revolution*
Ludmilla Jordanova	*The Representation of the Human Body: Art and Medicine in the Work of Charles Bell*
Nicholas Alfrey	*The Map and the Vista*
Andrew Hemingway	*Art Exhibitions as Leisure Class Rituals in early 19th-century London*
John Gage	*The British School and the British School*
Martin Postle	*In Search of the 'True Britain': Hogarth, Reynolds and the British School*
Peter Funnell	*William Hazlitt, Prince Hoare and the Institutionalisation of the British Art World*
Eric Shanes	*Dissent in Somerset House: Opposition to the Political Status Quo within the Royal Academy, 1800–1832*
Caroline Arscott	*Ramsgate Sands, Modern Life and the Shoring-Up of Narrative*
Julie Codell	*Artists' Professional Societies and Dealers' Galleries: Art Production, Aesthetics and the Image of the Artist*
Stella Tillyard	*The End of Victorian Art: W. R. Sickert and the Defence of Literary Painting*

19–20 November 1993
Albion's Classicism: The Visual Arts in Britain 1550–1660
(held at the Warburg Institute)

Nicholas Mann	*Opening Remarks*
J B Trapp	*Chairman's Remarks*
Lisa Jardine	*Books, Gifts and Amicitia: The Quentin*
Leonard Barkan	*Mute Poetry Speaking Pictures: European Visual Culture and the Elizabethan Scene*

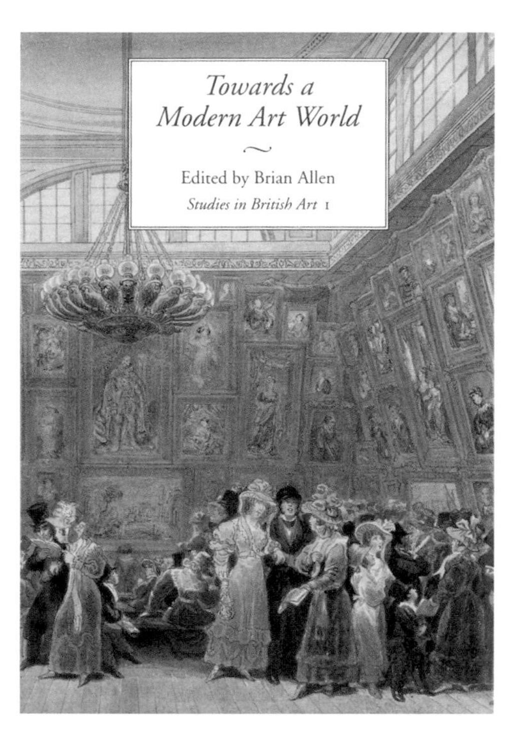

Maurice Howard	*Classicism and Civic Architecture in Renaissance England*
Christy Anderson	*Learning to Read Architecture in the English Renaissance*
Felicity Heal	*Chair's Remarks*
Lucy Gent	*The Rash Gazer: Alternative Economies of Vision c.1600*
Deborah Howard	*Scotland's 'Thrie Estates': Classicism and Class Identity in Scottish Architecture*
Paula Henderson	*The Loggia: The Adaption and Function of Classical Form*
Ellen Chirelstein	*Emblem and 'Recklesse Presence': The Drury Portrait at Yale*
Catherine Belsey	*Chairman's Remarks*
Thomas Greene	*Shakespeare's Richard II: The Sign in Bolingbroke's Window*
Elizabeth Honig	*Sir Philip Sidney: Maker's Voice and Woman's Vision*

CONFERENCES

3 July 1998
Angels and Urchins: The Fancy Picture in 18th-century British Art
(held at Kenwood)

Martin Postle	*Angels and Urchins*
Anne Higonnet	*Images of Children in the 18th Century*
David Alexander	*The Fancy Picture and Print Making*

6 October 1998
Town and Country: The Aristocratic London Town House and its Demise
(held at Syon House, Syon Park)

Joseph Friedman	*The Great London House: Rise and Fall*
David Cannadine	*The Socio-political Context*
Tim Knox	*Going the Round: The Planning of the State Apartments in the London Town House*
Treve Rosoman	*Servicing the Town House*
Joseph Mordaunt Crook	*The New Plutocracy*
James Yorke	*Stafford House*
Charles Sebag-Montefiore	*Dorchester House 1849–1928*
Gavin Stamp	*The Demolition of the Great Town Houses*
Clive Wainwright	*The Dispersal of Collections*

24 October 1998
Cross-currents: Fresh Perspectives on 19th-century 'New World' Landscape Painting
(held at the Wadsworth Atheneum, Hartford, Connecticut)

Moderators	Brian Allen, Elizabeth Kornhauser, Patrick McCaughey
Elizabeth Johns	*What I Learned in the Process: The Hazards of 'National Identity' in interpreting Landscape Painting*
Michael Rosenthal	*The Artless Landscape: Early Colonial Imagery in Australia*
Jos Hackforth-Jones	*Picturing Mountains in 'Old' Wales and New South Wales, c.1770–1850*
Timothy Bonyhady	*The Merits of Microscopism: The Environmental Significance of Eugene von Guerard's 'Tower Hill'*
Andrew Sayers	*Augustus Earle: Wandering Through the Colony*
H. Barbara Weinberg	*International Impressionism*

29–30 October 1998
The Special Relationship: American and British Architecture since 1945
(held at the Architectural Association and the Paul Mellon Centre)

Murray Fraser	*Reflections on the Anglo-American Relationship*
Robert A. M. Stern	*Britons at Yale in the 1960s*
John Winter	*From London to Yale and Beyond*
Norman Foster	*Personal Experiences*
Richard Rogers	*Personal Observations*
M. J. Long	*West to East*
Lionel March	*The Transshipment of Architectural Research Styles*
Colin Davis	*British Hi-Tech and America*
Allen Cunningham	*Marcel Breuer: Second Generation Modernist*
Adrian Gale	*Working with Mies*
Michael Wilford	*Stirling and Wilford in America*
Richard MacCormac	*Frank Lloyd Wright*
Zaha Hadid	*Alvin Boyarsky and the AA*
Adrian Forty	*Reyner Banham and his Context*
Martin Pawley	*Buckminster Fuller and Britain*
Peter Cook	*The British Avant-Garde and California*
Nicholas Bullock	*Reconstructing Modernism: The British Avant-Garde's Debts to America 1943–1950*
Ted Cullinan	*The Influence of the Los Angeles School*
Charles Jencks	*American versus British Postmodernism*
Kenneth Powell	*The American Big Boys in Britain*
David Childs	*SOM in Particular*
Raymond Seitz	*Concluding Overview*

6 November 1998
English Accents: The Uses of British Art in the USA, Russia and Australia 1776–1855 (held at Tate Britain)

Galina Andreeva	*The Role of British Portraiture and History Painting in Russia*
Rosalind Polly Gray	*'Help me to eclipse the celebrated Hogarth': The Reception of Hogarth in Russia*
Elizabeth Johns	*Sea Change: Genre Painting Crosses the Atlantic*
Andrew Sayers	*The Weird Scribblings of Nature: Australian and American Landscape Painting in the 19th Century*
Michael Rosenthal	*The Artless Landscape: Early Colonial Imagery in Australia*
William Vaughan	*Response to the papers*

2 July 1999
The Popular Print in England
(held at the Paul Mellon Centre)

Sheila O'Connell	*Introduction*
Margaret Aston	*'From Big Book to Broadside': Some early 17th-century Ballad Prints*
Nicholas Barker	*Thomas Trevillian's Great Book of 1616*
Malcolm Jones	*A Popular View of Relations between the Sexes. And how English is the 1628 Print Series?*
Margaret Spufford	*Disturbing Prints in the 17th Century*
V.A.C. Gatrell	*How Popular was the Satirical Print, 1770–1820?*
Diana Donald	*What is a Popular Print? Some Thoughts on Problems of Meaning and Definition*

10–11 September 1999
Performing Arts: Alliances of Studio and Stage in Britain, 1776–1812
(held at the Huntington Library, San Marino, California)

Robyn Asleson	*Opening Remarks*
Shelley Bennett	*Moderator: Women on Display: Beauty, Desire, Commerce*
Martin Postle	*'Painted Ladies': Sir Joshua Reynolds and the Female Studio Model*
Gillian Perry	*Flirting with the Muse: Metaphors of Sexuality in late 18th-century Imagery of the Actress*
Shearer West	*Body Connoisseurship*
Ann Bermingham	*Moderator: The Commodification of Celebrity: Biography, Criticism, Portraiture*

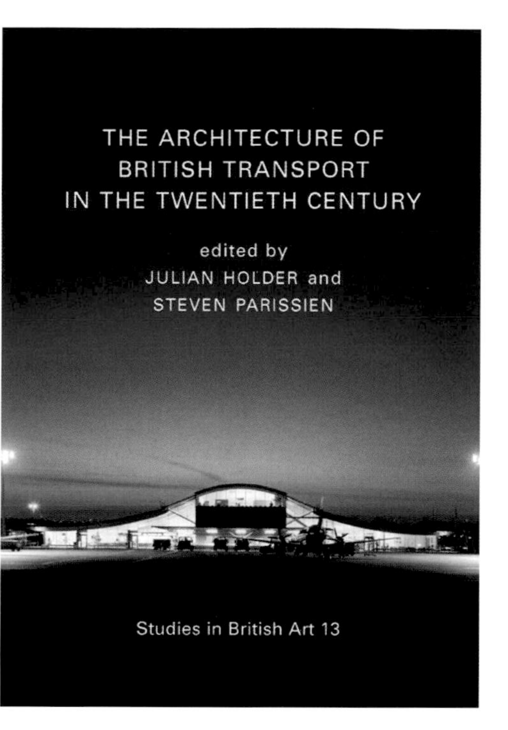

Kalman Burnim	*The Phenomenon of Theatrical Portraits and Prints in the Great Age of Painting in England*
Joseph Roach	*Patina: Sarah Siddons and the Depth of Surfaces*
Cheryl Wanko	*Rogues and Gentlemen: Early Player Biography in England*
Robyn Asleson	*Moderator: Counterfeiting the World: Stage and Studio Effects*
Frederick Burwick	*Gesture in Acting and Painting*
Aileen Ribeiro	*Costuming the Part: A Discourse of Fashion and Fiction in the Image of the Actress, 1776–1812*
Nancy Hazelton	*The Theatrical Landscape*
David Rodes	*Moderator: Sublime Representations: Tragedy and the Grand Manner*
Jonathan Bate	*Shakespeare and the Romantic Actress*
Michael Wilson	*Contested Terrain: The Art of the Actor's Body Politic*
Heather McPherson	*Painting, Politics and the Stage in the Age of Caricature*

CONFERENCES

October–November 1999
The Metropolis and its Image: Constructing Identities for London *c.*1750–1950
(a series of lectures held at the Paul Mellon Centre)

Elizabeth McKellar	*The View from the Hill: Alternative Aspects and Rural Presences in mid-18th-century London*
Lucy Peltz	*Aestheticizing the Accidental City: Antiquarianism, Modernity and the Representation of late 18th-century London*
Diana Donald	*'Beastly Sights': The Treatment of Animals as a Moral Theme of Representations of London, c.1820–1850*
Dana Arnold	*London Bridge and its Symbolic Identity in the Regency Metropolis: The Dialectic of Civic and National Pride*
Michael Port	*Ministers and the Metropolitan Image: Cabinet, Parliament and the Concept of a Capital City c.1850–1910*
Iain Black	*Re-building the Heart of the Empire: Financial Headquarters in the City of London 1919–1939*
Adrian Rifkin	*Benjamin's Paris? Freud's Rome? Whose London? Imaging London after World War II*

8 March 2000
Destinations Anywhere: The Architecture of Transport in the 20th Century
(held at the Paul Mellon Centre)

Elain Harwood	*Reappraising British Railways*
Susie Barson	*'A Little Grit and Ginger': The Impact of Charles Holden on the London Underground 1923–40*
Gavin Stamp	*Early 20th-century Stations*
Kenneth Powell	*The Jubilee Line Extension*
Neil Bingham	*Arrivals and Departures: Civil Airport Architecture in Britain during the Interwar Period*
Colin Davies	*The Contemporary British Airport*
David Jeremiah	*Roadside Services*
Stuart Evans	*House, Car, Countryside*
Julian Holder	*From Chaos to Control: The Development of the Bus and Coach Station in Interwar Britain*

25 May 2000
A Noble Art: Amateur and Drawing Masters in Stuart and Georgian Britain
(held at the Paul Mellon Centre)

Ann Bermingham	*Women Amateurs and the Language of Flowers*
David Alexander	*Amateur Etchers*
Dongho Chun	*Framing Cultural Hegemony: Sir John Fleming Leicester's Amateur Painting 1784–1827*
Katie Coombs	*The Portrait Miniature and the Amateur*
Lucy Peltz	*Amateurs, Authors and Artists: A Socioeconomic Look at Extra-Illustration in the late 18th Century*

22–23 September 2000
Georgian Geographies: A Conference on Space, Place and Landscape in the 18th Century
(held at the Paul Mellon Centre)

Opening Remarks	Miles Ogborn, Charles Withers
Stephen Daniels	*'Gothic Gallantry': Repton, Byron and the Sexual Politics of Landscape Gardening*
Vladimir Jankovic	*Arcadian Instincts: A Geography of Truth in Georgian England*
Mark Overton	*Geographies of Consumption in Early Modern England*
Dan Clayton	*Spaces of Cultural Engagement and Effacement on the Northwest Coast of North America in the Age of George III*
John Gascoigne	*Joseph Banks and Geographies of Natural Knowledge*
Michael Bravo	*Evangelicalism, Scientific Travel and Arctic Geography in Georgian Britain*
David Lambert	*Neither Slave nor Master: The Ambiguities of 'Freed' and 'Poor' in the Barbadian Colonial Order*
David Solkin	*Crowds and Connoisseurs: Viewing Genre Painting at the Royal Academy c.1790–1822*
Rosie Dias	*'The World of Pictures': Pall Mall and the Topography of Display, 1780–99*
Luciana Martins	*The Art of Tropical Travel, 1768–1830*
Paul Glennie	*Geographies of Time in Georgian Bristol*
Robert Mayhew	*Geography Books and the Character of Georgian Politics*
Cynthia Wall	*Geographies of Georgian Fictional Interiors*
Chloe Chard	*Laughter, Comedy and Imaginative Geography*
Karen Harvey	*Spaces of Erotic Delight in the 18th Century*

16–17 November 2000
Cultures of the West End
(held at the Tate Gallery)

Denys Cosgrove	*Keynote Address*
David Cannadine	*Social and Economic History: The Monarchy*
Michael Port	*Land Ownership and Architecture*
Elizabeth McKellar	*London's Social and Architectural Histories*
Dana Arnold	*London's Social and Architectural Histories*
Iain Black	*Private Banks*
Andrew Hanham	*The Court of George II*
Diana Donald	*Lampooning London*
Tim Clayton	*Prints of the West End*
Lynda Nead	*Shopping, Gender and the Display and Consumption of Goods*
Chris Breward	*Shopping, Gender and the Display and Consumption of Goods*
Tony Travers	*The West End Today*
Respondents	David Green, Miles Ogborn, Dana Arnold, Adrian Rifkin

5–7 July 2001
Art and the British Empire, c.1600–2000
(held at Tate Britain)

Opening Remarks	Tim Barringer, Geoff Quilley
Linda Colley	*Britain, Smallness and Otherwise: A Visual and Imperial Odyssey*
Barbara Groseclose	*Material Culture and Some Early American Paintings*
Eric F Gollannek	*Fractured Imperial Visions: George Stubbs' 'Cheetah with Two Indian Attendants'*
Romita Ray	*Storm in a Teacup? Visualising Tea Consumption in the British Empire*
Kariann Yokota	*Sowing the Seeds of Colonial Aspiration: The Transatlantic Exchange of North American Botanical Prints and British Patronage*
Amy Meyers	*A Work in Progress: Nexus of Exchange, Philadelphia and the Visual Culture of Natural History 1740–1840*
Sarah Thomas	*The Art of Science: Art of the Flinders and Baudin Voyages to Australia*
John Bonehill	*Confrontation and Conflicts: The Image of the British Soldier and the Fight for Empire c.1770–1790*
Stephen Vella	*'The Simple Garb for Truth': Imperial Fault Lines and the Aesthetic Economy of William Hodges' India*
David Solkin	*'Conquest, Usurpation, Wealth, Luxury, Famine': Mortimer's Banditti and the Anxieties of Empire*
Joan Coutu	*Fame and Fortunes: Funerary Monuments and the Definition of Self in the British West Indies*
Sarah Parsons	*Sexualising Slavery: Representing Black Femininity in the British Empire c.1800*
Pascal Dupuy	*Abolition and the English Caricature 1780–1810*
Maya Jasanoff	*The Nawab and the Nabobs: Collecting in Lucknow 1775–1800*
Natasha Eaton	*Gifting the Inalienable? The Presentation and Perception of British Portraiture in 18th-century India*
Beth Fowkes Tobin	*The English Garden Conversation Piece in India*
Eleanor Hughes	*Ships in the 'Line': Imagining Empire at the Royal Academy Exhibition of 1784*
Douglas Fordham	*Gentlemanly Capitalism and the Transformation of the London Art World 1750–1770*
Urmilla De	*'Empire of Colour': The Publishing World of Edward Orme*
Jordana Pomeroy	*Picturing their Empire: Victorian Women Artists Abroad*
Pamela Gerrish Nunn	*Derring-do and the Damsel Nation in Distress*
Kristina Huneault	*'The Mistress's Favourite': Paradigms of Race, Empire and Domestic Service in Edwardian Advertising*
Kurt M. Koenigsberger	*All Richness and Force: Elephants, Englishness and Empire at the Delhi Durbars*
Morna O'Neill	*Allegory, History, Tradition: Empire and Meaning in Charles Ricketts' 'Bacchus in India'*
Tapati Guha Thakurta	*The Empire and its Antiquities: A Pioneer's Discovery of the 'Ancient Architecture of Hindosthan'*
Roger Blackley	*Paper Landscapes: Colonial Trompe l'Oeil Drawings*
Rod MacNeil	*Colonisation by Art: Colonial Landscape Painting and the Construction of a White Australia*
Joanna Sassoon	*Imagining Western Australia*
Ian McLean	*First Art or Empire Art? 'Sydney Cove' 1794*

CONFERENCES

David Hanson	*Between the Big River and the Nile: John Glover and the Course of the Colonial Picturesque*
Jos Hackforth-Jones	*Westward Ho! Internal and External Colonialism in Wales and New South Wales and the Push Westwards c.1780–1830*
Kay Dian Kriz	*Marketing Mulatresses in the Paintings and Prints of Agostino Brunias*
Jeff Guy	*The Making of a Zulu Chief: Visual Images in the Creation of Ngoza kaLundaba*
Susan Lowish	*Then and Now: Perceiving Indigenous Art and Empire in the Discourse of Art History*
Mary Roberts	*The Politics of Portraiture: Behind the Veil*
Kenneth Bendiner	*Justifying Empire: John Frederick Lewis's Vision of the Near East*
Emily Weeks	*Imperial Peripheries: re-reading the 'Egyptian' Years of John Frederick Lewis*
Michael Gaudio	*Savage Marks: Engraving and Empire in Thomas Harriot's 'Briefe and True Report'*
Marcus Wood	*Exploding the Taboo: Pornography in the Visual Representation of Slavery*
Michael Hatt	*Uranians and Imperialists: Homoeroticism and Boyhood in late-Victorian Britain*
Catherine M Pagani	*Capturing the Picturesque: William Alexander and George Chinnery in China*
Luciana Martins	*Imperial Routes: British Visions of Rio de Janeiro*
Felix Driver	*Imperial Routes: British Visions of Rio de Janeiro*
Michael Godby	*Settlers and Travellers: Different Ideas of 'Home' in the Representation of the South African Landscape by Thomas Bowler and Thomas Baines*
Jeffrey Auerbach	*Art, Honour and the mid-19th-century Crisis of Empire*
Pramila Sharma	*The Tradition of London 'Punch' in India*
Catherine Speck	*A Not so Genteel Pen: Grace Cossington Smith's View of the Empire*
Sandra Klopper	*Gentlemen at Leisure: Riding Breeches in late 19th- and early 20th-century Portrait Photos of Black South Africa*
Leonard Bell	*Pictures in History: Settlement as Theatre: John Davis's Photo-Portrait of Robert Louis Stephenson and Family in Valima, Samoa, 1892*
Jonathan Black	*'The Price of Empire': British Sculpture and the Promotion of an Imperial Masculine Ideal 1920–33*
Elizabeth Rankin	*Africanising Christian Imagery in South African Missions*
Juliett Leeb-du Toit	*Preaching Back to the Centre*
Jordanna Bailkin	*Modern Ethnographies in South Africa*
Partha Mitter	*Murals of New Delhi and India House, London: Raj Patronage and the Contested Definition of Indian Nationhood*
Julie Codell	*Making Empire Modern: Re-visioning the British Empire in the Films of the 1930s*
Simon Faulkener	*Minton in Jamaica*
W.J.T. Mitchell	*Empire and Objecthood*
Concluding Remarks	Tim Barringer, Geoff Quilley

18 July 2001
The Interpretation of Georgian Towns
(held at the Paul Mellon Centre)

Orlando Ridout	*Annapolis*
Julian Holder	*Edinburgh*
Carl Loundsbury	*Williamsburg*
Eddie Booth	*Lewes*
Carter Hudgins	*Charleston, Fredericksburg and Alexandria*
Timothy Mowl	*Cheltenham*

19 October 2001
Painted Ladies: Women at the Court of Charles II
(held at the National Portrait Gallery)

Frances Harris	*Margaret Godolphin, John Evelyn and the Court Beauty*
Paulina Kewes	*Roman Heroines on the Restoration Stage*
Oliver Millar	*In Light of the Restoration*
Sheila O'Connell	*Love–Pleasant, Love–Unfortunate: Women in 17th-century Popular Prints*
Susan Shifrin	*'Subdued by a Famous Roman Dame': Picturing Foreignness, Notoriety and Prerogative in the Portraits of Hortense Mancini, Duchess Mazarin*
Andrew Walkling	*Music and the Programme of the Masque in Restoration England*
Steven Zwicker	*Sites of Instruction: Andrew Marvell and the Tropes of Restoration Portraiture*

2 November 2001
Turner Revisited
(held at the Paul Mellon Centre)

Chaired by Brian Allen and MaryAnne Stevens

John Gage	*The New Turner*
Cecilia Powell	*The Presentation of Turner in Public Collections*

11 January 2002
Art on the Line, Scholar's Study Evening
(held at the Courtauld Institute of Art)

Brian Allen — *Introduction*
David Solkin — *The Great Room in the Histories of British Art*
Giles Waterfield — *Somerset House and the 19th-century British Picture Gallery*
MaryAnne Stevens — *A Modern British Picture Gallery*
Alex Potts — *The Spectacle of Images*

14 March 2002
Art and Industry: The Life and Work of Matthew Boulton
(held at the Paul Mellon Centre)

Nicholas Goodison — *Introduction*
Jenny Uglow — *Vulcan's City: The Birmingham Boom of the mid-18th Century*
Nicholas Goodison — *Ormolu*
Kenneth Quickenden — *Design of Boulton Silver*
George Demidowicz — *The Development of Soho Manufactory and Mint*
Jenny Uglow — *Boulton and the Lunar Society*
Rita McLean — *Soho House*
Val Loggie — *Visitors to Soho*
Adam Green — *The Archives of Soho*

12–16 August 2002
Cursos de Verano: The Grand Tour from a European Perspective
(held at El Escorial, University of Madrid)

Introduction by José Mª Luzon Nogué, David Bindman, Brian Allen
Jeremy Black — *The Grand Tour: An Historian's Perspective*
Roundtable discussion with David Bindman, Mercedes Cerón, José Mª Luzon Nogué, Jeremy Black and Andrés Úbeda de Los Cobos
Brian Allen — *British Travellers in Italy in the 1770s*
Pedro Moleón Gavilanes — *Arquitectos españoles en la Italia del Grand Tour*
Roundtable discussion with Brian Allen, Moleón Gavilanes, María Dolores Sánchez-Jáuregui, Mª Luisa López Vidriero
José Mª Luzon Nogué — *El Westmorland y otras presas en el estudio del Grand Tour*
David Bindman — *The Westmorland from an English Point of View*
Roundtable discussion with José Mª Luzon Nogué, David Bindman, Ana Mª Suárez Huerta, Isabel Rodríguez López
Kim Sloan — *Sir William Hamilton and Naples*
Alison Yarrington — *Grand Tourists and the Collecting of Sculpture*
Carlo Knight — *Piccoli souvenirs del Grand Tour: Impronte di gemme antiche, vedute á la gouache e ventagli*
Roundtable discussion with Kim Sloan, Alison Yarrington, Carlo Knight, María del Carman Alonso Rodríguez, Alfonso Pleguezuelo Hernández
Andrew Wilton — *Watercolours for the Grand Tour*

24–26 October 2002
Facing the Eighteenth Century: New Approaches to British Portraiture
(held at the Huntington Library, San Marino, California)

Alex Kidson — *Opening keynote address. George Romney and the Operation of Fashion: A Case Study in late 18th-century British Portraiture*
Shelley Bennett — *Opening Remarks*
Moderators: John Brewer, Alex Kidson, Brian Allen, Ann Bermingham
Richard Wendorf — *Skating Around Raeburn*
Karen Stanworth — *Portraiture, Visual Culture and the Representation of Situated Identity in 18th-century Group Portraiture*
Malcolm Baker — *Making the Portrait Bust Modern: The Changing Role of Sculptural Portraiture in 18th-century England*
Gillian Forrester — *Some Elements of Painting with Crayons: John Russell's Scientific Portraits*
Elizabeth Barker — *Tokens of Affection and Esteem: Three 'New' Portraits from the Circle of Joseph Wright*
Carol Gibson-Wood — *Furnished With Faces: Portraits in London Houses at the Beginning of the 18th Century*
Katie Coombs — *The 'Disgrace' of Miniature Painting: Miniaturists and the Royal Academy*
Catherine Tite — *'The True Airs of Heads': High Art, Portraiture and the Cultural Exchange at Wilton and Stowe, 1768–1789*
Douglas Fordham — *Philosophy or Satire? Allan Ramsay and British Portraiture in the 1760s*
Lucy Peltz — *'Hydra-Headed Monsters': Engraved Historic Portrait Prints and the Rise of Extra-Illustration in the late 18th Century*
Michael Rosenthal — *Double Headed: Portraiture and Public Reputation*

CONFERENCES

17–18 October 2003
Regency Portraiture: Regarding the Regency, The Possibilities of Portraiture in 'this Age of Personality'
(held at the National Portrait Gallery)

Cassandra Albinson	*Sir Thomas Should Always Have Had Such Sitters*
John Bonehill	*Royal Games: The Duke of York, Graphic Satire and Rumours of War in the mid-1790s*
Fintan Cullen	*From Union to Repeal: Representing Ireland at Westminster, 1800–40*
Holger Hoock	*Military Heroics and the St Paul's Pantheon*
Ludmilla Jordanova	*Shaping the Regency*
Paul Langford	*Response to Shaping the Regency*
Jan Marsh	*Token and Touchstone: Representation of Black Sitters between the Ending of the Slave Trade and Abolition of Slavery in British Colonies*
Martin Myrone	*Biography as Art History: Writing the British School 1790–1830*
Steven Parissien	*Thomas Lawrence and the Iconography of Spin*
Gill Perry	*Performing the Feminine: Notoriety and Excess in Portraits of the Actress*
Marcia Pointon	*The Colour Crimson*
Angela Rosenthal	*The Fair Sex*
Shearer West	*The Romantic Portrait Revisited*
Vicky Whitfield	*Inventing the Industrial Nation*

11 November 2003
Thomas Jones Roundtable
(held at the National Gallery)

Ann Sumner	*Thomas Jones's Large Oil Paintings*
Chloe Chard	*Whimsical Incidents: The Adventures of Thomas Jones in Italy*
Michael Rosenthal	*Thomas Jones and the Fragmentation of Landscape*
Christopher Riopelle	*The Installation of 'Thomas Jones in Italy'*
Greg Smith	*Thomas Jones's Watercolours*

5 December 2003
Collecting and the Imagination: Horace Walpole at Strawberry Hill
(held at the Paul Mellon Centre)

Stephen Calloway	*Reality, Illusion and Effect at Strawberry Hill*
Katie Coombs	*Walpole and the Collecting of Miniatures*
Lucy Peltz	*A Friendly Gathering: The Social Politics of Presentation Books and Extra-Illustration in Horace Walpole's Circle*
Earle Havens	*Imagination and Tradition: Collecting Literary and Historical Books and Manuscripts in the Age of Walpole*
Bet McLeod	*Connoisseur or Collector: An Assessment of Walpole's Collection of Decorative Art and Sculpture*
Tim Knox	*Collecting Curiosities*
Stephen Clarke	*The Afterlife of a Collector: The 1842 Sale and Walpole's Posthumous Reputation*

10 January 2004
Painted from the Shadows
(held at the National Portrait Gallery)

Introduction by Giles Waterfield and Anne French

Jessica Gerard	*The Elite Below Stairs: Country House Service 1815–1914*
John Styles	*Servants and Costume*
Reyahn King	*Painted from the Shadows: Portraits of Black Servants, Identified and Unidentified*
Denise Bethel	*Servants in Photography: The Unexpected Dialogue*
Pamela Horn	*Maids on the Move: Servant Migration in Victorian and Edwardian England*
Alison Light	*The Class War in the Home: Live-in Service Between the Wars*

19–20 March 2004
Pre-Raphaelitism and Science: Painting, Photography and the Investigation of the Visible World
(held at Tate Britain)

James Second	*Victorian Sensation and the History of Naturalism*
Jennifer Tucker	*Painting, Photography and the Investigation of the Natural World*
Carol Jacobi	*W. H. Hunt, Truth to Nature?*
Heather Birchall	*Contrasting Visions: Ruskin, the Daguerrotype and the Photograph*
Jacqueline Ridge	*Pre-Raphaelite Techniques and their Consequences*
Christopher Newall	*'The Constancy of Change'*
Jonathan Ribner	*Three Concepts of Time from 'The Autumn'*
Tim Barringer	*On the Rocks: Geology and National Identity in Britain and America in the 1850s*
Jason Rosenfeld	*Architecture as Landscape: The Pre-Raphaelites, Benjamin Woodward, Richard St John Tyrwhitt and the Oxford University Museum*
Mike Hickox	*Science and Religion in the Pre-Raphaelite Work of John Brett*
Nicola Brown	*Imitations of Life: Photography, Pre-Raphaelitism and Taxidermy*
Paul Barlow	*Millais's Motiveless Veracity: Realism in Millais's Late Landscapes*

26 March 2004
The Crystal Palace at Sydenham
(held at Dulwich Picture Gallery)

Jan Piggott	*The Fine Arts Courts at the Crystal Palace and the Contemporary Response*
Rosemary Hill	*'The earnest enthusiasm and profound knowledge of one man': A.W.N. Pugin and the Medieval Court of 1851*
Shelly Hales	*Re-casting Antiquity: Classics and the Crystal Palace*
Kathryn Ferry	*'Monumental Architecture Under a Glass Roof': Owen Jones's Egyptian and Alhambra Courts*
Carol Flores	*'Beauty of Effect and Arrangement': The Exhibition Architecture of Owen Jones*
John Kenworthy-Browne	*The Sculpture at the Crystal Palace*
Charles Newton	*Owen Jones and Christopher Dresser: Their Responses to the Problems of Design in the Nineteenth Century*

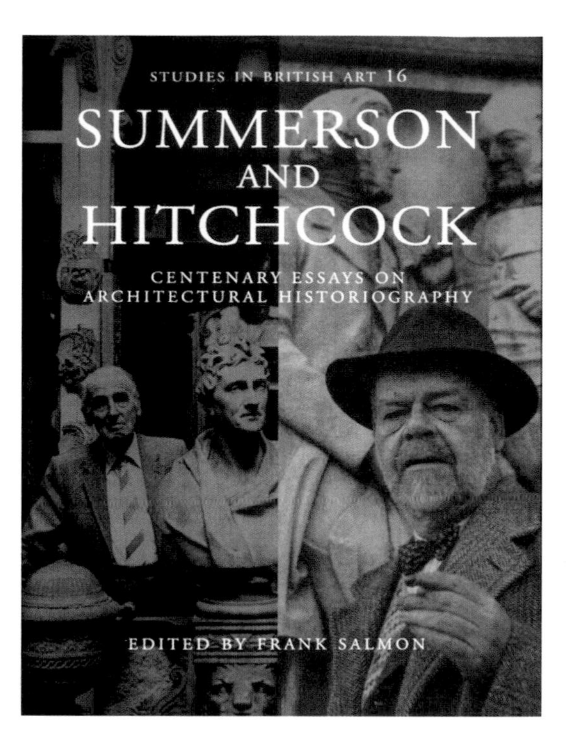

11–12 June 2004
Sir John Summerson and Henry-Russell Hitchcock
(held at the Paul Mellon Centre)

John Harris	*Personal Recollections of Working with Henry-Russell Hitchcock and Sir John Summerson*
Gavin Stamp	*Summerson, Hitchcock and Glasgow: The Emergence of Two Architectural Historians*
Mosette Broderick	*Hitchcock and Summerson on Tape*
Andrew Saint	*Hitchcock and Summerson on Tape*
Nina Stritzler-Levine	*Henry-Russell Hitchcock and Architecture Exhibition Practice at the MoMA*
Margaret Richardson	*Summerson and (The) Soane*
Michela Rosso	*Preserving Architecture: John Summerson and the Heritage of the Victorian Age*

CONFERENCES

Barry Bergdoll	*Romantic Modernity in the 1930s: Henry-Russell Hitchcock's Architecture: Twentieth and Nineteenth Centuries?*
Alan Powers	*Summerson, Hitchcock and Romanticism*
Marie Frank	*Formalism and Objectivity in American Aesthetic Thought c.1900*
Christy Anderson	*Not Quite the Renaissance*
Caroline Van Eck	*A Marriage of Classicism and Modernism: 'Artisan Mannerism' Revisited*
Frank Salmon	*The Eighteenth Century: 'Long' or just Episodic?*
Marlene Heck	*Mind the Gap: Rewriting Sir John Summerson's 'American Architectural History'*
Helen Searing	*Henry-Russell Hitchcock and Dutch Architecture*
Anthony Geraghty	*Summerson and Wren*
Ann Gilkerson	*Constructing the Modern Victorian: Henry-Russell Hitchcock's 'The Architecture of H H Richardson and his Times'*
Neil Jackson	*John Summerson and the View from the Outside*
Philip Goad	*Mischievous Analogy, Bureaucracy and Genius: John Summerson, Henry-Russell Hitchcock and Post-War Architectural Historiography*
Elizabeth McKellar	*The Critical Legacy: John Summerson and the Post-war Foundations of 18th-century Studies*
Nigel Whitely	*Hitchcock's 'Unfortunate Classic': Reyner Banham and the International Style*
David Van Zanten	*Discussion and closing comments*

18 June 2004
Art of the Garden
(held at Tate Britain)

Patrick Wright	*Introduction*
Anne Helmreich	*National Identity and English Garden Design, 1870–1914*
Ysanne Holt	*'The Veriest Poem of Art in Nature': E.A. Hornel's Japanese Garden in the Scottish Borders*
Stephen Bann	*Myths, Oppositions and Crossovers: The Garden, English and French*
Brent Elliott	*The Artificial Garden, 1820–1870*
Jason Rosenfeld	*Nature and Display: The Pre-Raphaelites, Wardian Cases and Natural History Collections in the 1850s*
John Lucas	*Some Poets' Gardens: Co-opting Nature*

14–16 July 2004
The Art of Exploration: European and American Artistic Responses to Exploration 1750–1860
(held at the National Maritime Museum)

Sir David Attenborough *Caird Medal Lecture*

Chaired by Margarette Lincoln, Nigel Rigby, Brian Allen, Amy Meyers

Sarah Monks	*Beyond the Sea: Desire, Fear and the Construction of Space in 18th-century British Marine Art*
Geoffrey Quilley	*The Pencil in the First Person: The Artist as Eyewitness on Voyages of Exploration*
Peter Brunt	*Et in Rapanui ego: An Allegory of Unnatural History in Two Paintings by William Hodges*
Pieter van der Merwe	*The Virtuous Swiss: The Legacy of John Webber*
David Mabberley	*Ferdinand Bauer's Australian Plant Drawings, 1801–3*
Leonard Bell	*Not Quite Darwin's Artist: The Travel Art of Augustus Earle and the Topography of Human Knowledge*
Simon Schaffer	*The Scientist as Artist: The Case of William Gooch and Vancouver's Voyage of 1791–95*
Michael Bravo	*The Whaler as Artist: William Scoresby's Arctic Visions*
Jordan Goodman	*The Naval Officer as Artist: Captain Owen Stanley and the Voyage of HMS Rattlesnake*
David Bindman	*A 'philosophical eye': The Forsters and Human Variety*
Michael Godby	*Samuel Daniell's Travels in South Africa, 1800–1803, and the Engravings he made from them*
Roy Bridges	*Did African Travellers Produce Attractive Illustrations or Visual Records? The Art of J.A. Grant on the Nile Expedition of 1860–63*
Barbara Groseclose	*Circum-Atlantic Aristocracy: The Image of the Indian Queen and Voyages of Discovery*
Natasha Eaton	*Landscapes of Interaction? Trafficking Mughal and British Images of Place in Early Colonial India*
Stephanie Pratt	*Contexts for the Images of American Indians in North American Expeditionary Art, 1778–1840*
Robert Peck	*Plates for the Book that Never Appeared: The Lost Visual Legacy of the Lewis and Clark Expedition*
Nicholas Thomas	*Cook, Hodges, Exploration and Art*

24 September 2004
The Edwardians: Secrets and Desires
(held at the Paul Mellon Centre)

Anna Gray	*The Exhibition and its Reception*
MaryAnne Stevens	*The Royal Academy in the Edwardian Era*
Hilary Fraser	*Vernon Lee and the Edwardian Art World*
Christine Riding	*'The Blue Boy' and Whistler*
Angus Trumble	*Edwardian Colonial Baroque: The Portrait of Sir Frank A. Swettenham by John Singer Sargent*
Ben Read	*Edwardian Public Sculpture: The Expanded Field*
Stephen Coppel	*Charles Candor, Lithography and 'A Taste for Literature'*
Ysanne Holt	*'Modern Idylls' and English Landscapes from before the Great War*
Kenneth McConkey	*British and American Artists in Paris 1890–1910*
Ann Galbally	*Decadence and Art Nouveau: Sourcing Charles Candour's European Reputation*

12 November 2004
George Frederic Watts Centenary Conference
(held at Tate Britain and the National Portrait Gallery)

Kenneth McConkey	*Introduction*
Colin Trodd	*Watts and Late Victorian Culture: Bodies of Enchantment and Experience*
Paul Barlow	*Making and Remaking Watts's 'Sistine Chapel'*
Stephanie Brown	*Watts and Sculpture*
Veronica Franklin-Gould	*Good and Evil Interwoven: Watts's Dual Vision*
Peter Funnell	*Introduction*
Barbara Bryant	*G.F. Watts: The Art of Portraiture*
Lara Perry	*Thinking of England: Watts's Art for the Nation*
Shelagh Wilson	*Watts and Women*
Andrew Wilton	*Watts Abroad: The Symbolist Legacy*
David Stewart	*Chair, Discussion*

15–16 April 2005
Turner, Whistler, Monet: Aesthetics, Pollution and the City
(held at Tate Britain)

Victoria Walsh	*Turner and Whistler: The Aesthetics of Ambiguity*
Elizabeth Prettejohn	*Whistler and Art for Art's Sake*
Suzanne Singletary	*Whistler and France*
Katharine Lochnan	*Whistler and Monet: Impressionism in Britain*
John House	*When Monet met Whistler: The Question of Evidence*
Sam Smiles	*Turner on Display: The Making of a Modern Artist*
Jonathan Ribner	*Imagining Purity in the Age of the Great Stink*
Julia Thornes	*Monet's London Series and the Climate of London 1899–1904*
Barry Venning	*Turner's London*
John Stewart	*Thames and Variations: Cosmopolitan Performance in Whistler's London Landscape*
David Gilbert	*Imperial Highway: London, Empire and the Thames*

22–23 April 2005
International Arts and Crafts
(held at the Victoria & Albert Museum)

Linda Parry	*William Morris and the Arts and Crafts Movement*
Peter Stansky	*'Meet me at St. Louis': William Morris and the Louisiana Purchase*
Karen Livingstone	*'Moot Points': Art, Industry and the Arts and Crafts Exhibition Society*
Jan Marsh	*The Back to the Land Impulse*
Alan Powers	*1884 and the Arts and Crafts Movement*
Wendy Hitchmough	*Lifestyle and Design in the Arts and Crafts Home*
Elizabeth Cumming	*Home and Away: British Arts and Crafts across the World*
Edward Bosley	*From East to West: The Arts and Crafts Movement in America*
Renate Ulmer	*An Artists' Community, Mathildenhöhe, Darmstadt*
Edyta Supinska-Polit	*Stanislaw Wyspianski and the Polish Arts and Crafts Movement*
Edmund de Waal	*Cultured Living: Japan and the Model Room*
Tanya Harrod	*Paradise Postponed: What Happened to the Arts and Crafts Movement in Britain*

CONFERENCES

28 June 2005
Stubbs and the Horse
(held at the National Gallery)
Short presentations by Malcolm Warner, Judy Egerton, Deanna Petherbridge, Michaela Giebelhausen

23 September 2005
Restoring Hawksmoor
(held at the Paul Mellon Centre)

Kerry Downes	*Hawksmoor in Perspective*
Michael Ramirez	*Hawksmoor's Design Process and Achievement in the Early Commission Churches*
Pierre du Prey	*Hawksmoor and Halicarnassus*
Jason Ali	*Orientation in Hawksmoor Churches*
Kevin Rogers	*The Hawksmoor Archive*
Alan Powers	*A Different 'Modern': H.S. Goodhart-Rendel on Hawksmoor*
Gavin Stamp	*Hawksmoor Redeemed? The Fates of his Churches since 1945*

Tour of St George's Bloomsbury

2 December 2005
John Talman's Collection of Drawings: A Historia of Art from Antiquity to Christianity
(held at the Paul Mellon Centre)

Dmitrios Zikos	*John Talman and Italian Sculpture*
Christopher Baker	*John Talman and Henry Aldrich's Collection of Prints*
Antonella Capitanio	*John Talman and the Liturgy of the Catholic Church*
Marco Collareta	*John Talman and the Italian Middle Ages*
Louisa Connors	*Topham's Collection of Drawings*
Peter Davidson	*British Catholic Culture in the late 17th and early 18th Century*
Elizabeth Kieven	*John Talman and Italian Baroque Architecture*
Edward Olszewski	*Cardinal Ottoboni and the European Arcadia*
Cinzia Sicca	*The Making and Unravelling of Talman's Collection of Drawings*

13 January 2006
Samuel Palmer: A British Romantic Artist Reassessed
(held at the Paul Mellon Centre)

Samuel Smiles	*From the Valley of Vision to the M25: Samuel Palmer and Modern Culture*
Greg Smith	*Ancients and Moderns: Samuel Palmer and the 'Progress of Water Colours'*
Christiana Payne	*Dreaming of the Marriage of the Land and the Sea: Samuel Palmer and the Coast*
Timothy Wilcox	*Critical Responses to Palmer's Later Career*
Paul Goldman	*Samuel Palmer: Poetry, Printmaking and Illustration*
Martin Postle	*Palmer and the British Academic Tradition*
Simon Shaw-Miller	*Palmer and the Persistence of the Pastoral in 20th-century English Music*

3–4 February 2006
Ascribing Value: The Production and Collection of Architectural Drawings
(held at the Victoria & Albert Museum)
Chaired by Frank Salmon, Michael Snodin, Irena Murray, Wim de Wit

David Chipperfield	*Keynote Address*
Mariet Willinge	*Collecting Dutch Architectural Archives in a Changing World*
Alan Powers	*An Architect Collects: Albert Richardson*
Paul Brislin	*Design and Collection: The New Fluid Dynamic between Design and Electronic Retrieval Systems*
Jo Ronaldson	*Design and Collection: The New Fluid Dynamic between Design and Electronic Retrieval Systems*
Howard Shubert	*If the Architect is Dead can the Connoisseur be far behind? Connoisseurship in the Digital Age*
C.J. Lim	*Architecture for Drawing's Sake*
Aaron Betsky	*Collecting in an Architectural Field*
Marie-Ange Brayer	*New Statuses for Architectural Drawing and Collecting*
John Harris	*History of the Market: Public and Private Collecting*
Charles Hind	*History of the Market: Public and Private Collecting*
Niall Hobhouse	*Can there be a Market without a Marketplace?*
Tom Avermaete	*Archives in Formation: Defining Concepts and Models for a new Collection of Architectural Archives*
Gerald Beasley	*Drawing to a Close: Collecting in a Digital Age*

Margaret Richardson	*Edwin Lutyens*
Eleanor Gawne	*Edwin Lutyens*
Colin Cunningham	*Alfred Waterhouse*
Michael Snodin	*Alfred Waterhouse*
Adrian Forty	*Philip Webb*
Sally Watson	*Philip Webb*
Howard Burns	*Andrea Palladio*
Charles Hind	*Andrea Palladio*
Eammonn Canniffe	*Unusual Graphic Techniques*
Mary Guyatt	*Unusual Graphic Techniques*
Robert Elwall	*Erno Goldfinger*
Gavin Stamp	*Erno Goldfinger*
Gordon Higgott	*Inigo Jones and John Webb*
Susan Pugh	*Inigo Jones and John Webb*

15–18 February 2006

Roma Britannica: Art Patronage and Cultural Exchange in 18th-century Rome (held at the British School at Rome)

Chaired by Susan Russell, Joseph Connors, Brian Allen, Christopher Johns

Edward Corp	*Il Palazzo Del Re: Cultural Forum and Surrogate Embassy*
David Marshall	*Introduction to the conference*
Edward Chaney	*Before the Eighteenth Century*
Elizabeth Bartman	*Egypt, Rome, and the Concept of Universal History*
Malcolm Baker	*Commemoration 'in a more grave and durable manner': Portrait Busts for the British*
Clare Hornsby	*Was Gavin Hamilton an Archaeologist?*
Andrew Wallace-Hadrill	*From the Villa Negroni to Ickworth: Romanizing Frescoes*
Tommaso Manfredi	*Roma communis patria: Juvarra e i britannici*
Katrina Grant	*Planting 'Italian gusto' in a 'Gothick country': the influence of Filippo Juvarra on William Kent*
Elizabeth Kieven	*The other way round. Alessandro Galilei and his British Patrons*
John Wilton-Ely	*'My Holy See of Pleasurable Antiquity': Robert Adam and his Associates in Rome*
Francis Russell	*James Byres and Lord Bute: a postscript*
Letizia Tedeschi	*Vincenzo Brenna e i disegni dell'Antico per Charles Townley*
Karin Wolfe	*Acquisitive Tourism: Francesco Trevisani's Roman Studio and British Visitors*
Edgar Peters Bowron	*From Homer to Faustina the Younger: Representations of Antiquity in Batoni's Grand Tour Portraits*
Peter Kerber	*Lord Arundel, Pompeo Batoni and the Art of Catholic Recusancy*
Alastair Laing	*Gian Paolo Panini's English Clients and their Use of his Pictures*
David Marshall	*Panini and the Stuarts in Rome*
James Holloway	*John Urquhart of Cromarty: A little known collector of Roman paintings*
Carol Richardson	*Andrea Pozzo and the Venerable English College, Rome*
Wendy Wassyng Roworth	*Between 'Old Tiber' and 'Envious Thames': The Angelica Kauffman Connection*
José María Luzón Nogué	*Travelling through Italy with Books*

CONFERENCES

Margaret Stewart	*'Metaphysical Scots': Scottish Intellectual and Architectural Creativity in the 18th Century*
Stana Nenadic	*Patronage and Professional Identitities: Scottish Architects in 18th-century London*
Alistair Rowan	*The Adam brothers: Builders from North Britain*
Peter Guillery	*Scottish Dock Builders in Late Georgian London*
Ted Ruddock	*Engineers Southbound after 1760*
Paul Bradley	*William Burn, Scottish Export*
David Walker	*Edwardian Scots and Public Building in London*
Miles Glendinning	*Robert Matthew and his Circle*

Tour: St Katherine Docks (Telford); 99 Aldwych (Burnet); St Mary le Strand (Gibbs); Scottish Church, Crown Court (Balfour & Turner); Chandos House (Robert Adam); Knightsbridge Barracks (Spence); Cadogan Square (Shaw, Stevenson, Young); Chelsea Town Hall (Brydon); Oakhill Road, Putney (William Young); Sudbrook Park, Petersham (Gibbs); St Michael & All Angels, Bedford Park (Shaw).

19–21 September 2007
Artistic Links between the Early Tudor Courts and Medicean Florence
(held at Villa I Tatti, Florence)

Chaired and opening remarks by Joseph Connors, Brian Allen

Stephen Gunn	*Anglo-Florentine Contacts 1485–1547: Political and Social Contexts*
Cinzia Sicca	*Giorgio Vasari and the Progress of Italian Art in early 16th-century England*
Alan P. Darr	*Pietro Torrigiano and his Sculpture in Henrican England: Sources and Influences*
Louise Waldman	*Benedetto da Rovezzano in England and after*
Francesco Caglioti	*Benedetto da Rovezzano in Inghilterra: novita sulla tomba del cardinale Wolsey e poi di Enrico VIII*
Giancarlo Gentilini	*Baccio Bandinelli e il progretto della tomba per Enrico VIII*
Tommaso Mozzati	*Baccio Bandinelli e il progretto della tomba per Enrico VIII*
Philip Lindley	*Why were Italian Sculptors successful in early 16th-century England?*
Maurice Howard	*Italian Architects and Military Engineers under Royal and Courtier*
Thomas Campbell	*From Papal Rome to Tudor London: The Context and Significance of Henry VII's Raphael Workshop Tapestries*
Susan Foister	*Antonio Toto and the Market for Italian Painting in early Tudor England*
Martin Biddle	*The Palace of Nonsuch*

Site visits: San Salvi, Cappella Pandolfini alla Badia, Museo del Bargello, Santa Trinità, Santi Apostoli, Il Carmine and the Uffizi

18 January 2008
A Passion for British Art: Collecting in the 20th Century
(held at the Paul Mellon Centre)

David Cannadine	*Father and Son as Collectors and Philanthropists: Andrew W. Mellon and Paul Mellon compared*
Shelley Bennett	*Henry and Arabella Huntington: Collecting and Cultural Philanthropy in America c.1900*
Andrew Wilton	*Collecting British Watercolours and Drawings in the 20th Century*
Alison Smith	*Modern Collectors of Victorian Art*
Angus Trumble	*From Hubert von Herkomer to Kenneth Clark: Buying British Art for Australasia, 1899–1954*
Louisa Buck	*From Saatchi to Frieze: the Reception and Acquisition of Contemporary British Art at Home and Abroad*

16 May 2008
Pompeo Batoni 1708–1787
(held at the Paul Mellon Centre)

Chaired by Christopher Johns, Edgar Peters Bowron

Paolo Coen	*Imperiali and Batoni, Batoni and Imperiali: The Historical and Social Background*
Peter Bjorn Kerber	*Seamless: Sartorial Theology in Batoni's Alterpieces*
Christoph Frank	*Batoni's Russian Patrons*
Nicola Figgis	*Batoni and his Irish Patrons*
Clare Hornsby	*Serving the 'Lovers of the Virtu': Batoni, Barazzi and the Dealers*
Stephen Lloyd	*Batoni and the Portrait Miniature*
Aileen Ribeiro	*Batoni and the Arts of Fashion*

14–16 July 2008
Vauxhall Revisited: Pleasure Gardens and their Publics 1660–1880
(held at Tate Britain)

Victoria Walsh	*Introduction*
John Dixon Hunt	*'Theatres of Hospitality': The Forms and Uses of Private Landscapes and Public Gardens*
Stephen Daniels	*Grounds for Pleasure*
Michael Symes	*Pleasure Gardens and the English Landscape Garden*
Paul Elliott	*Victorian Provincial Public Parks: The Pleasure Gardens of the 19th Century?*
Peter Borsay	*Pleasure Gardens and Urban Culture in the Long 18th Century*
Roey Sweet	*Pleasure Gardens Outside London*
Jon Stobart	*The Provincial Pleasure Gardens of Georgian England*
Katy Layton-Jones	*'Agreeable elevations' and 'healthful situations': Liverpool's Walks and Gardens in the Long 18th Century*
Wolfgang Cilleßen	*Exoticism and Commerce: Vauxhalls in Pre-Revolutionary Paris*
Aileen Ribeiro	*Transformations: Dress and Disguise in 18th-century London*
Martin Postle, Chair	*Patriotic Visions*
Eleanor Hughes	*Guns in Gardens: Peter Monamy's Supperbox Paintings at Vauxhall*
Nebahat Avcioglu	*'Vauxhall Gardens or a Turkish Paradise': Princely Politics and the Architecture of the Other*
Belinda Beaton	*Vauxhall Meets its Waterloo: Wellington, Heroism and History*
Brian Allen	*Introduction*
Rachel Cowgill	*Performance Alfresco: Music-making in English Pleasure Gardens pre-1880*
Simon McVeigh, Chair	*Divisions on a Ground*
Berta Joncus	*'To Propagate a Sound for Sense': Music for Diversion and Seduction at Ranelagh Gardens*
Bonny H. Miller	*Poetical Essays, Pleasing Strains: Pleasure Garden Music in the Popular Periodical Press*
William Weber	*The Evolving Canon of British Vocal Pieces, 1750–1890*
Penelope Corfield, Chair	*An Inclusive Space? Class, Gender and Race*
David Hunter	*The Real Audience at Vauxhall*
Hannah Greig	*'All Together and All Distinct': Social Exclusivity and the Pleasure Gardens of 18th-century London*
Lake Douglas	*Pleasure Gardens in New Orleans, 1810–1830*
Marius Kwint, Chair	*Light and Dark*
Alice Barnaby	*Light Entertainment: The Role of Illumination, 1780–1860*
Deborah Nord	*Gaslight, Daylight and the Decline of Carnivalesque: Egan, Dickens and Thackeray*
Margaret MacDonald	*'The evening mist clothes the riverside with poetry, as with a veil': Whistler and Cremorne*
John Brewer, Chair	Final comment and discussion

28–29 November 2008
Living with the Royal Academy: Artistic Ideals and Experiences in Britain, 1768–1848
(held at the Centre for Eighteenth Century Studies and the Department of History of Art, University of York)

Mark Hallett	*The Academy Quartet: Joshua Reynolds in 1769*
Matthew Craske	*The Making of the Royal Academy and the Concept of Imperial Peace*
Martin Postle	*The Sandbys and the Royal Academy*
Sarah Monks	*'Un peu gascon': Dominic Serres and Alienation in the Academy*
John Bonehill	*The Eye of Delicacy: Joseph Wright of Derby Reviewed*
Iain McCalman	*Slipping between Two Academies: Philippe de Loutherbourg's Channel Crossing*
John Barrell	*Thomas Banks as Radical Activist*
Anne Bermingham	*Apocalypse at the Academy: The Revelation of Benjamin West*
Rosie Dias	*Venetian Secrets and Secret Venetians: Colour and the Royal Academy*
Aris Sarafianos	*Polite Anatomies for Gentlemen in the Age of Counter-Revolution: Sir Anthony Carlisle at the Royal Academy*
Martin Myrone	*A Child of the Royal Academy: William Etty as Perpetual Student*
Jason Edwards	*'By Abstraction Springs Forth Ideal Beauty?' John Gibson's Modernity*
Sarah Monks	Closing remarks

CONFERENCES

4 December 2008
Architecture, Diplomacy and National Identity: Sir Basil Spence and mid-century Modernism
(held at the British School at Rome)

Andrew Wallace-Hadrill *Welcome*
Gavin Stamp *Lutyens and Spence*
Louise Campbell *Introductory remarks*
Jane Loeffler *Architecture of Diplomacy: the Changing Face of America Abroad*
Eeva-Liisa Pelkonen *Eero Saarinen: Three Embassies*
Robin Skinner *Sorting out the hornet's nest: Sir Basil Spence and the New Zealand Parliament Building*
Brian Edwards *Spence at Expo '67: Modernism and the Search for National Identity*
Miles Glendinning *A Modern Palazzo: Designing and Building the Rome Embassy*
Maristello Casciato *Neo-Liberty and Post-war Architecture in Italy*
Giorgio Piccinato *Rome in the Fifties: Architecture and Ideology*

27 March 2009
The Intimate Portrait
(held at the Paul Mellon Centre)

Kim Sloan *Introduction*
Chaired by Lucy Peltz, Peter Funnell
Hanneke Grootenboer *'Kisses springing from her eye': On Intimate Vision of Eye Miniatures*
Katherine Coombs *The 18th-century Miniature as 'intimate portrait': A Consideration of the Diminutive and the Minute*
Marcia Pointon *Thinking about Intimacy and Portraiture*
Constance McPhee and Elizabeth Barker *Fancy Piece or Portrait Study? A Pastel Head by Wright of Derby in the Metropolitan Museum of Art*
Ruth Kenny *The Intimate and the Commercial: Hugh Douglas Hamilton and Pastel Portraiture c. 1760–1790*
Jacob Simon *Marketing and Displaying Portraits on Paper in 18th-century Britain*
Stephen Lloyd *Experts and Plutocrats: The Revival in the International Art Market for British 18th-century Portrait Drawings and Miniatures c.1890–1935*
Shearer West, Chair *Discussion*

2 September 2009
John William Waterhouse 1849–1917
(held at the Paul Mellon Centre)

Ronald Hutton *Languages of Paganism in Victorian Britain*
Christina Bradstreet *Wicked with Roses: Waterhouse's 'The Soul of the Rose'*
Simon Goldhill *Sex in the Afternoon: The Ancient World and Desire in Waterhouse*
Nancy Marshall *Nymphs in the City: Waterhouse in the Context of late 19th-century London*
Stefano-Maria Evangelista *Ladies of Shalott: Waterhouse and Victorian Poetry*
Roundtable discussion with Elizabeth Prettejohn, Peter Trippi, Robert Upstone, Patty Wageman

15–17 October 2009
Transatlantic Romanticism
(held at the Royal Academy, the Paul Mellon Centre and University College London)

Alan Wallach *Thomas Cole and Transatlantic Romanticism*
Dell Upton *The Urban Ecology of Art in Antebellum New York*
William Vaughan *'The pit of modern art': Ambitions and Practices in the London Art World in the early 19th Century*
Mark Ford *Cooper's Frontier*
William Truettner *Painting Indians and Building Empires in North America, 1710–1840*
Sarah Monks *A Werewolf in London: Benjamin West's American Accent*
Andrew Hemingway *The Politics of Style: Allston's and Martin's 'Belshazzars' Compared*
Kenneth Myers *William Dunlap's 'A Trip to Niagara' (1830) and the Cultural Construction of Landscape Experience in Jacksonian New York*
David Bindman *John Martin and Thomas Cole*
Leo Costello *'Gorgeous but altogether false': Turner, Cole and Transatlantic Ideas of Decline*
Paul Giles *Washington Irving and the Ghosts of Colonialism: From Transatlantic to Transpacific*
Wendy Ikemoto *John Quidor and Memories of Revolution*
Matthew Beaumont *Broad Ways, Narrow Ways: The Transatlantic City in Poe's 'The Man of the Crowd'*

28–29 January 2010
Antiquity at Home
(held at the British Museum and the Paul Mellon Centre)

David Watkin — Keynote lecture *From Antiquity to Enlightenment: the origins of the British Museum*
Tribute to Ilaria Bignamini by Andrew Wallace-Hadrill
Introduced and chaired by Kim Sloan, Edward Chaney
Ian Jenkins — *The Townley Discobolus*
Elizabeth Angelicoussis — *The Hope Dionysus*
Eloisa Dodero — *Clytie before Townley: the Gaetani d'Aragona Collection of Sculptures and its Neapolitan Context*
Dolores Sánchez-Jáuregui Alpañés — *Sculptures on board 'The Westmorland': A Cross-section of Grand Tour Collecting*
Jonathan Yarker — *The 'Paper Museum' of Charles Townley*
Thorsten Opper — *Lyde Browne – The House Museum as Sales Room*
Jason Kelly — *The Society of Dilettanti and the Planning of a Museum*
Anna Seidel — *Display and Dispersal of the Montalto-Negroni Marbles*
Adriano Aymonino — *A Roman Columbarium on the River Thames: Robert Adam's Library–Gallery at Syon House*
Ruth Guilding — *Sir Richard Worsley, Connoisseur of the Parthenon*
Clare Hornsby — *Collecting or Accumulation? Thoughts on Motivation*
Tim Knox — *Soane and the Antique, and some Reflections on House Museums Then and Now*
Closing panel chaired by Frank Salmon

18–19 March 2010
Paul Sandby and the Geographies of 18th-century British Art
(held at the Royal Academy and the Paul Mellon Centre)

John Bonehill — Introduction to the exhibition *Paul Sandby. Picturing Britain*
Bruce Robertson — Keynote address *Paul Sandby: Father of English Watercolour?*
Tim Wilcox — *Burying the Hatchet: Paul Sandby at Luton Park*
Finola O'Kane — *'A Genuine Idea of the Face of the Kingdom'? Jonathan Fisher and Paul Sandby's portrait of Ireland within the frame of Great Britain*
John Barrell — *A Common in Wales: Edward Pugh, the Pastoral, and Progress*
Gillian Forrester — *'No Joke Like a True Joke'? Sandby's 'Twelve London Cries'*
Nick Grindle — *Living in London and Windsor: The Sandby Brothers' Residences, c.1752–1809*
Carolyn Anderson — *'The art of depicting with a soldier's eye': The Military Mapping of 18th-century Scotland*
Stephen Daniels — *'Great Balls of Fire': Representing the Remarkable Meteor of 18th August 1783*

15–16 April 2010
Curious Specimens: Enlightenment Objects, Collections, Narratives
(held at the Royal College of Surgeons, Victoria & Albert Museum and Strawberry Hill)

Pamela Smith — Keynote lecture *Curious Modes of Production: Making Objects in the Early Modern World*
Walpole and Delaney, chaired by Amy Meyers.
Panel discussion by Michael Snodin and Alicia Weisberg Roberts
Cutting, Sampling, Extra-illustrating, chaired by Alicia Weisberg Roberts
Lucy Peltz — *An Author Extra-illustrates his Books: Thomas Pennant and Horace Walpole*
Janice Neri — *Paper Kingdoms: Mary Delany, the Duchess of Portland, and the Consequences of Collage*
Collectors, Predisciplinarity, Divisions of Knowledge, chaired by Brian Allen
Stacey Sloboda — *Material Displays: Porcelain and Natural History in the Duchess of Portland's Museum*
Adriano Aymonino — *A mirror of the Enlightenment: The Collections of Elizabeth Seymour Percy, 1st Duchess of Northumberland*
Craig Hanson — *Collecting Virtue: The Patronage and Acquisitions of Dr Richard Mead in Early Georgian London*
Stephen Bann — *Curiosity future and past: Siting Horace Walpole*

CONFERENCES

Malcolm Baker — *Walpole and Sculpture*

Aesthetic and/or Antiquarian Collecting, chaired by Tim Knox

Cynthia Roman — *Collecting Copies, Surrogates, and Misattributions*

Rosemary Sweet — *'Contrary to my System and my Humour': Horace Walpole and Antiquarian Collecting in the 18th Century*

George Haggerty — *Eccentric Collectors: Walpole, Beckford, and the Erotics of Things*

Museums, Collecting, Predisciplinarity, chaired by Luisa Calè.

Panel discussion by Malcolm Baker, Tim Knox, Kim Sloan, Michael Snodin

18 October 2010
Salvator Rosa in Britain
(held at Dulwich Picture Gallery)

Introduced and chaired by Claire Pace, Susan Jenkins, Christoph Vogtherr

Wendy Wassying Roworth — *The Legacy of Genius: Salvator Rosa, Joshua Reynolds and Painting in England*

Elinor Shaffer — *The Lives of Artists: William Beckford and Salvator Rosa*

Cinzia Maria Sicca — *'One of the most excellent Masters that Italy has produced in this century': The Circulation of Salvator Rosa's Works through the English Community in Leghorn*

Alexis Ashot — *'Unbounded capacity': A 1778 Vita of Salvator Rosa by the London Connoisseur, Charles Rogers*

Jonathan Yarker — *Joseph Goupy and the Imitation of Rosa in early 18th-century England*

Helen Langdon — *Belisarius in Norfolk*

Panel and audience discussion chaired by Claire Pace

18–19 November 2010
Thomas Lawrence: Regency, Power and Brilliance
(held at the National Portrait Gallery and the Paul Mellon Centre)

Lawrence, Gender and Representation Introduced and chaired by Lucy Peltz

Sarah Monks — *Slippery Blisses: Lawrence's Male Portraiture and the Structure of Desire*

Marcia Pointon — *Lawrence's Teenagers*

Shearer West — *A Royal Performance: Lawrence's Portraits of the Siddons Family*

Richard Holmes Keynote lecture — *How the Romantic Generation Discovered the Beauty and Terror of Science*

Lawrence in Practice: The Studio and the Print Shop Introduced and chaired by Kim Sloan

Jacob Simon — *Sir Thomas Lawrence and the Process of Portrait Painting*

Sally Doust — *The Perfect Facsimile: Thomas Lawrence and his Engravers*

Cassandra Albinson — *Thomas Lawrence and the Group Portrait: In and Out of the Studio*

Lawrence's Contemporary Influence and Reputation Introduced and chaired by Fintan Cullen

Viccy Coltman — *Lawrence vs. Raeburn: The 'knotty' Business of Portrait Painting*

Martin Myrone — *'His Pupil still': Lawrence, Etty and Academic Unease*

Lawrence's Posthumous Reputation and Historiography Introduced and chaired by Peter Funnell

Philippa Simpson — *An Ornamental Figurehead: The Problem of Lawrence as National Hero*

Pat Hardy — *Thomas Lawrence: The Shaping of his Legacy*

Roundtable discussion with Mark Hallett, David Solkin, Ludmilla Jordanova

STUDY DAYS

In May 2000 the first of a series of Country House Study Days was organised in collaboration with the Rothschild Trust at Waddesdon Manor and study days have also been held at Arundel Castle, Welbeck Abbey and Castle Howard. These events, usually consisting of about fifty scholars with relevant expertise, are by invitation.

9 May 2000
The Dix-Huitième: The Enduring Popularity of the Ancien Régime Interior in Europe and America 1850–1920
Waddesdon Manor

Philippa Glanville — *Welcome*
Jon Whiteley — *The Taste for 18th-century Art*
John Tschirch — *The Vanderbilts and the Ancien Régime*
Joseph Mordaunt Crook — *London Houses of the Nouveaux Riches*
Carolyn Sargentson — *French Furniture in British Contexts*
Charles Sebag-Montefiore — *Dealers and the Taste for the Ancien Régime*
Ulrich Leben — *Paris Boiseries*
Selma Schwartz — *Sèvres*
Alastair Laing — *The Drawings Collection*
Martin Meade — *The Drawings Collection*
Giles Barber — *French Books and Bindings*

22 May 2001
Buying British: The Fashion for collecting 'Golden Age' British Painting
Waddesdon Manor

Philippa Glanville — *Welcome*
Christopher Lloyd — *George IV and 'Golden Age' Painting*
Alastair Laing — *The 19th-century Market for 18th-century Paintings*
Martin Postle — *Buying and Selling Reynolds*
Julius Bryant — *Lord Iveagh and the Influence of Agnews*
Shelley Bennett — *Henry Huntington's British Painting Collection*
Alison McQueen — *The Frick and Mellon Collections and British Art*
Colin B. Bailey — *Henry Clay Frick and Grand Manner Portraits*
Michael Hall — *Late Georgian Pictures as Decorative Elements at Waddesdon*
Martin Postle — *Rothschild and Reynolds*
David Mannings — *Rothschild and Reynolds*
Alastair Laing — *Assembling the Waddesdon Collection*

19 September 2002
French Without Tears: Collecting French Decorative Arts in Britain and America 1880–1920
Waddesdon Manor

Philippa Glanville — *Welcome and Introduction to the Powerhouse*
Rosalind Savill — *The 19th-century Taste for Sèvres*
Simon Jervis — *Rococo Revival in the Early Victorian Period*
Charles Truman — *Gold Boxes*
Ulrich Leben — *Rothschild Preferences in 18th-century Objects*
Rachel Akpabio — *Works on Paper*
Ulrich Leben — *18th-century Objects: New Discoveries*
Ian Gow — *To Match the Furniture: Lorimer Goes Louis in a Fife Drawing*
Bertrand Rondot — *Nissim de Camodo*

17 September 2003
The Jardin Anglais, A Rediscovery of the 19th Century
Waddesdon Manor

Therese O'Malley — *Sources for early 19th-century American Gardens*
Elizabeth Barlow — *Frederick Olmsted*
Melanie Aspey — *Archival Sources for 19th-century Rothschild Gardens*
Chris Sumner — *Redesigning the Rothschild Gardens at Gunnersbury Park*
Anthony Fleming — *Restoring Nesfield's Work at Witley Court, Worcestershire*
Martin Meade — *Object Session: Garden Drawings*
Peter Fuhring — *Object Session: Gabriel-Hippolyte Destailleur's Books*
Michael Walker — *Tour of Waddesdon Gardens*

2 November 2004
Furniture and Armour from the Norfolk Collections
Arundel Castle

John Martin Robinson — *Introduction to the Arundel Collections and their Backgrounds*
Simon Jervis — *Charles Davis and the Collection of European Renaissance Furniture in the 19th Century*
David Edge — *The Collecting and Display of Arms and Armour in Victorian Britain*
Rosemary Baird — *Seventeenth- and 18th-century Furniture from Norfolk House*

STUDY DAYS

8 November 2005
Lions Rampant
Arundel Castle

John Martin Robinson	*Introduction*
Richard Marks	*Late Medieval Collegiate Foundations*
Ann Payne	*Heraldry in English Illuminated Manuscripts*
David Skinner	*Liturgy*
John Goodall	*Examination of the Fitzalan Tombs*
Heather Warne	*Examination of Medieval Manuscripts*
Tessa Murdoch	*Examination of Chapel Plate*
Thomas Woodcock	*Examination of the Drawing Room*

9 November 2006
The Collector Earl and Regency Dukes
Arundel Castle

John Martin Robinson	*Introduction*
Edward Chaney	*The Collector Earl in Italy*
Nick Savage	*Georgian Colour Plate Books*
Rachel Elwes	*The Paul Storr Dinner Service*
Marjorie Trusted	*François Diessart's Busts of Charles I and Prince Charles Louis of the Rhine*
Christopher Brown	*Van Dyck's Portraits commissioned by Lord Arundel 1636–39*
Robert Harding	*Colour plate books*

28 September 2007
Welbeck Abbey

Derek Adlam	*Introductory Talk*
Pete Smith	*The Architecture of Welbeck Abbey*
Derek Adlam	*Tour of State Rooms*
Philippa Glanville	*Silver*
Katharine Coombs	*Miniatures*

19 September 2008
Welbeck Abbey

Derek Adlam	*Introduction to Welbeck*
Alastair Laing	*Tour of the State Rooms*
Derek Adlam	*Tour of the State Rooms*

16 November 2009
Castle Howard

Christopher Ridgway	*Introductory lecture*
Charles Beddington	*Italian Paintings*
Christopher Ridgway	*Architecture*
Jeremy Musson	*Architecture*
Alison Brisby	*George Howard, 9th Earl of Carlisle and the Castle Howard Chapel*

13 September 2010
Castle Howard

Christopher Ridgway	*Introductory lecture*

Walking tour of the Castle Howard Estate

Castle Howard Study Day September 2010

30 September 2010
Ham House

Simon Jervis	*In Institutional Hands: The Study and Display of Ham House by the Victoria & Albert Museum and the National Trust*
Alastair Laing	*Disentangling the Lauderdale Inventories: The Hanging of a Caroline Picture Collection*
Jacob Simon	*Picture Framing at Ham House in the 17th Century*
Reinier Baarsen	*Seventeenth-century ébénisterie at Ham House*
Adam Bowett	*Baldassare Artima's scagliola at Ham, related furniture and monuments*
Charles Avery	*Sculpture at Ham House*
Helen Wyld	*Seventeenth- and Eighteenth-century Tapestries at Ham House*
Michael Hall	*Bodley & Garner and Watts & Co.: Repairs and Renovation for William Tollemache, 9th Earl of Dysart*

Tour of Ham House

THE PAUL MELLON LECTURES

THE PAUL MELLON LECTURES were inaugurated in 1994 when Professor Francis Haskell (1928–2000) delivered the first series at the National Gallery in London. They have always been held at the Sainsbury Theatre in the National Gallery, London except in 2000 when they were held at Tate Britain. The model for the series was the Andrew W. Mellon Lectures, established in 1949 and named in honour of Paul Mellon's father, the founder of the National Gallery of Art in Washington, DC. The lectures are given biennially by a distinguished historian of British art.

1994 (The National Gallery)
Francis Haskell
The Dispersal of the Collections of King Charles I and his Courtiers

11 Oct. *Art Collections in London on the Eve of the Civil War (1)*
18 Oct. *Art Collections in London on the Eve of the Civil War (2)*
25 Oct. *'Scandalous Monuments and Pictures'?*
1 Nov. *Exiles and Exports*
8 Nov. *The Royal Sale*
15 Nov. *Final Departures and First Returns*

1996 (The National Gallery)
Lisa Tickner
Modern Life and Modern Subjects

6 Oct. *Walter Sickert: The Camden Town Murder and Tabloid Crime*
13 Oct. *Augustus John: Gypsies, Tramps and Lyric Fantasy of Kermesse*
20 Oct. *Wyndham Lewis: Dance and the Popular Culture of Kermesse*
27 Oct. *Studland Beach, Nursery Tea, Domesticity and 'Significant Form'*

1998 (The National Gallery)
William Vaughan
The Making of the British School

28 Oct. *Hogarth: The Problem Parent*
4 Nov. *Why Landscape?*
11 Nov. *Trash or Treasure? The National Gallery of British Art*
18 Nov. *Going Modern and Being British*
25 Nov. *The Eccentric Island*

2000 (Tate Britain)
Marcia Pointon
Brilliant Effects

28 Sept. *Fault Lines and Points of Light: What have History and Art to do with Jewels?*
5 Oct. *Portraits as Jewels: Bridging Distances in Visual and Material Culture*
12 Oct. *Jewellery as Excess: Luxurious Expenditure and the Imagery of the Tragic Heroine*
19 Oct. *Jewellery and Transvaluation: on Shrines, Museums and Protestant Painting*
26 Oct. *Jewellery, Geology and Morality: John Ruskin's Lapidary Loves*

2002 (The National Gallery)
Paul Binski
The Living Church: Art, Architecture and the Religious Imagination in 13th-century England

28 Oct. *Becket and the Aesthetics of Martyrdom: The Cult of Becket at Canterbury and its Role in the Formation of this Early Gothic Church*
4 Nov. *Architecture, Morality and Emancipation: The Theories which may have Influenced the Spread of English Gothic Architecture*
11 Nov. *The Cult of Saints: The Role of Saints as Models of New Ideals in the Church*
18 Nov. *Gothic Expressivities: A History of Facial Expression in English Gothic Art, and of the Range of Religious Sentiment*
25 Nov. *Crisis: A Final Lecture on the Origins of the Decorated Style and its End*

2004 (The National Gallery)
David Solkin
The Epic of Common Life: Genre Painting and Social Change in early 19th-century Britain

25 Oct. *New Adventures in Space and Time: Reconfiguring Rural Life in the Age of Revolution*
1 Nov. *Trouble in Arcadia*
8 Nov. *The Subjects and Spaces of Surveillance*
15 Nov. *The Colonisation of Carnival*
22 Nov. *The End of Olde England: Remaking the Nation after Waterloo*

THE PAUL MELLON LECTURES

2007 (The National Gallery)
Giles Waterfield
For an Excellent Purpose: Museums and their Publics in Britain from 1850 to 1914

10 Jan.	*Memories of the Art Museum*
17 Jan.	*The Rise of the Regional Museum in Victorian Britain (1)*
24 Jan.	*The Rise of the Regional Museum in Victorian Britain (2)*
31 Jan.	*Beyond the Crystal Palace: Museum Exhibitions in 19th-century Britain*
7 Feb.	*Explaining the Museum*
14 Feb.	*Architecture and Display*

2009 (The National Gallery)
Duncan Robinson
Pen and Pencil: Writing and Painting in England, 1750–1850

21 Jan.	*'Subjects I consider'd as writers do.' William Hogarth*
28 Jan.	*'He can never be a great artist who is grossly illiterate.' Joshua Reynolds*
4 Feb.	*'From the window I am writing I see all those sweet fields…' John Constable*
11 Feb.	*'Painting and Poetry…reflect and heighten each other's beauties.' JMW Turner*
18 Feb.	*'I dare not pretend to be anything other than the Secretary; the Authors are in Eternity.' William Blake*

BIBLIOGRAPHY

Ralph Edwards, 'The Mellon Foundation and British Art : a stimulus to public appreciation', *The Connoisseur*, August 1967, pp. 230–31

Basil Taylor, 'The Paul Mellon Foundation for British Art: A Report on Progress', *Contemporary Review* 211:1222, November 1967, pp. 264–67

Editorial, 'Mellon Foundation Books', *The Burlington Magazine*, Vol. 110, No. 778 (Jan. 1968), pp. 3–4

Marina Vaizey, 'The Paul Mellon Foundation for British Art', *Arts Review*, 16 August 1969, pp. 526–27

Editorial, 'The Future of the Mellon Foundation', *The Burlington Magazine*, Vol. 112, No. 806 (May 1970), pp. 267–68

Editorial, 'The Mellon Centre', *The Burlington Magazine*, Vol. 126, No. 979 (Oct. 1984), p. 603

John Wilmerding, ed., *Essays in Honor of Paul Mellon: Collector and Benefactor* (Washington: National Gallery of Art), 1986.

Paul Mellon with John Baskett, *Reflections in a Silver Spoon: A Memoir* (New York: William Morrow), 1992

Brian Allen, 'Paul Mellon and scholarship in the history of British Art', in John Baskett et al., *Paul Mellon's Legacy: A Passion for British Art: Masterpieces from the Yale Center for British Art* (New Haven; London: Yale University Press, 2007), pp. 43–53